PANZERS
IN THE SAND

Volume 2: 1942–1945

PANZERS
IN THE SAND

The History of Panzer-Regiment 5

Volume 2: 1942–1945

Bernd Hartmann

Pen & Sword
MILITARY

Dedicated to the Soldiers of
Panzer-Regiment 5 **and** *Panzer-Abteilung 5.*

English Translation © 2011 by Battle Born Books and Consulting

First published in English in the United States of America by Stackpole Books in 2011

Republished in this format in the United Kingdom in 2011 by
Pen & Sword Military
An imprint of
Pen & Sword Books Ltd
47 Church Street
Barnsley
South Yorkshire
S70 2AS

Copyright © Bernd Hartmann 2002, 2011

ISBN 978 1 84884 506 0

Printed and bound in the United States of America.

Pen & Sword Books Ltd incorporates the Imprints of Pen & Sword Aviation,
Pen & Sword Family History, Pen & Sword Maritime, Pen & Sword Military, Wharncliffe Local History,
Pen & Sword Select, Pen & Sword Military Classics, Leo Cooper, Remember When, Seaforth Publishing and
Frontline Publishing

For a complete list of Pen & Sword titles please contact
PEN & SWORD BOOKS LIMITED
47 Church Street, Barnsley, South Yorkshire, S70 2AS, England
E-mail: enquiries@pen-and-sword.co.uk
Website: www.pen-and-sword.co.uk

CONTENTS

FOREWORD

After more than half a century since the end of the Second World War, the writing of the history of *Panzer-Regiment 5* and *Panzer-Abteilung 5* was a difficult undertaking, especially with regard to the detail in which it is presented. The author, who did not take part in the war, was compelled to study the sources in his work. Many gaps in the narrative and even contradictory statements made the work more difficult. Particularly unfortunate was the fact that the names of many members of the formations in leadership roles, such as battalion and company commanders, could not be determined completely. Despite those deficiencies, it was high time for the history of the regiment to be written, since all previous efforts at a comprehensive portrait had failed for one reason or another, and the only thing available were individual contributions or broad portrayals.

The time frame under discussion here was relatively short, but it was marked by important events that still influence us today. The soldiers of the regiment fulfilled their duties bravely and in a self-sacrificial way for our German fatherland. They fought in Poland, France and North Africa. Reconstituted as *Panzer-Abteilung 5*, they landed in the middle of the collapse of *Heeresgruppe Mitte* on the Eastern Front in the summer of 1944. Reconstituted anew, they were first committed on the Western Front, before they fought outside of Berlin and in Mecklenburg at the end of the war. The author made every effort to present events truthfully, since history is obligated to the truth. Consequently, the unfortunate and annoying tendency to load up any treatment of historical events with ideology—especially from the German viewpoint—is avoided. In addition, it was important not to observe the history of the oldest formation of the *Panzertruppe* in an isolated manner but to present it in the context of the war and military history.

This work is not intended to appeal just to veterans. Instead, it is designed to inform members of the younger generation about those times. Graphics are kept as simple as possible, with the aim of making the situation and conduct of the fighting understandable even to non-military professionals.

Bernd Hartmann, *Oberstleutnant a.D.*
Spokesman for the Veterans Association of Former
Panzer-Regiment 5

A Word of Introduction

Thanks to tremendous effort and a great deal of professionalism, the author has assembled a history of *Panzer-Regiment 5*—a regiment that led the way for the *Panzertruppe* in all of the theaters of war—that honors and memorializes all members of the regiment, the living and the dead. This book is a fitting tribute to my old regiment.

Werner Grün, *Major a.D.*
Former Battalion Commander in *Panzer-Regiment 5*

CHAPTER 1

Panzer-Regiment 5 in the Campaign in North Africa, 1942

1. 25 January–25 May 1942: Counterattack and Recapture of Cyrenaica; Preparations for the Attack on the Gazala Line

The communications center of the British 22nd Armoured Brigade radioed the following to Cairo on the first day of the New Year:

> The *DAK* sang the German national anthem in its positions last night. It may be the case that Rommel's formations no longer have any tanks, but to speak of a beaten army is premature. We should not deceive ourselves into believing that these soldiers, led by an unbroken general, are inclined to give up. They will continue to fight like the devil.[1]

At the beginning of 1942, the regiment was with its parent division, the *21. Panzer-Division*, *Generalmajor* Böttcher commanding, in the vicinity of the high ground around Belaudah, some 20 kilometers southeast of Agedabia. On 4 January, the future Oak Leaves recipient, *Oberleutnant* Rolf Rocholl, assumed command of the 6th Company.[2]

By 7 January, the division had been pulled back to the Marsa el Brega position in the area around El Agheila. The positions there favored the defense due to the marshy terrain and the sandy desert, which was difficult to negotiate, that adjoined it to the south.

The British operation, "Crusader," ended at that point and, correspondingly, the withdrawal movements of *Panzergruppe Afrika*. The British had not been successful in their effort to envelop and destroy the Axis forces. In addition, they were then burdened with a long logistics line of communications; it was nearly 1,200 kilometers to Alexandria. The enemy ceased their advance in order to receive more reinforcements. Of paramount importance for *Panzergruppe Afrika* was the battlefield reconstitution of its troop elements.

✠

The *Luftwaffe* forces on Sicily were reinforced, with the result that the British naval forces and the island of Malta could be engaged more effectively than previously. That enabled the Axis to be resupplied almost without interference across the Mediterranean. At the beginning of January, large amounts of materiel arrived in Tripoli, especially armored vehicles. The *DAK* had 139 tanks at its disposal on 19 January, after 220 had been written

---

1. Author's Note: Kühn, *Mit Rommel in der Wüste, Kampf und Untergang des Deutschen Afrika-Korps, 1941–1943*, 94.

2. Author's Note: Werner Trodler, correspondence dated 19 October 2000 concerning participants in the fighting in North Africa from the regiment.

off during the winter fighting. The Italian XX Corps (Motorized) had ninety armored fighting vehicles of Italian origin.

The widely dispersed elements of the British 8th Army facilitated the commander-in-chief of *Panzergruppe Afrika, General der Panzertruppen* Rommel, in his intention to conduct a counterattack to retake Cyrenaica. By doing so, he hoped to beat them to the punch in their approach and attack. Remaining idle in the Marsa el Brega position would have meant handing the initiative over to the enemy and inevitably led to the lost of Tripolitania. To deceive the enemy, Rommel had a few decrepit huts and the hulk of a stranded ship set on fire during the evening of 20 January. What he intended to do was accomplished: The British leadership concluded from the fires that *Panzergruppe Afrika* was continuing its withdrawal to the west. Instead, under the cover of rain and a sandstorm, the Germans moved out to attack.

On the morning of 21 January, Rommel had the military police put his order for the attack on display at all of the road maintenance buildings in Tripolitania and the Syrte Bend:[3]

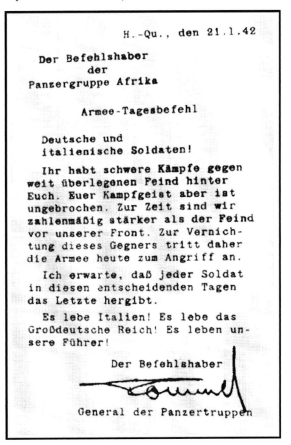

Headquarters, 21 January 1942

The Commander-in-Chief of *Panzergruppe Afrika*

Army Order-of-the-Day

German and Italian Soldiers!
You have difficult fighting against vastly superior enemy forces behind you. Despite that, your fighting morale remains unbroken. At present,

Pocket calendar for 1942 for members of *Panzergruppe Afrika*. The calendar was presented to the soldiers by the German propaganda ministry.

3. Author's Note: Münnich, *Panzer in Nord-Afrika 1941– 1943,* 47.

we are numerically stronger than the enemy to our front. Therefore, the field army is moving out today to attack to destroy that enemy.

I expect that every soldier will give his all during these decisive days.

Long live Italy! Long live the Greater German *Reich*! Long live our leaders!

The Commander-in-Chief

/signed/ Rommel

General der Panzertruppen

On that same morning, two radio messages from the *Führer* Headquarters arrived.[4] In one message, *Panzergruppe Afrika* was redesignated as *Panzer-Armee Afrika*. In the other, Rommel was awarded the Swords to the Oak Leaves to the Knight's Cross of the Iron Cross. A few days later, he would also be promoted to *Generaloberst*.

The redesignation did nothing to change the organization of the forces in the field.

Panzer-Armee Afrika attacked with elements along the *Via Balbia* and with the *DAK* through the desert to the northeast. *Panzer-Regiment 5* was employed as the main effort of the *21. Panzer-Division* along the right wing. *Stuka* dive bombers effectively supported the attack. The enemy was completely surprised by the attack, and his positions were broken through on the first attempt. The British troop elements were scattered and started to withdraw to the east.

The *21. Panzer-Division* advanced to an area approximately seventy kilometers east of El Agheila by the evening of the first day of the attack. It continued its attack in the direction of Saunu the next day.

---

4. Author's Note: Aberger, *Die 5. (lei.)/21. Panzer-Division in Nord Afrika 1941–1943*, 174.

On 23 January, *Panzer-Regiment 5*, advancing about two kilometers in front of the main body of the division, encountered strong enemy armor forces. In the engagement at Saunu, the regiment, supported by 8.8-centimeter *Flak* and antitank elements, was able to eject the enemy, despite its own numerical inferiority. The German forces were also able to inflict heavy casualties on their opposing number.

The success was made possible primarily through adroit tactical maneuvering. Protected on the flanks by the *Flak* and an antitank company, *Oberleutnant* Sandrock's tank company opened fire on the advancing enemy tanks—initially sixteen—from partially concealed positions on a ridgeline. In the face of the effective tank fire, the enemy pulled back, only to run into the guns of the antitank company. When the enemy started to withdraw yet again, *Oberleutnant* Rocholl's company was employed, which initiated an immediate counterattack from its partially concealed positions. Rocholl's tanks were able to complete the destruction of that enemy tank company. The Germans were then attacked by a force of forty tanks. That attack was also turned back in the face of the combined arms fires. When the enemy attacked with yet more reinforcements, *Oberleutnant* Rocholl's tanks attacked it in the flanks while the *Flak* fixed the force from the front. *Kampfgruppe Mildebrath* was thus able to turn back all enemy attack efforts—in all, some eighty tanks. All further efforts by the enemy to turn the engagement at Saunu to his favor also failed. Exploiting the fires of the support weapons, the tank companies of the regiment were able to conduct flank attacks while suffering few friendly loses, interdicting the enemy and destroying him.

The *DAK* attacked Msus on 25 January. The logistical elements of the 8th Army were located there. Large stocks were captured, which were able to supply the *DAK* for several weeks.

During the period from 21 to 26 January, the German forces destroyed or captured 600 wheeled

Rolling forward again!

vehicles, 280 tanks or armored vehicles and 126 field pieces, decisively weakening the combat power of the 8th Army. *Panzer-Regiment 5* was able to report that it had captured or destroyed 122 tanks or armored vehicles, 37 field pieces, 2 aircraft and 312 wheeled vehicles in the period from 21 to 25 January. In addition, it took 492 prisoners.[5]

5. Author's Note: Aberger, 178.

On 29 January, *Panzer-Armee Afrika* was able to recapture Bengasi with large amounts of all types of supplies. Approximately 1,300 vehicles were captured, temporarily solving the transportation problems of the field army. By 6 February, all of Cyrenaica was back in the hands of the Axis forces.

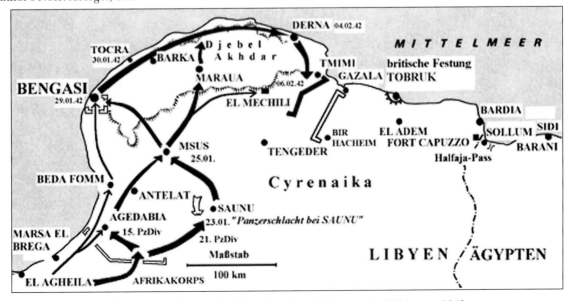

Counterattack to regain Cyrenaica from 21 January to 6 February 1942.

Personnel	Officers	Noncommissioned Officers	Enlisted personnel	Totals
Authorized	82	441	1,920	2,443
On Hand	42	373	1,574	1,989
Shortfall	40	68	346	454

On 6 February, the regiment reported the personnel strength as above.[6]

The main body of the *21. Panzer-Division* remained in the Msus area until 8 February without encountering significant enemy resistance.

The 8th Army evacuated Cyrenaica after the loss of Msus and Bengasi and taking considerable losses. It occupied positions along the western edge of Marmarica to the south of Gazala. For the British, the planned attack to retake Tripoli had failed before it had even started.

On 9 February, the *21. Panzer-Division* marched through Maraua to the north and reached the *Via Balbia* on 10 February. The division then remained in an assembly area in the vicinity of Derna for the remainder of the month. *Generalmajor* Böttcher transferred acting command of the division to *Oberst* von Bismarck on 18 February.

Replacements—very young and still insufficiently trained—arrived to the division in several march groups. The deficiencies in weapons and combat training were intensively targeted. There was also time to present deserving soldiers with awards. In addition to the well-known awards, such as the Iron Cross, the Armor Assault Badge and the Wound Badge, soldiers of the regiment also received Italian awards for the first time—for example, the Italian Bravery Medal (awarded in silver to *Oberleutnant* Grün, for instance) and, above all, the Italian Africa Commemorative Medal.[7]

The cooperation between the German and Italian formations was more intense in the North African theater than anywhere else and more publicly acknowledged. As thanks and recognition for the achievements of the German soldiers,

who bore the main burden of the fighting, and in order to visibly demonstrate the commonalities of the two nationalities, the Italians established the Remembrance Medal for the Italian-German campaign in Africa. In the jargon of the German troops, it was referred to disrespectfully as the "Orange Order," the "Sardine Order," the "AM medal," the "*Avanti* Order" or the "Sandstorm Order." The first medals were presented to soldiers of the regiment on 19 January 1942. Not every soldier in Africa received the award automatically. The award conditions specified a longer period of time in the African theater of war.

Obverse of the medal (approximately three times larger): The bronze medal had the *Arco dei Fileni* triumph arch in its center. To the right was the German swastika with the Italian fasces on the other side. To the bottom was a figure-eight knot, symbolizing the inseparability of the brothers-in-arms.

6. Author's Note: Aberger, 182.

7. Author's Note: Aberger, 183.

Reverse of the medal: Two armored warriors, recognizable as a German and an Italian by the shape of their respective helmets, pull the teeth out of the symbolic British crocodile. The ribbon for the medal contained the colors of the two states: green, white and red for the Italians and black, white and red for the Germans. The common element—red—was in the middle of the ribbon. The medal was worn on the uniform in the form of a ribbon bar on the left breast.

At right are certificates for the award of the Italian Commemorative Medal. It was issued in two European standardized sizes, DIN A5 (top) and DIN A4 (bottom). The more elaborate award certificate has the signature of *Hauptmann* Otto-Friedrich von Senfft zu Pilsach, who had been awarded the Knight's Cross to the Iron Cross as an *Oberleutnant* on 27 June 1941, while serving as the company commander of the 4th Company. In January 1942, he was the acting commander of the regiment's 1st Battalion.

During the night of 27–28 February, the *21. Panzer-Division* relieved the *15. Panzer-Division* in the Tmimi position. *Panzer-Regiment 5* occupied an assembly area as the divisional reserve.

Major Mildebrath, who had been the acting commander of the regiment since 25 November 1941, turned over command to *Oberst* Müller on 1 March. Mildebrath, who was then soon promoted to *Oberstleutnant*, assumed command of the 1st Battalion.

The new regimental commander, *Oberst* Müller, at his command post.

During the first half of March, there were only occasional encounters with British reconnaissance elements, which felt their way forward against the Tmimi position. Otherwise, it was quiet along the front.

On 14 March, the enemy took an important hill in the area between the *21. Panzer-Division* and the *90. leichte Division*. On 16 March, the *21. Panzer-Division* retook the hill. On 21 March, the enemy took an important strongpoint. On 22 March, the penetration by the enemy was sealed off and cleaned up. *Panzer-Regiment 5* played an important role in that counterattack.

During the time from April until the issuance of the attack order on 20 May, the division enjoyed relative calm. It was in an assembly area, only attacked occasionally by fighter-bombers. Once again, replacement personnel arrived and important materiel was issued, for example, tentage (to replace that lost in the winter fighting), but also armored cars, antitank guns, signals and engineer equipment and, most importantly, additional tanks.

Among the new tanks were the *Panzer III* with the longer-barreled (L60) 5-centimeter main gun, and the first *Panzer IV's* with the longer-barreled (L43) 7.5-centimeter main gun. With the arrival of the 3rd and 7th Companies, the regiment almost reached its authorized strength levels based on the table of organization and equipment (TO&E) of 1 February 1941.

Organization and Commanders of the *21. Panzer-Division,* as of 1 April 1942 (minus command & control and logistical forces)

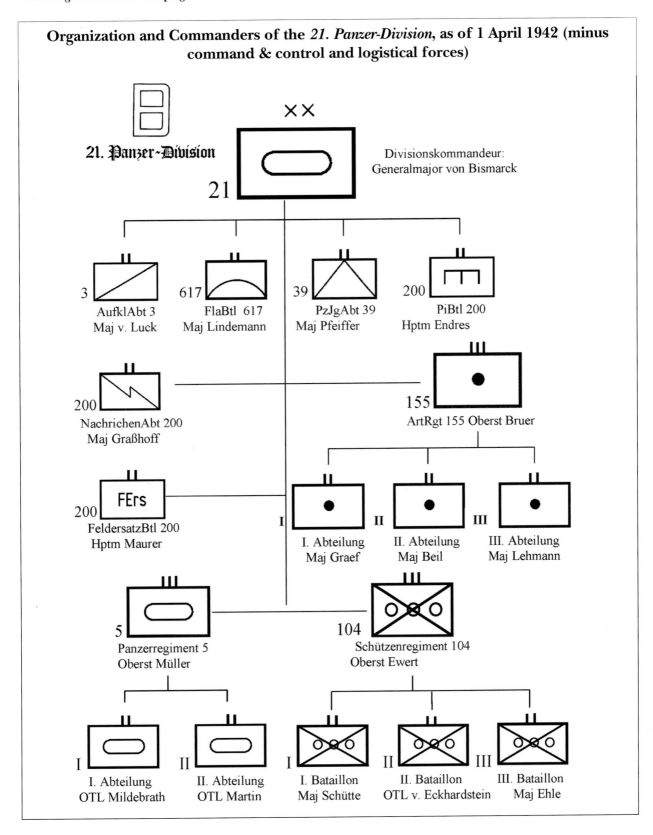

21. Panzer-Division

21

Divisionskommandeur:
Generalmajor von Bismarck

3
AufklAbt 3
Maj v. Luck

617
FlaBtl 617
Maj Lindemann

39
PzJgAbt 39
Maj Pfeiffer

200
PiBtl 200
Hptm Endres

200
NachrichenAbt 200
Maj Graßhoff

155
ArtRgt 155 Oberst Bruer

200 FErs
FeldersatzBtl 200
Hptm Maurer

I
I. Abteilung
Maj Graef

II
II. Abteilung
Maj Beil

III
III. Abteilung
Maj Lehmann

5
Panzerregiment 5
Oberst Müller

104
Schützenregiment 104
Oberst Ewert

I
I. Abteilung
OTL Mildebrath

II
II. Abteilung
OTL Martin

I
I. Bataillon
Maj Schütte

II
II. Bataillon
OTL v. Eckhardstein

III
III. Bataillon
Maj Ehle

The battalion physician of the 2nd Battalion, *Dr. Alfons Selmayr*, wrote about the time frame in his memoirs:[8]

The enemy had evacuated Cyrenaica. We pursued and went into rest positions east of Derna. From Msus, we proceeded north to the *Via Balbia* . . . Derna was bypassed to the south on the new bypass road. We encamped a few kilometers north of the road at Kilometer Marker 39 east of Derna. As was normally the case, the terrain was flat and rocky; to the south were the *dschebbel* and the airstrip at Martuba. The battalion was reconstituted. Initially, it was led by *Oberleutnant* Rocholl. The Headquarters Company [was commanded by] *Leutnant* Schorm, Signals Officer *Leutnant* Wendorff, and Adjutant *Leutnant* Schumann. The platoon leader of the light platoon was *Leutnant* Dohani. The 6th Company, *Oberleutnant* Rocholl; the 8th Company, *Oberleutnant* von Hülsen . . .

There was a small operation. Our engineers emplaced mines at Signali, and we were directed to cover them. Both of the battalions took off; I was in a staff car with an ambulance. That evening, we crossed old scenes of fighting. In one of our knocked-out tanks, there was still a driver, carbonized and half decomposed at his driver's station. A horrifying picture. We had to leave him in his steel grave . . .

Tents finally arrived. We received a large tropical tent and set it up a bit off to the side of the battalion. Our two vehicles were parked near it . . .

The new regimental commander, *Oberst* Müller, had lost his lower left arm in the campaign in Poland. A *Leutnant* Gehring arrived at the 8th Company; he had had his left leg amputated to the upper thigh. I was completely upset and told him that I thought it was inappropriate that

he was employed here, since he would never be able to use his prosthesis in the summer during a sandstorm. He didn't take offense at my comments, but he stayed. That I should later be proven right will be stated at the outset . . .

Large celebration on the occasion of the first year's anniversary for the regiment in Africa . . .

The best times for me was the daily training for my people. I was fortunate to have men who thought like me to instruct. The people were also really good and willing. Otherwise, the usual infirmary grind with immunizations, etc. A nighttime storm practically tore down our tent. *Unteroffizier* Werner and I held on to the tent poles for nearly two hours, so at least we were able to keep dry. That's how four weeks passed. Occasional, bombers would fly over us, but they only dropped bombs on the airfield at Martuba.

Broke camp and headed south through Martuba into the desert. But this time, it offered a view as in paradise. The downpours have caused it to sprout everywhere and we took up positions in a pretty meadow full of daffodils. The 5th Company went forward to an outpost line for a few days . . . Orders were received to check the entire regiment for amoebas. . . . Rocholl and Hülsen received the German Cross in Gold. We received alcohol; a big drink fest at our location, then it moved on to the Headquarters Company . . . We received a certain *Major* Martin as the new battalion commander. Instruction for the entire battalion, company by company, in first aid. I was busy the entire day, but it was all really enjoyable and the work paid off, as would later be seen . . . The preparations for the attack were completed. We received two new *Panzer IV's* with the long gun, which made us very happy. The 7th Company also finally arrived from the continent and brought a lot of medical equipment with it . . .

8. Author's Note: Selmayr, *Meine Erlebnisse im Weltkrieg 1939–1945,* 18ff.

With the introduction of the long main gun for the *Panzer IV*, that tank became the standard armored fighting vehicle of the German Army for the remainder of the war. It was more than adequate against all enemy armor employed in Africa.

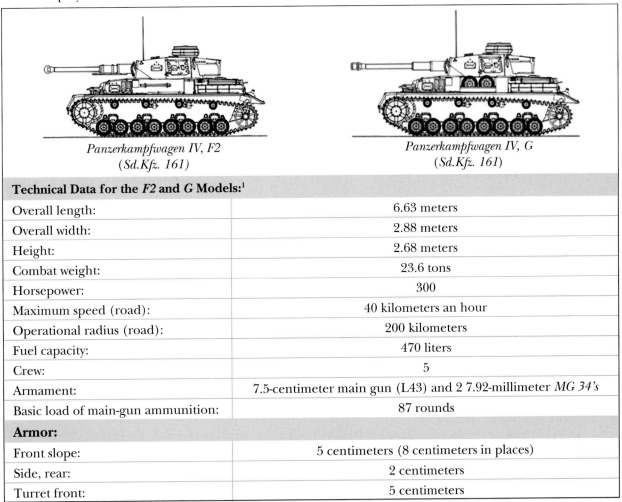

Panzerkampfwagen IV, F2
(Sd.Kfz. 161)

Panzerkampfwagen IV, G
(Sd.Kfz. 161)

Technical Data for the *F2* and *G* Models:[1]

Overall length:	6.63 meters
Overall width:	2.88 meters
Height:	2.68 meters
Combat weight:	23.6 tons
Horsepower:	300
Maximum speed (road):	40 kilometers an hour
Operational radius (road):	200 kilometers
Fuel capacity:	470 liters
Crew:	5
Armament:	7.5-centimeter main gun (L43) and 2 7.92-millimeter *MG 34's*
Basic load of main-gun ammunition:	87 rounds
Armor:	
Front slope:	5 centimeters (8 centimeters in places)
Side, rear:	2 centimeters
Turret front:	5 centimeters

In the time between January and May 1942, a total of 328 tanks were delivered to the *DAK*. Individually, they numbered: 4 *Panzerbefehlswagen III's*; 30 *Panzer II's*; 245 *Panzer III's*; and 49 *Panzer IV's*.[2]

On 25 May, just before the attack on the British Gazala Line, *Panzer-Regiment 5* had the following tanks in its inventory:[3]

Tank Type	On-hand (25 May / 8 Tank Companies)	TO&E Authorizations (1 February 1941)
Panzerbefehlswagen III	4	6
Panzer II	29	59
Panzer III (short and long main gun)	122	111
Panzer IV (short and long main gun)	19	30
Total	174	206

1. Author's Note: Senger und Etterlin, *Die deutschen Panzer—1926–1945*, 45ff.
2. Author's Note: Jentz, *Die deutsche Panzertruppe*, vol. 1, 177.
3. Author's Note: Jentz, 178.

Panzertyp	Ist-Bestand PzRgt 5 am 25. Mai 1942 mit 8 Panzerkompanien	Soll-Bestand PzRgt 5 gem. K.St.N. gültig ab 01.02.1941
PzBefWg III	4	6
Panzerkampfwagen II	29	59
Panzerkampfwagen III 5 cm kurz und lang	122	111
Panzerkampfwagen IV 7,5 cm kurz und lang	19	30
	174	206

2. 26 May to 21 June 1942: The Fighting For the British Gazala Position (Operation "Theseus") and the Capture of the Fortress of Tobruk

The British Gazala position stretched from the coast at Gazala across eighty kilometers of desert to Bir Hacheim.

Extensive minefields had been laid, some 500,000 mines in all. In between the minefields were strongpoints—the British referred to them as "boxes"—that had a diameter of between two and four kilometers. The "boxes" were manned by infantry, artillery and antitank forces. Strong armor forces were positioned east of Gazala as a reserve.

Auchinleck, the British commander-in-chief, had intended to attack and destroy the German and Italian forces from those positions in June. The British objective for the offensive was Tripoli. In the middle of May 1942, the 8th Army had 994 tanks—242 Grants, 219 Stuarts, 257 Crusaders, 166 Valentines and 110 Matildas.[9] That represented

9. Author's Note: Aberger, 191.

considerably more tanks than the Axis forces had at their disposal. With regard to artillery, the force rations were also unfavorable for the Axis forces. Despite all that, Rommel decided to beat the British to the punch with his own attack.

✠

Rommel's operation envisioned:
- frontal feint in the north with German and Italian forces, reinforced by the 1st Battalion of *Panzer-Regiment 5*;
- simultaneous envelopment of the Gazala Line in the south by the DAK, the *90. leichte Afrika-Division* and the Italian XX Armor Corps (*Ariete* and *Trieste* Divisions); and
- following that, an advance into the rear of the Gazala Line to the north in the direction of the coast, so as to cut the enemy forces in two.

A *Panzer IV* with the longer main gun advances. The main gun has been depressed, so that the longer main gun cannot be immediately identified.

The attack started on 26 May. The *21. Panzer-Division* initially reached the area around Segnali and then marched to the southeast as part of the *DAK* after the onset of darkness with the 2nd Battalion of *Panzer-Regiment 5* in the lead. The entire formation deployed in a *Flächenmarsch*, which was a shallow, rectangularly shaped formation moving on a broad front.

Around 0800 hours on 27 May, the attack formations enveloped the Gazala Line from the south. The *Trieste* Division swung inward too soon, however, and its forces bogged down in front of the British positions. In the area southeast of Bir Hacheim, the first firefights started with around 80 British tanks. During the fighting, the new commander of the 2nd Battalion, *Oberstleutnant* Martin, was badly wounded. He later died of his wounds.

The enemy was forced to pull back, and the attack was continued to the north. The *90. leichte Afrika-Division* swung to the northeast and advanced in the direction of El Adem. Until the evening of 27 May, the British conducted repeated attacks against the German attack wedges, with both sides taking considerable losses.

A three-kilometer-wide kill zone was established with eighteen 8.8-centimeter *Flak* to counter a flanking maneuver by British Grants. The *Flak* were able to eliminate the enemy threat.

An especially unpleasant surprise for the Axis forces was the appearance of the Grant, an American tank delivered to the British under the provisions of the Lend-Lease Agreement. In addition to a 3.7-centimeter secondary main gun in a revolving turret, there was a 7.5-centimeter main gun in a sponson located on the right front hull. The 7.5-centimeter gun was capable of penetrating German tanks from the front at distances up to 1,200 meters. Only the 8.8-centimeter *Flak* and the *Panzer IV* with the longer-barreled 7.5-centimeter main gun were superior to the Grant. Both were capable of knocking it out at a distance of up to 1,500 meters.

In the face of strong enemy resistance, *Panzer-Regiment 5* was able to take the high ground between the Trigh Capuzzo and Acroma by evening on 27 May. At that point, the *DAK* transitioned to the defense temporarily, oriented west, north and east. A rapid advance of the British formations east of the Gazala Line to the sea could not be executed.

On 28 May, the British formations advanced between the *DAK* and the *90. leichte Afrika-Division* to the west and cut the *DAK* off from its logistics lines of communications. As a result, the German forces in the field were in a critical situation.

On 28 May, the 1st Battalion of *Panzer-Regiment 5* rejoined the regiment from the feint it helped conduct in the north on 26 May.

During the evening hours of 28 May, the regiment reported the following tank strengths: 3 *Panzerbefehlswagen III's*, 13 *Panzer II's*, 43 *Panzer III's* (short), 8 *Panzer III's* (long), 12 *Panzer IV's* (short) and 4 *Panzer IV's* (long). That totalled 84 vehicles.[10] That meant that roughly 50 percent of the on-hand tanks of the regiment had been lost in the space of three days as the result of battle damage or for other reasons.

On 29 May, the regiment found itself in a firefight with numerically superior enemy tank forces, but it was able to claim the battlefield after knocking out 30 of the enemy's number.

The logistical situation for the German and Italian forces east of the Gazala Line remained

10. Author's Note: Aberger, 179.

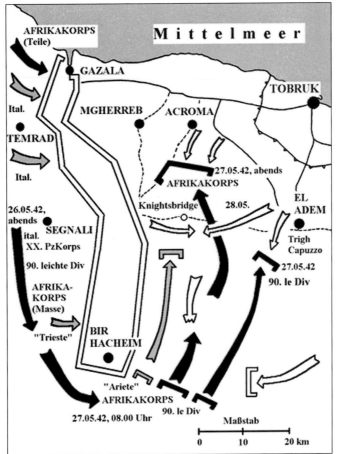

The attack on the British Gazala Line: Development of the situation from 26 to 28 May 1942.

critical and not only because the gap between the *DAK*, the *90. leichte Afrika-Division* and the *Ariete* Armor Division was dominated by British forces. In addition, the southern bulwark of the British defenses, the desert fort of Bir Hacheim, could not be taken, and the British were launching attacks on the Axis supply routes from it.

As a result, the supply columns initially had to cut a wide swath around Bir Hacheim and were exposed to enemy fires as they made their way north, resulting in painful losses in fuel and ammunition trucks.

✠

After the German forces had been forced back to the Gazala Line in the so-called *Wurst* pocket and fuel and ammunition became ever scarcer, Rommel ordered his forces to attack and break through from east to west in an effort to shorten the supply routes for his forces.

Leading the *21. Panzer-Division, Panzer-Regiment 5* attacked the Got el Ualeb strongpoint south of Sidi Muftah on 30 May. The regiment ran into heavy defensive fire. It lost 11 tanks and was turned back. The attack also failed the following day as well.

On 1 June, the *15. Panzer-Division* arrived as a reinforcement. At that point, the attack was successful. By midday, some 100 tanks and 124 guns had been captured or destroyed and around 3,000 prisoners taken. The attack punched a hole in the Gazala Line. The area that had been taken was held in the days that followed in the face of repeated enemy counterattacks. The *90. leichte Afrika-Division* was pulled back from the area south of El Adem and attacked Bir Hacheim, which was being held by a French brigade. In seesaw fighting, in which elements of *Panzer-Regiment 5* participated, the fort was taken on 11 June.

After the middle of the line had been penetrated and the southern bulwark taken, the Gazala Line

was rolled up in the days that followed in a series of individual actions. On 12 June, the main body of withdrawing British armor was defeated in fighting around the Knightsbridge strongpoint. The critical situation of *Panzergruppe Afrika* had not only been eliminated by the taking of Got el Ualeb, Bir Hacheim and Knightsbridge, but, contrary to expectations, it put the Axis forces in a decisively advantageous position.

On 15 June, the *DAK* took the roads leading from the mountains down to the coastal plain and took the enemy forces withdrawing east under effective fire. The Gazala Line no longer existed. The remnants of the 8th Army were scattered across the desert.

Since *Panzerarmee Afrika* was faced with a catastrophic situation in the course of the fighting for the Gazala Line and still achieved a notable victory in the end, closer examination of the reasons for the dramatic turn of events is necessary.

Out of a number of factors, the following stand out:

- the abilities, bravery and unbelievable combat morale—at least from a modern standpoint—of the German soldiers;
- a highly qualified officer and noncommissioned officer corps on the part of the Germans; and, above all
- the leadership abilities of the commander-in-chief, *Generaloberst* Rommel.

While the British prepared and planned their operations down to the last detail, Rommel was of a mind with Moltke in believing that no plan survives the first encounter with the enemy. Once the battle had started, Rommel allowed his plan to remain a plan and then fought based on the demands of the situation and in accordance with his tactical sense. In contrast to the enemy's troop leaders, Rommel disregarded routine and did not remain in a command post far behind the front. Instead, he went to the hot spots of the fighting and led from the front. As a result, he was able to decisively influence

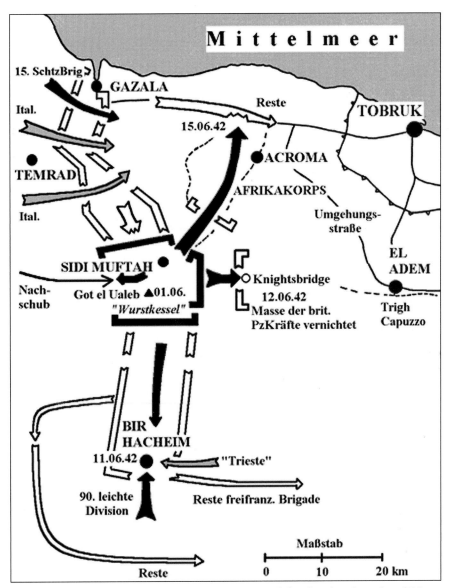

The destruction of the Gazala Line: Development of the situation from 1 to 15 June 1942.

a number of engagements and battles to his favor, because he was best able to judge the situation at the scene of the fighting, where he could determine which measures were best suited for the situation and translate his decisions into orders without delay. He was thus able to directly influence his troop elements.

The discussions concerning the advantages and disadvantages of the leadership style of this commander-in-chief continue to this day. Back then, success proved him right.

The fighting of the regiment in Africa was also chronicled by war correspondents of the time. The battle for the British positions along the Gazala Line

The commander-in-chief of *Panzerarmee Afrika*, *Generaloberst* Rommel, studies a map during an engagement.

was documented by Lutz Koch, a war correspondent with the rank equivalent of a *Leutnant*. His article, *Weg frei nach Agypten*—"Path Clear to Egypt"—appeared in the *Berliner Illustrierte Zeitung*, a Berlin-based illustrated weekly. Here are some excerpts:[11]

> On the morning of 26 May, the longed for D-Day, the heavy behemoths of our tanks moved out after weeks of quiet, which were used to good advantage for careful training. At this point, there was still no fighting. Instead, it was imperative to reach the assembly areas.
>
> "My tank regiment is as strong as it's ever been," the one-armed commander of the regiment from Brandenburg declared.[12]

His eyes lit up. They followed the proud approach of his battalions and companies. Many new tanks with new and heavy weapons were among them. The scars, which had been delivered by Tommy during the fighting withdrawal of November and December—which, in the end, only attest to the victories of our tanks—have long since been forgotten. Today, a completely outfitted regiment was moving against the enemy.

"A good thing that it's happening. We'll give it to Tommy!" The person who called that out to me was *Oberleutnant* R,[13] a recipient of the German Cross in Gold. He's a specialist in the engagement of enemy artillery positions and a terrific tank cracker, no matter how the British employ them.

The tankers are full of trust. Powerful clouds of dust, dirt and sand are raised by their tracks. They practically rise vertically

11. Author's Note: *Berliner Illustrierte Zeitung*, No. 27/1942, 394; No. 28/1942, 402ff.; and No. 29/1942, 417ff.

12. Author's Note: In the interest of operational security, commanders and formation were frequently not named. In this case, the author of the article is referring to *Oberst* Müller.

13. Author's Note: *Oberleutnant* Rochell.

to the heavens. Despite the dust clouds, the tankers laugh. Finally . . . they're advancing against the enemy, against Tommy, whom they had hunted so often before . . .

It is a captivating picture to race past the hundreds of vehicles during their nighttime approach march. Rommel's wild hunting party has taken off. The night has become a protector of our actions, enabling the enemy to be completely surprised. Compass and map, a cardinal direction of march and sharp eyes . . . that's all that that can guide us this night. As the new day dawns, we are to the south of Bir Hacheim. Rommel has reached his first objective. The master of desert fighting is leading his assault divisions around the southern anchor point of the British front and stands ready to advance into the British divisions in an attack wedge as the sun rises on the eastern horizon . . .

We move with the lead elements of the tanks to the north. The engines are at full throttle. After a short halt by our forces, the first engagement of the new Rommel advance starts at the battlefield around Bir el Harmat, which will draw us into its spell, both near and far, over the next three weeks . . .

General von B,[14] a Knight's Cross recipient from the East, pushes his way forward in his personnel carrier, which will take him to the forward-most positions over the next few days, to the regimental commander. *Oberst* M gives the last instructions to his tanks.

Oberstleutnant M[15] leads the attack of one of the battalions, while the other one is brought forward quickly so as to stand by to reinforce the attack at a later hour.

Batteries draw up close to us; heavy *Flak* is brought forward to cover the tanks, while the long and ponderous trains, hundreds of vehicles, wait impatiently to the rear. Only the vehicles of the maintenance services follow closely behind the attacking steel phalanx, so as to be ready right away in case a tank is hit and lost.

While the tanks press forward, death holds his first harvest among our ranks. Solid shot comes hissing and screaming towards us, mostly from the vehicles we see massed in front of us. They impact with a deafening roar like deceptively large rocks that constantly cascade over one another between our vehicles. The rounds land hot and threatening that miss the tanks, their course leading us, next to us . . .

While one tank after the other stops to fire in front of us, a terribly bitter fight erupts in the fortified encampment, which is one of the first of the enemy's camps. With almost the first round, the battalion commander's tank receives a direct hit from a concealed English 7.5-centimeter antitank gun,[16] a very rapidly firing *Ratsch-Bum.* The battalion commander is badly wounded; the signals officer is killed in the tank. A young company commander, *Oberleutnant* R, assumes command on the battlefield and employs his companies against Tommy, who is fighting in rare form. The enemy repeatedly attempts to draw our tanks towards the gun positions to knock them out at pointblank range. "We have to attack in the flank!" That's the order that comes over the radio for the 5th Company of *Oberleutnant*

---

14. Author's Note: *Generalmajor* von Bismarck, the commander of the *21. Panzer-Division. Oberst* M, later in the paragraph, refers to *Oberst* Müller.

15. Author's Note: *Oberstleutnant* Mildebrath, the commander of the 1st Battalion.

16. Editor's Note: This was most likely a 6-pounder (57-millimeter) antitank gun.

R.[17] The company immediately swings in that direction, takes the batteries under fire from the side and harries the enemy tanks from the flank. The battle rages for hours. The tanks slowly box their way forward—kilometer by kilometer—to the north . . .

In the face of the English tanks, vastly superior in number and attacking again and again, and the artillery, which is firing with extraordinary precision from excellent hilltop positions that offer many options around the contested terrain, it is fortunate that the tank battalion of *Oberstleutnant* M arrives in time after a forced march. After the first assault, 30 enemy tanks remain victims on the battlefield, even though he [the battalion commander] has to lead the attack against an extremely well-positioned field position that initially could not be identified.

And so our tanks attacked into the afternoon hours against enemy defenses that continued to grow ever stronger along the heavily occupied ridgelines and against a broad minefield. They break through again and the English pull back, but they close the gates behind the [German] tanks and artillery racing through and attack the elements of the rifle regiment and the trains elements that have been brought forward.

On this first day, Ritchie has lost more than 100 tanks, but our losses are also not inconsiderable against an enemy that is fighting tougher than ever before, because he knows that Tobruk and much more hang in the balance.

But Rommel also knows his divisions. He trusts his tankers, who move out against the enemy with tanks than he has. He puts morale ahead of numbers, and he is not disappointed. In the first difficult days of the attack, Rommel's tankers prove that they are the same men who had been at Sidi Rezegh, at Agedabia and at Mechili. They know how to fight, and they do not grumble, even when it's one against three . . .

"We're heading north!" *General* von B announced that morning. The advance to cut off Gazala from Tobruk is continued, even though the pressure from Tommy's tanks in the east continues to grow by the hour. We'll turn them back . . .

The 28th of May sees new and difficult defensive operations against the attacking English armored divisions and brigades, who are so certain of victory that they ride to their deaths in some places with open eyes . . .

On the evening of the third day of the advance, we could see the blue sea like an invitation twelve kilometers away. In front of us is the brilliant strip of the *Via Balbia*. All along the road, collections of vehicles and movements of vehicles in both directions. Vehicle after vehicle is hit under the thunder of our guns. The first round of the heavy *Flak* landed in the middle of a truck, which blew apart, splintering in a single surge of flame . . .

Rommel himself provides the example for heroic daredevilry. He leads threatened trains elements out of harm's way from a large number of approaching Tommy tanks and through minefields—even though he has few armor-defeating weapons himself—and into the protective cover of our own lines. In a few days, the combat elements of the *Generaloberst*—led by *Hauptmann* K[18]—destroy dozens of enemy tanks by means of antitank guns and *Flak*, blow apart numerous guns and take hundreds of prisoners.

---

17. Author's Note: *Oberleutnant* Riepold.

18. Author's Note: *Hauptmann* Kiehl.

A *Panzer III* in the attack. A burning British truck can be seen in the background.

Rommel then turned his attention to Tobruk. He initially awakened the impression among the British that he was going to leave Tobruk alone. The Germans conducted a feint in the direction of the Egyptian border. On 15 June, the lead elements of the *21. Panzer-Division* attacked east and, by the afternoon, were located south of El Adem. Employed on the flanks, the British strongpoint at Bir Battruna was taken by the 2nd Battalion of the regiment. On 16 June, the enemy-occupied forts and ridgelines at El Duda and Bel Hamed were taken. The next day, the *21. Panzer-Division* prepared to attack Sidi Rezegh. Enemy air attacks led to losses in personnel and materiel. Flank attacks by the enemy were turned back. On 17 June, Sidi Rezegh fell. The tank regiment, together with *Panzerjäger-Abteilung 39*, was able to turn back British immediate counterattacks.

The next attack objective was Gambut, with its air strip and extensive supply depots. On the evening of 17 June, *Oberst* Müller was personally ordered by Rommel to attack Gambut.

At that point, the regiment had 3 *Panzerbefehlswagen III's*, 10 *Panzer II's*, 30 *Panzer III's* (short), 9 *Panzer III's* (long), 3 *Panzer IV's* (short) and 2 *Panzer IV's* (long).[19] That was a total of 57 armored vehicles, representing only a third of the original strength of the regiment on 25 May. Early on the morning of 18 June, the regiment, supported by the 3rd Battalion of *Schützen-Regiment 104*, took the airfield and then the town of Gambut proper. The British losses were considerable. As a result, the area between the bypass road from Tobruk to Gambut was clear of the enemy and the encirclement of Tobruk reestablished.

19. Author's Note: Aberger, 208.

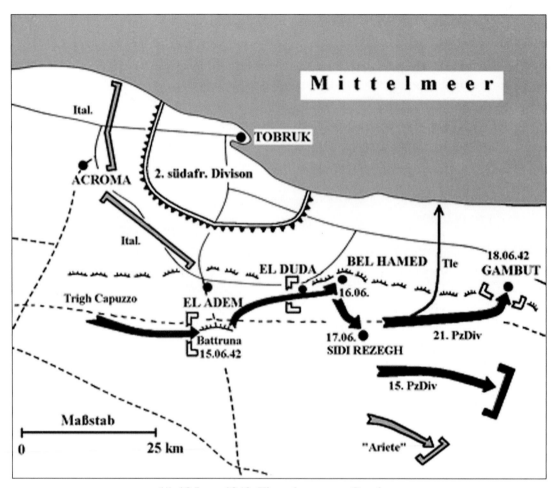

15–18 June 1942: The advance on Gambut.

Dr. Selmayr, the battalion physician of the 2nd Battalion of the regiment, wrote about his experiences in the fighting for the Gazala Line in his memoirs:[20]

It started on 26 May. Moving quickly, we took a swing to the south. A fantastic view. *Panzer-Regiment 5*, widely dispersed, the three medium companies up front, the heavy company behind. Somewhat behind it was the commander and, about 150 meters away, my non-entity. Behind me were the other vehicles of the light platoon. A short distance away, the artillery, whose observer vehicles crossed between and among us. That was followed by the division headquarters, the infantry and the combat trains, where there was also a light platoon from the medical company. The antitank companies moved along the flanks of the division. It was in that configuration that we almost always moved through the desert, not only when attacking, but also when withdrawing . . .

We encountered the first English tanks at Bir Hamat. The collision was bloody. *Oberleutnant* von Hülsen was immediately killed by a round to the head. The com-

---

20. Author's Note: Selmayr, 23ff.

mander rammed a field piece and also took one. He and his adjutant were dead . . .

Rocholl assumed command of the battalion. Right at the beginning of the fighting, one of the vehicles was hit and I was called forward. I moved up, jumped out of my vehicle and dressed the people in the open (burns). Then moved back a bit and gave the wounded over to a *Panzer II* for onward transport; moved back forward again. I had to search for a long time until I found the battalion again . . .

I ran into my ambulance. It as full of wounded and had been commandeered by the [medical] light platoon. We had been cut off to the rear. No fuel, no water, no ammunition resupply, but also no evacuation for the wounded. We captured an English brigade order that stated that no German prisoners were to be given water until they had talked. And that at 40 degrees in the shade [104 Fahrenheit]. Rommel then ordered that issuance of water to English prisoners was to stop until the [English] order had been rescinded. These gentlemen, who appear to have borrowed their humanity from elsewhere, soon came to their senses . . .

The next few days saw small skirmishes followed by hours of remaining stationary under a blazing sun. You'd almost think your head would burst in the blazingly hot iron crate . . .[21]

One time, the Tommies tried to surprise us at first light. For some reason, I did not take the alert too seriously and was really shocked when I saw enemy tanks approaching as I was in the process of folding up my blankets. But our tanks were more on the ball and, in the

blink of an eye, thirty-five tanks were knocked out. Wherever you looked, you saw knocked-out tanks. Later, we knocked out another three tanks, and I took the crews, which were running around the desert helplessly, aboard my tank. We ran into an English troop transporter that had been blown apart by a high-explosive round. A horrible picture. Badly wounded, ripped off limbs and dead and, between and among them, cans of preserves. My people were no slouches; they immediately began to collect the cans. That disgusted me so much that I forbade them from collecting and told them I would not eat anything from those cans. But two hours later, the peaches from a can tasted really good; it was only afterwards that they told me where the can had come from . . .

I went back with one of our youngest soldiers, who had been badly burnt. It was very moving how he told me about his grandmother and his home area, neither of which he would ever see again . . .

Attack on Gambut. A wild firefight, then we stopped in front of a minefield, in which a tank from the 1st Battalion had already driven. I was busy on my tank, when there was a terrible crash, a large column of smoke and dirt and then the call: "Doctor up front!" Riepold and another officer had been hit by shrapnel from mines. Riepold's face was peppered with shrapnel; one, about the side of the nail on a small finger, had wounded the carotid artery. Before I could do anything, he was dead. Once more, one of our best one was dead; we buried him at the cemetery at Gambut . . .

On 19 June, the *DAK* received orders to attack the British fortress of Tobruk. It was directed that

---

21. Author's Note: Selmayr's vehicle was a *Panzer II*. It bore the turret number *II/05*.

the attack take place from the southeast, with the main effort on the right in the sector of the *21. Panzer-Division.*

Early in the morning of 20 June, the elements of the rifle regiment and the engineer battalion that were up front occupied their assembly areas. That was then followed by an air attack by 80 *Stukas* and 100 bombers. Right after the first wave of aircraft had departed, the supporting fires from the artillery commenced on the designated narrow sector. That was followed by a second wave of aircraft, which attacked the enemy bunkers. At 0600 hours, the riflemen and engineers moved forward. By 0700 hours, the first British prisoners had been taken; the riflemen had broken into the enemy positions to a depth of one kilometer.

Panzer-Regiment 5 then launched its attack, followed by additional engineer forces, *Flak*, artillery and the remaining elements of the rifle regiment. Moving rapidly, the tank regiment soon reached the attack spearheads, which were far to the front. They then continued the attack through and past the motorized riflemen. The tanks advanced to Tobruk's eastern air strip. A threat from the flanks from Fort Solaro was eliminated by the *15. Panzer-Division*, which was also able to take Fort Pilastrino.

Soon, there was no longer any cohesive defense being put up in the sector of the *21. Panzer-Division.*

Just before 1800 hours on 20 June, the first tanks of the regiment entered Tobruk proper and advanced to the harbor. Several small boats attempted to put out to sea. Six of them were sunk, as was a gunboat in the harbor.

At 1900 hours that day, *Generalmajor* von Bismarck, the division commander, reported the capture of the city and its harbor.

The successful attack was continued west the next day into the depths of the fortified zone. With *Panzer-Regiment 5* in the lead, the division advanced through the western edge of the fortification zone.

At 0940 hours that day, the fortress commander, Major General Klopper, the commander of the South African 2nd Infantry Division, surrendered his command and its 33,000 soldiers.

For the first time, an armored corps had taken a strong fortress by means of a surprise attack, aggressively led. In the process, the *Luftwaffe* had worked perfectly with the forces on the ground and contributed greatly to the attack's success. Large quantities of fuel, rations, equipment of all types, vehicles and weapons were captured by the Axis forces, thus creating vital prerequisites for the continuation of the offensive into Egypt. *Panzer-Regiment 5* even received a number of captured operational tanks.

20 June 1942: Elements of the *21. Panzer-Division* follow *Panzer-Regiment 5* during the attack along the mountain ridgeline in the direction of Tobruk.

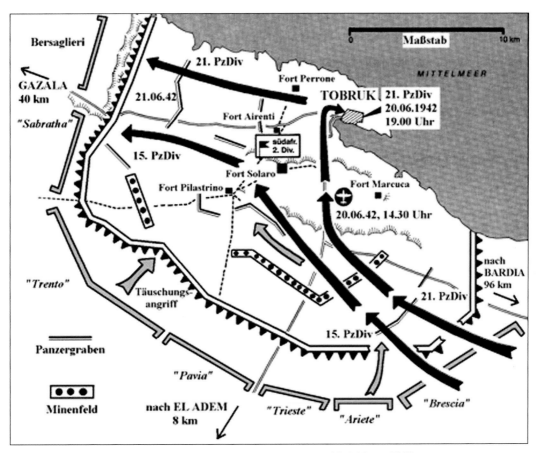

The conquest of the Tobruk Fortress on 20–21 June 1942.

On 21 June, *Panzerarmee Afrika* released the following order-of-the-day:[22]

Soldiers!

The major fighting in Marmarica reached its crowning point with the rapid taking of Tobruk. In all, more than 45,000 prisoners were taken; more than 1,000 tanks and almost 400 guns were destroyed or captured. Through your incomparable bravery and toughness, you have delivered blow after blow to the enemy in hard fighting over the last four weeks. As the result of your offensive spirit, the enemy has lost the core of his field army—most of all, his strong tank forces—which had been poised in front of us to attack. My special recognition goes out to the leadership and the troops for their magnificent performance.

Now it is imperative to completely destroy the enemy. We do not want to rest until we have defeated the last elements of the 8th Army. In the coming days, I ask great efforts from you again, so that we can reach our objective.

/signed/ Rommel

22. Author's Note: Kühn, 136.

How did the average tanker experience this round of fighting for Tobruk? *Dr.* Kurt Wolff, a *Leutnant* in the tank regiment, wrote down him impressions on 23 June (excerpts):[23]

The desert stretches in front of our eyes—yellow, glimmering, immeasurable—and our main guns point to the east again. The wire fence of the Egyptian border is not too far ahead of us, which we will move through tomorrow. Every day is a new revelation. My men lay under the tanks and sleep. We have two difficult night marches behind us, and my eyes burn from the clouds of dust and dirt that the tracks kick up.

But I will never forget the 19th of June 1942, the evening before the 20th, the day we entered Tobruk late in the afternoon and, while the sun sank red in the west, we sank fleeing English ships. That had been a fight that none of us had ever dared to dream.

On the afternoon of 19 June, our commander moved with the *General* as far as the area right outside the fortress.[24] There wasn't much to reconnoiter—the desert contains no points of orientation—but attack sectors were assigned, assembly areas allocated and, at the same time, the magic of the day to come was conjured up through this and that statement. When the tank leader called his officers to the large English map of Tobruk afterwards and, in the evening twilight—Lilli Marlene was just starting to sing her sad song in Belgrade—

explained the situation and the intent to take Tobruk in a few plain words, no one had any questions.

We wrote one more letter to Germany on that evening of the 19th. Around 0200 hours, early on the morning of 20 June, the riflemen began to advance into the outer attack terrain under the protection of batteries that had been brought forward. They moved forward more rapidly than had been assumed, if only advancing step-by-step. When they reached the first broad tank ditch, which the English had dug along a length of twelve kilometers, the sun was in the process of rising.

At that moment, the engineers moved forward. Even the heavy artillery fire from the concrete bunkers in front of the fortress could not hold up the men, who removed the wire obstacles, leveled the banks of the ditches with heavy charges and thus created a path for the tanks. A short while later, we marched through the broad English minefields and across the ditch and penetrated into the actual fortification zone.

What a picture as the tanks advanced in a long column behind the radiantly rising sun and slowly spread out. The rattle of machine-gun fire echoed across the battlefield; the *Flak* went into position off to the right. To the left behind us, the light artillery pulled up; the main guns thundered.

I almost forgot one thing: the moment when the *Stukas* appeared above us. While the engineers created gaps in the mine obstacles and the riflemen continued to advance, the gray birds swooped down from their blue heights, and we observed

---

23. Author's Note: *Dr.* Kurt Wolff, *"Wir nahmen Festung, Stadt und Hafen Tobruk."*

24. Author's Note: *Oberstleutnant* Mildebrath (battalion commander) and *Generalmajor* von Bismarck (division commander).

as we stood on the cupolas of our fighting vehicles how the bombs plowed up one fortress work after the other. Few escaped from the chaos that broke over them. Once the *Stuka* attack was over, the spell was broken and the tank commander issued his attack order. We then crossed the first part of the fortress and were in front of the second tank ditch faster than we would have thought possible. Our companies overran enemy battery and antitank-gun positions while they were still reeling from the attack of the German aviators, and knocked out several heavy English tanks that had threatened our flanks. They burned brightly and showed the following riflemen the path of our attack.

Finally, the smaller fighting vehicles following behind our first wave started collecting the prisoners, whose dull, empty eyes showed what kind of hell they had escaped.

The second tank ditch could be crossed without a great deal of preparation on the part of the engineers. The general was driving the attack of the division forward so rapidly that the batteries following us barely had a chance to get off a salvo against the enemy batteries blocking our route, before they had to limber up again and move out. The heavy *Flak*, the platoons of antitank guns and the artillery raced behind us, in the open and without cover. No one was thinking about covered positions, everyone had only one thought: Stay forward!

The spirit of the attack had gripped everyone so thoroughly, and the thought of Tobruk let them forget everything else—even their lives—that the attack more resembled an assault as opposed to a deliberate attack against a fortress. In my mind's eye, I can still see the *Oberleutnant* of the heavy cannon battery following us, as he stood on his prime mover and, disregarding the hacking English machine-gun fire, directed the fires of his guns on the enemy bunkers.

When I went to him one time to ask for his support against an especially difficult English position, he and his battery moved up front to the forward line of tanks and fired so well, so damned good, that the two tanks companies moving on the left could no longer contain themselves and took the last, decisive fortification in a *coup de main*.

The desert around Tobruk is some of the most desolate of Libya. The sun burned and the men sat in the tanks, soaked in sweat, covered in dust, dirty, greasy—only their eyes shone in their faces. No one was really sure: Was this the beginning? Was this the first major decision?

A few knew that we were in the area which we had been directed to reach in the course of the first day of the attack. Almost no one knew how much the hard fighting of the previous weeks had shaken the English divisions. We were finally harvesting the fruit of the previous, difficult days and harvesting it in this most decisive of all battles.

It was not quite noon when the white ribbon of the *Via Balbia* shone in front of us. Amazed and shaken at the same time, the tankers looked at the almost legendary road, which was supposed to take us into the middle of the objective. It did not matter what the kilometer markers said or what was to come, since once we reached the road, the end must be near.

The fighting continued. Initially, the tanks were unable to make any forward progress, since they were receiving antitank-gun fire from the flanks that blocked the route. The advance had moved so rapidly that the commander had to stop his companies and wait until all of the forces arrived whose support was needed for the success of such an ambitious undertaking. The commanders of the artillery battalions came forward with their artillery observers; the commanders of the attached *Flak* batteries were briefed. Antitank guns were emplaced on the wings. I had never experienced anything that was so dependent on chance.

There were mines in front of the road; they were bypassed to the right. Enemy batteries were positioned behind a ridgeline behind the *Via*. They were eliminated. When a few enemy tanks appeared off to the left in front, our heavy company, which was a little farther back in reserve, moved forward and drove them back and to the west after sending a few of them up in flames. The fighting certainly lasted more than an hour, but you lose all sense of time in war. When the sun had reached its apex, the tanks rolled on the famous Libyan road towards the northwest and towards the long-sought-after objective.

The general was up front. In the course of the day, his voice had grown hoarse and fragile; so much had assailed him, he had had to issue so many orders.

Shells burst all around and the engines of the tanks howled. You had to shout to be understood. The advance had not been planned so far forward; meter by meter, almost every movement had to be identified and ordered. Minefields bordered the road

on the left and right. Then the broad plateau of the airfield of Tobruk appeared off to the right and the tank battalion was sent off in the direction of that decisive objective. That was open country.

But our eyes were constantly being deceived. In front of the high ground of the airfield, there was a broad depression, in which vast quantities of vehicles were located. The enemy appeared to have been surprised. He had probably not considered it possible that the German tanks would advance as far as this hill. Although some British commander committed some tanks against our left wing in a desperate immediate counterattack, they pulled far back after the 2nd Company had knocked out four of them. In the meantime, the English had set the thousands of vehicles in the depression on fire; a gigantic cloud of smoke hovered over the blue Mediterranean skies.

The cannon battery had moved aggressively up to the road. The observer stood on one of the high English observation towers, which had been in British service two hours ago. They directed the fire of their guns into the middle of the giant mass of vehicles. I have seldom seen artillery fire with such precision in the middle of enemy fire.

The tanks then advanced in the direction of Tobruk. Many narrow *wadis* appeared, which were difficult to move through, but the company commanders basically acted on their own. For periods of time, the entire battalion was scattered; there was scarcely any contact between the platoons. But it then continued its cohesive attack after a few minutes in a broad formation. The enemy tanks, on the other hand, just continued to pull back. We were already in the midst of the English trains vehicles, shot up or burnt out. No one counted the vehicles, no one counted the abandoned guns, no one counted the prisoners. The tanks had to continue forward. The confusion of the enemy was our success.

We slowly took the high ground of the airfield. The enemy then assembled his last remaining artillery forces and attempted to destroy the advance with final concentrated fires. The garish muzzle flashes of the batteries formed a seemingly endless front. Should we run up against them there?

Our own batteries helped us without receiving orders to do so. It was especially the heavy cannon battery that once again helped out decisively. It received additional ammunition during the last few minutes and started firing as if the cannoneers were possessed by the devil, even as the ammunition vehicles were still unloading. As soon as the other heavy weapons had registered and the fires started to concentrate more and more, the enemy began to see the futility of his undertaking and started to flee for a final time, inasmuch as his guns and limbers were not destroyed. It must have been around 1400 hours when the tanks rolled across the airfield in a broad inverted wedge, and the commander reported the completion of the mission to the general.

We finally had a free hour. Talk about catching your breath! The English vehicles were burning all around and the prisoners were collected.

The tankers had known for some time that they had moved past a large rations dump and used the order to rest for half an hour to supply the tanks for a number of days with all conceivable sorts of rations. There were pears from Australia; apricots, peaches and pineapple from California; cigarettes from Egypt; chocolate from England; milk, beer, ham and mountains of corned beef. We could live for two weeks from those crates.

Camp life in the middle of the enemy. The tank that was next to me found a gramophone and played English tunes from the hit parade. Relaxed and smiling, the men sat around the small player and smoked cigarettes from Virginia.

A little while later, the general came by again. Situation brief. Maps were spread out; messengers headed out in all directions. In the meantime, the tanks got ready for combat operations again.

Afterwards, the commander summoned me and gave me the last reconnaissance mission for the day. Where is Tobruk? How far away and where is the enemy? My tank was already rolling slowly forward, passing two large burning hangers, as I folded my map together.

When I reached the high ground and, positioned up there on the crest and looking down into the plain below, I was deeply moved. And many others may have felt the same emotions when I gave my report to the battalion waiting impatiently behind me: In front of me—distance: 3,000—city and harbor of Tobruk!

The combat forces of the Axis had spent a long half a year in front of Tobruk. We had run up against that bulwark again and again in vain. The enemy was able to turn back the attacks with a laugh from his impregnable positions. No German soldier had ever heard more than the name of this city. Initially, it appeared like a mirage in front of me, and it would have been easy for my eyes to glaze over and my heart to stop for a while when I thought about that past year and now this day!

There was no more stopping us. The forces of the division were organized; the general issued his orders. The tanks rolled out again.

There was a road that led into the city from the south. One of our tanks was knocked out on it right at the very beginning. But we bypassed the city in a wide arc and, moving across hills and through valleys, the battalion rolled and rattled against the city from the west. There were antitank-gun positions and batteries along the route of advance that were overrun. Coastal batteries and naval ships fired from the sea; the extent of the enemy's fire almost confused us, but the more we advanced, the more our own artillery was able to be effective and the enemy succumbed to the momentum of the attack. The arc we traced must have been about five kilometers before we were at the first houses of the city, bright eyed, and entered the city, firing.

It was *Leutnant* P who was fortunate to be the first one to move into Tobruk. A roadblock first had to be eliminated before three tanks rolled along the harbor road as far as the exit. Behind them were the commander and the entire battalion.

Tobruk! Tobruk! As had been the case at Abbéville, there was something that crowned the fighting with burning fire after all the wonderful things of the day: Remnants of the garrison had fled onto boats in the harbor and attempted to escape that way. They had not counted on the German tanks.

As soon as the fields of fire were clear, the tank main guns barked at the English ships. And even while the trail tanks advanced slowly to close up with everyone else, the first two transporters were burning ahead. One cannon boat sank in the harbor. When all of the main guns of the tanks were finally aiming out into the harbor and heavy *Flak*, which had advanced directly to the harbor, joined in firing from the other side, only a few ships were able to escape to the open sea through the thick fog that they were firing. The fires from six boats glowed in the evening twilight that gradually settled. The rear portion of the harbor, where a tanker had been set alight, was a giant mass of flames.

A short while later, the battalion assembled in an open area in the city.

The riflemen had closed up. Antitank forces screened along the roads; the general set up his quarters in front of the Mussolini School and issued his last directives for security for the night.

What a night! Our commander had his birthday that day. We assembled around the command tank and drank Scotch in the shimmer of innumerable fires. To our left, a gigantic oil depot was on fire. The English had set it on fire themselves. The red light flickered in our faces, which were dirty and full of oil. Only our eyes continued to gleam.

What a night! And what a day! Tobruk, which the *Afrika-Korps* had struggled so hard to take, was in our hands! Fire all around . . . burning ships . . . but the circled wagons of a tank battalion in the middle, a tank battalion that had earned the highest laurels.

Someone talked about the previous year. Dead men stood next to us. Pale, but living nonetheless. Who wanted to be sad on such a day? We had decided a battle; victory was in our hands now.

Everyone thought of his homeland. We were so far away, and yet the longing united us more intimately than the reality. Later, the moon rose. The sky rose even higher. We sang our national anthem from our hearts.

After Tobruk was taken, the "Rommel boxes" behind the turrets were filled with rations. A *Panzer IV* of the 1st Platoon of the 4th Company, the "heavy" company.

3. 21–30 June 1942: From Tobruk to El Alamein

By late afternoon of 21 June, the *21. Panzer-Division* was already marching along the *Via Balbia* in the direction of Bardia. That evening, it had reached an area fifty kilometers east of Tobruk. That same evening, the Armed Forces Daily Report announced that Rommel had been promoted to *Generalfeldmarschall*. Walter K. Nehring, the commanding general of the *DAK*, was promoted to *General der Panzertruppen*.

Rommel wrote:[25]

> We had achieved the victory at Tobruk by harnessing all of our strength, since the weeks of extremely heavy fighting against an enemy superior in both personnel and materiel had also not gone unnoticed on my formations. But now the gigantic spoils of war in ammunition, fuel, rations and materiel of all types made it possible to outfit the forces for an additional offensive thrust.—That reinforced me in my decision to exploit the British weakness after the Battle of Tobruk and to advance as far as possible into Egyptian territory.

On 22 June, the *21. Panzer-Division* changed its direction of march. It left the *Via Balbia* and advanced south. During the night of 22–23 June, *Panzer-Regiment 5* set up all-round defensive positions in the desert west of Sidi Omar. The division then moved in a *Flächenmarsch* to the area south of Sidi Omar so as to turn in the direction of the Libyan-Egyptian frontier from there. During the afternoon of 23 June, *Panzer-Regiment 5* defeated British strongpoints along the Egyptian boarder. The headquarters of the 2nd Battalion moved back to Tobruk so as to organize the integration of repaired tanks that were being returned.[26] After night had fallen, the division was already forty kilometers deep into Egyptian territory.

25. Author's Note: Kühn, 138.
26. Author's Note: Selmayr, 32.

32

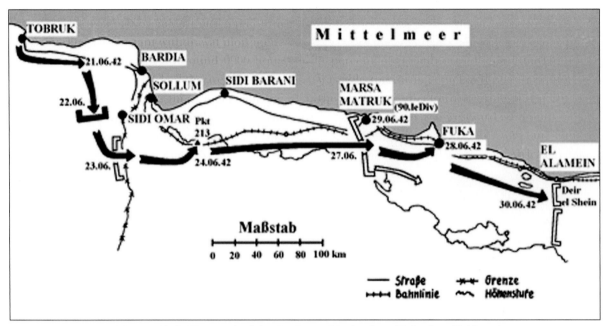

21–30 June 1942: The attack of the *21. Panzer-Division* from Tobruk to El Alamein.

On 24 June, British supply depots were taken at Point 213 along the desert railway from Marsa Matruk (Mersa Matruh) to Sollum. Large quantities of fuel, ammunition and rations could be captured. Most of the wheeled vehicles of the *21. Panzer-Division* consisted of captured vehicles by then, with the result that during the continued advance, there were constant errors on both sides concerning friend or foe. The rapid advance of the division was brought to a temporary halt on 26 June south of Marsa Matruk. On 27 June, the division penetrated enemy positions. A counterattack conducted by approximately forty British tanks was turned back by *Panzer-Regiment 5*. Strong enemy forces were encircled, but most were able to break through the encircling forces the following night and escape to the east. On 28 June, the division continued to advance east. The taking of Marsa Matruk, which had been transformed into a strongpoint, was left to the *90. leichte Afrka-Division*, which was following. By that evening, *Panzer-Regiment 5* had reached the airfield at Fuka. In cleaning up around the airfield, more British supply depots

with fuel, ammunition and rations were captured. The division advanced as far as the coastal road and blocked it. During the afternoon of 29 June, the division continued its attack in the direction of El Alamein from Fuka.

On 30 June, the tank regiment was southwest of El Alamein and reported the following tanks as operational: 1 *Panzerbefehlswagen III*, 1 *Panzer II*, 15 *Panzer III's* (short), 6 *Panzer III's* (long) and 1 *Panzer IV*.[27] That was a total of 24 armored fighting vehicles, or only 14 percent of the force strength on 25 May. In addition to the losses sustained through battle damage, losses due to mechanical problems also increased. Insufficient maintenance as the result of daily marches and combat actions, as well as the extreme weather conditions and the difficult terrain, all extracted their toll.

In the span of only ten days, the regiment had covered nearly 600 kilometers of desert. Considering the difficult terrain and the enemy situation, it was an extraordinary achievement. General Auchinleck,

27. Author's Note: Aberger, 227.

The commander-in-chief of *Panzerarmee Afrika*, *General-feldmarschall* Rommel, and the commanding general of the *DAK*, *General der Panzertruppen* Nehring.

Summer 1942: A signpost pointing to the command post of the *21. Panzer-Division*.

the commander-in-chief in the Mideast, had assumed personal command of the 8th Army from General Ritchie. He ordered the establishment of a 65-kilometer-long defensive front from El Alamein in the north and the impassable Qattara Depression in the south. The sector was criss-crossed by *wadis* and, correspondingly, restrictive terrain for armored forces. In that last line of defense outside of Alexandria, the British emplaced numerous bunkers, surveyed artillery positions, and set up wire obstacles and minefields. The withdrawing British forces assembled along the blocking position. The Commonwealth withdrawal movements were effectively supported from the air, and the Royal Air force was especially effective in engaging the supply columns of the Axis forces with low-flying aircraft. The British fighters carried bombs for the first time, signaling the birth of the fighter-bomber. Rommel had the following forces at his disposal outside of El Alamein: 2,000 infantry, 55 armored fighting

vehicles, 15 armored cars, 77 guns of all calibers and 65 antitank guns.[28]

The distance from El Alamein to Alexandria was about 100 kilometers. With shortened lines of communications, the British resistance stiffened considerably. *Panzerarmee Afrika* was in desperate need of reinforcements. But few convoys were reaching Africa at the time. In June, Rommel's forces received only 3,000 tons of the necessary 600,000 tons of logistics. The *Luftwaffe*, with its meager forces, was not in a position to accomplish three missions at the same time: suppress Malta; protect the convoys across the Mediterranean; and support the forces on the ground. The planned air landing on Malta—*Unternehmen "Herkules"*—was abandoned. The main effort of the supreme German command was unmistakably the Eastern Front, which demanded all of the Germans' attention.

Despite the enemy's materiel superiority, Rommel ordered an attack.

28. Author's Note: Piekalkiewicz, *Der Wüstenkrieg in Afrika 1941–1943*, 206.

4. 1–27 July 1942: The First Battle of El Alamein

The first attack on the British positions started on 1 July. Around 0700 hours, the *21. Panzer-Division* encountered the strongpoint of Deir el Shein, which was occupied by an Indian brigade. The strongpoint was taken by the afternoon, but the attack then stalled in the face of British artillery fire.

On 2 July, a critical situation developed when the New Zealand 2nd infantry Division counterattacked. The New Zealanders broke through the positions of the *Ariete* Division, which lost almost all of its tanks, and attacked the *DAK* in the right flank. The objective of the British counterattack was to advance through Deir el Shein towards the coast and then west, so as to cut off *Panzerarmee Afrika* from its logistical lines of communications. *Panzer-Regiment 5*, working closely with riflemen and antitank forces, was able to turn back the British forces, inflicting heavy losses on them.

Although the *DAK* and the *90. leichte Afrika-Division* were able to take back terrain by 3 July, they were unable to achieve the decisive breakthrough to the coast east of El Alamein.

On 4 July, *Panzer-Regiment 5* reported it had only 63 percent of its authorized personnel end strength of 2,443 men. *Schützen-Regiment 104* had shrunk to only 37 percent of its authorized strength.

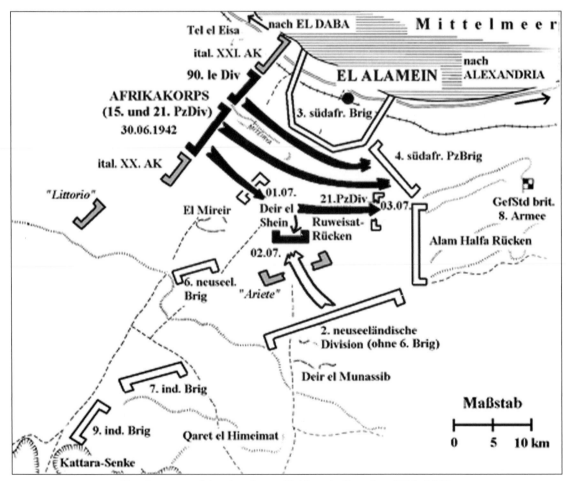

Development of the situation at El Alamein from 1 to 3 July 1942.

While the overall situation can be portrayed in a few sober words, what went on in terms of personal experiences can only be relayed by firsthand accounts, such as the one by *Dr.* Kurt Wolff, who was the adjutant to the commander of the 1st Battalion at the time, *Oberstleutnant* Mildebrath. Here are the events of 2 July (excerpts):[29]

That's a gigantic organization, a tank regiment. Over there are ammunition columns—and a few of them have been shot to pieces up front in the firefights—over there are fuel columns heading forward . . . field kitchens and rations trucks try to find their tank companies by following the tank tracks. Finally, and most importantly, the maintenance sections move forward when it starts to turn twilight and the enemy can no longer observe the terrain: men who look after the engines, get carburetors working again, mount springs and roadwheels, change out track, repair main guns and machine guns. There's a lot of hammering and, most likely, some cursing in the cold night. But when the sun rises out of the morning mist, the regiment rolls again: slowly, placidly, yet irresistibly.

There are a thousand other things that run together before a battle has been won. I see the long columns move forward on the black coastal road under the yellow moonlight. Occasionally, when the English bombers race in, they swing off to the sides, but then move on out again: forty or fifty kilometers an hour on their tachometers . . . water, fuel, ammunition resupply. Everything in motion . . . forward . . . and the darkest night is no different than the hottest, most glowing day.

But the best part is the attack! Dear God, when I think about the 2nd of July, my eyes start to burn! Just in our area alone, there were more than 100 tanks: knocked out, burning, like a huge pilgrimage of steel giants! And the day started that could cause you to despair! The maintenance company, which was sixty kilometers to the rear, had moved the barely mobile tanks to the road so as to perhaps still hold up an English breakthrough.

But the German tanks! Our magnificent, wide, rumbling tanks! We are still secretly proud that everyone calls for us whenever the danger is the greatest! Tank . . . tanks . . . up front!

During the night, New Zealanders entered the sector of the friendly forces to the right. How many? No one knew. The hedgehog was drawn tighter; two men were put on guard on each tank—one at the weapons, one outside with a submachine gun, straining his ears and staring into the night. The moon went down early; you couldn't see twenty meters in front of you.

I was next to the commander on the ground for a long time. The messengers and couriers next to me; the telephone that connected us to the division. Would the New Zealanders also attack us? Occasionally, English fighters and bombers appeared and illuminated the countryside near and far with parachute flares. Were they trying to show their own forces the way? Far to the rear, in the area of the trains, the long sticks of bombs were falling. Initially, not a lot happened. Because the artillery was silent, however, it made us a little uneasy . . .

---

29. Author's Note: *Dr.* Kurt Wolff, *"Panzer in Afrika."*

But at 0300 hours, orders suddenly came: to the south, on the far side of the hill, which we had been familiar with for several days, an English rifle brigade had penetrated and needed to be destroyed. Immediately. Our own riflemen had been overrun; tanks were the last hope!

The companies were combat ready in a flash. The engines were warmed up; orders rang through the radios. A few minutes later, the commander organized his force. The battalion marched. It was starting to dawn. In the east was the morning star, pale, slowly being extinguished, and the ground fog which formed for a while when it was early began to move in the morning winds. Otherwise, it was quiet. Only the noise of the tanks echoed in the yellow, lifeless land . . . But hard orders in between!

And then we took the hill, which was off to our right, slowly and carefully. There was no sun yet, but there was light. A short while later, when the patrols reported English vehicles at 1,200 meters, the gunners started to identify the targets in their optics. The fight started. The New Zealanders, who must have just gotten up, were walking around as if there were no German positions in this area. By the time they finally started to aim their guns at us, the first vehicles were burning off to the right.

The fight developed rapidly. When we had approached to within 800 meters—slowly, always covering each other, since we had often run up against previously unidentified English antitank-gun positions—we saw how to the right of us, that is, in the left flank of the surprised enemy, German antitank guns moved up and went into position. While the left-hand company knocked out

the first couple of English antitank guns, the German antitank forces opened fire, creating complete confusion among the enemy. I don't recall quite how it came about any more, but as I was in the process of knocking out an English carrier and was observing the hit with my binoculars, a high-explosive round from an American [Grant] impacted next to me. I was able to pull in my head in time, reflexively, and then I felt a small, biting pain on my right arm and saw that a little bit of blood was dripping on the shoulder of my loader. But my loader had already pulled out the first-aid box from his area, rolled up my sleeve and, two minutes later, had placed a field dressing on it. I had been lucky. A small piece of shrapnel was embedded a centimeter above my elbow.

My commander called me on the radio to ask whether something had happened to his adjutant. I had ordered my driver to stop for a minute, with the result that we hung back some. The attack was proceeding with such speed that the other fighting vehicles were already about 400 meters ahead. But I was able to close up to him, show him my small dressing with a smile, and continue to move.

What happened next was like a mirage. While one company continued to roll and attacked a few [Grants] off to the left at about 1,500 meters, the rest of the battalion moved into the English positions. Where there had previously been only a few guns, antitank guns and transport vehicles, yellow and brown Tommies started to rise from previously unseen holes . . . first 10, then 50, then 100 and finally probably about 600. They waved to us, half as a greeting, half defensively. A few ostentatiously tossed away their weapons; a few came towards us in a column. The entire New Zealand battle group surrendered, since we were already in the middle of it.

Our commander was laughing. Finally, a catch after all those long days of English artillery fire. Finally, something palpable: four burning tanks, perhaps ten shot-up prime movers, eight guns, a number of carriers, machine guns, antitank rifles . . .

The commander held up the battalion to reorganize the units and then an attack [with Grants] against the slope of a hill farther to the south. The company up front reported fourteen of them. The rounds were already starting to impact among the ranks of the withdrawing New Zealanders.

But at that moment, we received radio traffic from the division that initially caused confusion. To the south of Hill 63—that was approximately the area where we rested at night—a strong English tank brigade had broken through (that was more than 100 fighting vehicles), and the lead elements were already engaged in a firefight with *Flak* that had been posted to protect the flanks of the division . . .

We discovered later on from captured tankers that they had been given the mission to advance to the coastal road and then march on Tobruk with follow-on forces.

Our commander took in the big picture. Today, I know that it was one of his great hours. There was no longer a general there . . . no antitank gun . . . no *Flak* . . . no artillery . . . only a shrunken tank battalion that had advanced and fought from an area around Derna as far as El Alamein . . . well more than 1,000 kilometers . . . a tank battalion that had knocked out more than 250 enemy

tanks, not including a number of guns, cannon, antitank guns and carriers and now had the enemy in front of it, to its left and in its rear. An enemy, who was stronger than ever before, in a better position than perhaps at any time during the entire campaign, confident of its superiority—and despite that, the step must be taken. And it succeeded!

Initially, the battalion turned around, which sounds simpler than it was—why worry about the fact that there were twelve or twenty [Grants] to our rear? Then, platoon after platoon was pushed forward on the left and right, always with the enemy in their rear, full of uncertainty. In between there were the pressing radio messages from the division that reminded us to hurry, to advance, to attack at any price. Finally rolling—while all of this was happening and the heavy tanks were pulled back from the battlefield where they had just fought and reorganized themselves—the entire battalion fell forward and on the ridgeline with the yellow and red rising sun to its right and finally landed in such a masterful fashion—it was as if we were intoxicated—into the flank, exactly into the flank of the English tank brigade that was slowly advancing west. No more orders were needed! Since the approach had succeeded—calmly, very calmly and in a deliberate fashion, without haste and arranged . . . formed . . . ordered with cool, calm intellect—the battle could begin. No one needed to worry about the encounter. While the loaders were slamming the second rounds home in the breeches, the first fires were already rising.

The commander and I—I was at his side—breathed easier. What a picture! You have to imagine this shallow hill that runs from west to east[30] and, on the far side of that hill, running in the same direction, a depression about 800 meters wide. The English were marching in that depression and encountered our fire. The acting commander of the 4th Company knocked out seven tanks, another tanker five. Practically everyone could report two or three kills. By contrast—besides the laughable shrapnel in my arm, which I did not think about until later and which was cut out of me two days ago—we suffered two dead and two wounded. What was that compared to the more than sixty tanks that we later counted? The majority had been knocked out and set alight; the rest, who had been hit by an unexpected and virtually unseen enemy—we were behind the hill and only our main guns jutted over the top—fled and found their end in a minefield, which the tanks had probably crossed, feeling their way forward in a small lane at first light, and which now sealed their fate. An hour later, we slowly descended the hill and moved through the battlefield to the east, practically overcome by our victory, which was so visible. When we reoccupied our old security sector, as if the entire morning had never happened—the [Grants], which had initially been to our rear, had been driven off by antitank guns and a battery of howitzers—the sweat ran down our exhausted faces, but it was well earned and came after great work had been accomplished . . .

And tomorrow will be another day: hot and oppressive. You do not know how you will be able to take it. Hundreds of thousands of flies crawl around on your face; we have long since lost our mosquito nets, who knows where. The only thing left is patience.

The armor plating became glowing hot; the water was almost undrinkable. If the sandstorm comes around noon—yellow, impenetrable—the only thing left is hope . . . It is still night, and we pull guard. Tired, unwashed, greasy, faces moistened by the nightly dew of the desert. We pull guard for Germany in the middle of a star-filled African night.

✠

Under the pressure of the Axis forces, the British abandoned their strongpoints at Qaret el Abd and, farther to the south, at Abu Dweiss on 10 July.

Rommel came to the conclusion that it would be possible to break through the southern portion of the enemy's defensive line, thus causing the collapse of the British positions southeast of El Alamein. But Rommel's assessment was overcome by events when the enemy attacked the same day in the north. The enemy was able to achieve a deep penetration in the Italian sector and took the high ground around Tel el Eisa. It was only by means of a hurriedly assembled *Kampfgruppe* that the attack was interdicted.

It was intended for a counterattack to not only clear up the penetration but also take the strongpoint of El Alamein. After a *Stuka* attack and an artillery preparation by *Artillerie-Regiment 155*, the *21. Panzer-Division* and the *90. leichte Afrika-Division* moved out against the El Alamein strongpoint around noon on 13 July. British infantry, supported by armor, hit the *21. Panzer-Division* in the right flank and brought the German attack to a halt. After fending off the British attack, the division, with *Panzer-Regiment 5* in the lead, continued its advance, but the attack bogged down for good within visual range of the mosque at El Alamein. The forces of the *21. Panzer-Division* had been largely chewed up. The combat strength of the division that evening was only about 3,500 men.[31] The attack of the *90. leichte Afrika-Division* was also unsuccessful.

30. Author's Note: The Ruweisat Ridge.

31. Author's Note: Aberger, 237.

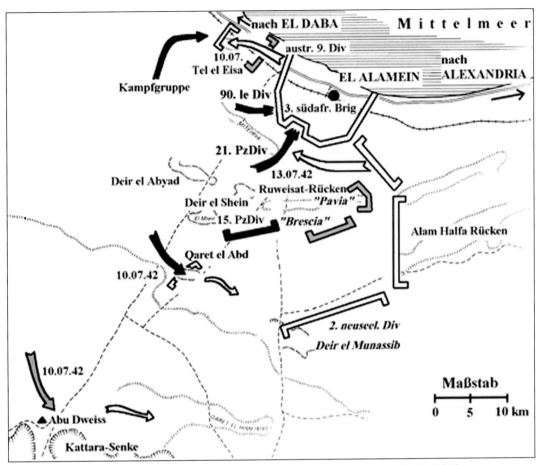

Development of the situation at El Alamein from 10 to 13 July 1942.

On 15 July, the New Zealand 2nd Infantry Division took Ruweisat Ridge in a night attack. The *Pavia* and *Brescia* Divisions took heavy casualties. A *Flak* battery was overrun at Deir el Shein. A large portion of the strongpoint at Deir el Shein, which was taken on 1 July, was lost.

On 16 July, the *21. Panzer-Division* was employed against those forces. *Panzer-Regiment 5*, together with mechanized infantry and engineers, took back Deir el Shein, but it was unable to regain the decisive Ruweisat Ridge. Around 18 July, it was temporarily quiet along the front. The Axis forces had not succeeded in breaking through the British positions and forcing a way to the Nile Delta. The German

divisions, which had been in action without a break for three months, were exhausted.

As a consequence of increased sorties on the part of the *Luftwaffe*, the supply columns of the Axis forces were able to make it through to the divisions without significant losses. Replacements also arrived. There was a distance of 400 kilometers between the fighting forces of the Axis and the closest supply dump. The route from Bengasi to the front—constantly threatened from the air—was more than 1,000 kilometers. The unimpeded supply routes of the British, in contrast, were less than 100 kilometers. A column moving from Bengasi to the front and returning needed seven or more days;

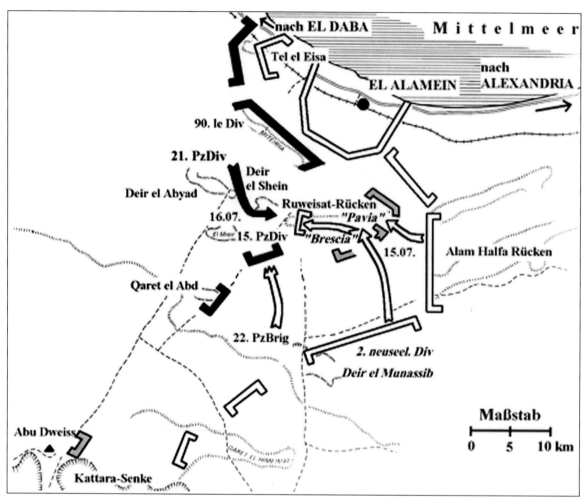

Development of the situation at El Alamein from 15 to 18 July 1942.

from Tripoli, the columns needed twice as much time, even though the trucks were driven up to 12 hours daily.

In accordance with orders from the Army High Command dated 5 July 1942,[32] all sub-elements of armored divisions were to have the term "armored" added to their designation. As a result, *Aufklärungs-Abteilung 3 (mot.)* of the division became *Panzer-Aufklärungs-Abteilung 3*. The redesignations were analogous for all of the troop elements that had not heretofore had *Panzer* as part of their designation.

32. Author's Note: Daily logs of the High Command of the Armed Forces, Volume 2/2, and Army Announce-ment 1942/No. 581, dated 5 July 1942.

Dr. Alfons Selmayr, whose firsthand account as the battalion surgeon for the 2nd Battalion of the regiment has already been quoted extensively, discusses the period of July 1942:

In the middle of July, there were so many tanks ready that we formed a battalion again. Rocholl went to the division; *Hauptmann* Grün assumed command of the 2nd Battalion. The heat grew ever more intense; it was especially unbearable at midday. Thirst became unbearable, despite doing nothing during the noon hours and despite tentage

In July 1942, *Schützen-Regiment 104* was redesignated as *Panzergrenadier-Regiment 104*, a redesignation that was analogous for all of the other troop elements of the division.

against the sun. It was only too good that we had a lot of captured tea and coffee. And the greatest plague was the flies!

About eighty people reported to sick call daily. Usually, it was diarrhea and wounds that only healed poorly, but there was also a few cases of diphtheria that appeared. Starting at 0900 hours, the flies became terrible. The dressings were only removed when the people were standing directly in front of me. But I frequently had to take the little beasts out of the wounds with tweezers, only to have them creep into our eyes and the corners of our mouths—simply disgusting. When eating bread, you always had to chase them off the topping first.

Of course, I also suffered from diarrhea. By the end of sick call, I was completely worn out. The "old Africans" among us were all complaining of pains in their chests around the area of their hearts and of heart pains. With the means at my disposal, I was unable to determine the cause, but since I knew they were all good people who were really not trying to put one over on me, I sent a few people to the internal medicine specialist in the field hospital at Marsa Matruk. They were returned immediately. Nothing found . . . During my daily rounds of the battalion during the afternoon, I also had powerful pain in the area around my heart, so that I was only able to return to my tent with difficulty . . . What was it? In my opinion, it was coronary disturbances caused by the heat that affected not only the men but also me. I could understand the men but, basically, I was powerless to act. I had no treatment; I could not send them home. The people were very reasonable. They understood my position and trusted me . . .

The rations were miserable. For lunch, bacon (captured goods), along with bread. However, the bread, which was intended for three days, started to get moldy after two days. The bacon would have been great, but there was too much fat to be able to eat it in 50 degrees of heat (122 degrees Fahrenheit). In the evening, there was *Sauerkraut* with dried potatoes, dried vegetables or beans. The latter was never received soft, that is, we placed them in water in the evening in accordance with instructions. In the morning, they were soft, but they became hard as a rock again when they were cooked . . . One time, there was supposed to be fresh meat. It turned out to be a few bones covered with a few shreds of dried, tough meat that

came from a sheep and a camel. You could only put the stuff through a meat grinder to get it to be palatable. We also received fruit occasionally, but the grapes turned bad as a result of the transport through Cyrenaica. Only the melons could be eaten.

The combat power of the 8th Army was increased by the introduction of new troop elements. The apparent weakness of the Axis forces in the El Alamein area caused General Auchinleck to launch an operation—"Lightfoot"—at the behest of Churchill. It was intended to attack Rommel's forces between Miteirija and El Mireir, breaking through the lines there and creating the prerequisites for an advance to the coast west of El Alamein and then on to Fuka and Marsa Matruk. As had been the case on 2 July, the Commonwealth forces wanted to separate the Axis forces from their lines of supply and then deny them the ability to withdraw to the west.

Operation "Lightfoot" started during the evening hours of 21 July. The infantry of the new Zealand 2nd Infantry Division encountered the positions of the *21. Panzer-Division* at El Mireir and was stopped. The Indian 5th Infantry Brigade attacked along the

Summer 1942: tank fighting in the desert. A *Panzer III* of the 1st Battalion moves past a clearing station.

Ruweisat Ridge. The 23rd Armoured Brigade of the recently introduced 1st Armoured Division (brought over from England) wanted to penetrate the positions of *Panzergrenadier-Regiment 104* between Deir el Shein and El Mireir on 22 July. *Panzergrenadier* Halm, a nineteen-year-old antitank gun gunner, knocked out seven tanks of the lead attack elements at a critical time, later becoming the first *Panzergrenadier* to be awarded the Knight's Cross (29 July 1942). At that point, *Panzer-Regiment 5* arrived. Working together with antitank forces, *Flak* and even *Stukas,* the regiment knocked out 146 British armored fighting vehicles in the fighting that followed. All of the enemy attacks were turned back.

The German losses, especially among the ranks of *Panzergrenadier-Regiment 104,* were also not inconsiderable. On the evening of 23 June, *Panzer-Regiment 5* reported 23 operational tanks—1 *Panzerbefehlswagen,* 4 *Panzer II's,* 12 *Panzer III's* (short), 5 *Panzer III's* (long) and 1 *Panzer IV.*

On 27 July, the effort by the Australian 9th Infantry Division to take the German forces in the rear in the El Miteirija failed. General Auchinleck thereupon called off the offensive. The intended breakthrough had failed and *Panzerarmee Afrika* had scored a considerable defensive success.

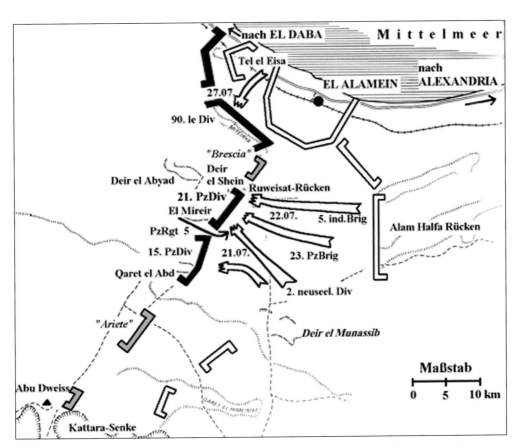

Development of the situation at El Alamein from 21 to 27 July 1942 (British Operation "Lightfoot").

On 28 July, it turned quiet all along the El Alamein front. July 1942, a bloody and event-filled month, came to an end. The series of fighting would become known as the First Battle of El Alamein. Neither side had been able to achieve a decisive success. But *Panzerarmee Afrika* had been weakened for a long time, while the British, who were able to draw from nearly limitless materiel sources, could make up their losses rapidly.

✠

In the days of quiet that followed, the Axis forces improved their defensive positions. The units and formations prepared after-action reports. In the period from May to the end of July, *Panzerarmee Afrika* completely wrote off 233 tanks. In approximately the same time period, the field army knocked out 1,388 armored vehicles. *Panzer-Regiment 5* was able to lay claim to 345 of them.[33] The *21. Panzer-Division* wrote the following about the enemy's use of armor:[34]

Enemy Armor Usage

Massed employment of large armored formations was only observed on 27 July 1942.

The enemy command is apparently still not in a position to lead armored formations in a quick and agile manner.

In general, it was observed that the enemy divided up his armored formations. The effort was noted to use tanks in the defense in greatly overlapping lines in order to get into the flanks of the attacker. It is striking how little the well-known Mark IV, V and VI tanks were employed over the last few weeks. To conduct the firefight, U.S. tanks with 7.5-centimeter main guns were generally used.

Changes and Recommendations

The larger antitank gun calibers and the range of the U.S. tanks necessitate a larger number of *Panzer IV's* (long).

The *DAK* reported on its experiences with the *Panzer IV* (long):[35]

From the very first, the 7.5-centimeter L43 main gun proved to be superior to all previously mounted tank weapons due to its higher penetrative power and precision. The armor-piercing round penetrated all British and American tank models that have been employed in Africa up to this point at distances up to 1,500 meters. Hit probability falls off at distances greater than 1,500 meters, because target acquisition is degraded by the shimmering air. Lighter tank models have been destroyed at distances up to 2,000 meters.

The enemy quickly realized that the *Panzer IV* "Special" was very dangerous. Because of its distinctive shape (longer main gun), it drew concentrated fire from all vehicles, artillery and antitank guns. It is therefore necessary to screen the *Panzer IV* "Special" with *Panzer III's*. In general, the *Panzer IV* "Special" should not be employed until valuable targets—for example, the [Grant]—appear in the fight. Flank security is especially important at that point.

---

33. Author's Note: Jentz, 182.

34. Author's Note: *21. Panzer-Division*, Operations, File 34, dated 5 August 1942.

---

35. Author's Note: Jentz, 182ff.

5. 29 August to 3 September 1942: The 2nd Battle of El Alamein (The "6-Day-Race")

General Auchinleck ordered the positions around El Alamein to be improved and expanded in depth to the east. The field fortifications in the center and northern sectors received the most attention. New British infantry and armor formations arrived in Egypt. The artillery was also reinforced. British logistical efforts went largely undisturbed.

Churchill, who was unhappy with developments in Africa, had Auchinleck relieved on 4 August and summoned General Alexander to be the new commander-in-chief in the Near East. On 13 August, Lieutenant General Montgomery assumed command of the 8th Army.

In August, two formations were sent to reinforce *Panzerarmee Afrika*: the *164. leichte Afrika-Division*, which had previously served as an occupation force on Crete as the *164. Infanterie-Division*, and *Fallschirmjäger-Brigade Ramcke*.[36] Both of those formations were not motorized and, therefore, poorly suited for employment in the desert.

---

36. Translator's Note: Airborne Brigade "Ramcke."

The German divisions, which had been in action without interruption for months, as well as the *Littorio* and *Ariete* Armored Divisions and the Italian XX Corps (Motorized), were pulled out of the line and occupied assembly areas to the rear. At the beginning of August, the eighty-kilometer front was occupied by the *164. leichte Afrika-Division*, the *Trieste*, *Brescia* and *Bologna* Infantry Divisions and *Fallschirmjäger-Brigade Ramcke*.

Rommel saw his last opportunity for success, perhaps even a thrust to the Nile Delta and the Suez Canal, by attacking by the beginning of September before the 8th Army received even more reinforcements, which made the prospects for success even more unlikely. Rommel's attack plan foresaw a thrust by the *DAK* to the east from the edge of the Qattara Depression. It would then swing north in the direction of the Alam Halfa Ridge, encircling the 8th Army. That would open the way to Alexandria. The *90. leichte Afrika-Division* and elements of the Italian corps were to conduct secondary attacks to fix the enemy and protect the left flank of the *DAK*. On 29 August, the attack forces occupied their assembly areas. The attack was scheduled for the next day.

29 August 1942: moving up for the "6-Day-Race."

On 30 August, *Panzer-Regiment 5* reported the operational tank strength outlined below, based on the arrival of new tanks and the repair of many others.[37]

---

37. Author's Note: Daily logs of the *21. Panzer-Division*, Operations, dated 12 September 1942.

The same day, *Panzer-Regiment 8* of the *15. Panzer-Division* reported an on-hand strength of 110 tanks, with the *DAK* thus having a total of 238 tanks on the day of the attack.

During the evening of 30 August, the *21. Panzer-Division*, divided into six attack groups, was guided

Panzertyp	Ist-Bestand PzRgt 5 am 30. August 1942 mit 8 Panzerkompanien	Soll-Bestand PzRgt 5 gem. K.St.N. gültig ab 01.02.1941
PzBefWg III	4	6
Panzerkampfwagen II	14	59
Panzerkampfwagen III 5 cm kurz und lang	50	111
	39	
Panzerkampfwagen IV 7,5 cm kurz und lang	7	30
	14	
	128	206

Type	On-Hand Strength (with 8 Companies)	Authorized Strength (TO&E dated 1 February 1941)
Panzerbefehlswagen III	4	6
Panzer II	14	59
Panzer III (short)	50	
Panzer III (long)	39	111 (both short and long)
Panzer IV (short)	7	
Panzer IV (long)	14	30 (both short and long)
	128	206

through lanes in the minefields that had been created by *Panzer-Pionier-Bataillon 200*. Bomber attacks and artillery fire made it clear that the enemy had identified the attack and there was to be no element of surprise.

The division commander, *Generalmajor* von Bismarck, was killed by shrapnel from bombs on the morning of 31 August, and the commanding general of the *DAK*, *Generalleutnant* Nehring, was wounded. *Generalmajor* von Vaerst assumed acting command of the *DAK*, while *Oberst* Lungershausen assumed acting command of the division.

Although the British 7th Armoured Division was driven back thirty kilometers, the terrain difficulties (long stretches of sand), the mines and the constant enemy bombing attacks considerably slowed the attack. The *15. Panzer-Division* was able to advance farther east than the *21. Panzer-Division*, and found itself to the south of the Alam Halfa Ridge.

The overall success of the attack then hinged on whether the efforts to eliminate the enemy positions along the ridgeline succeeded. There were 300 tanks positioned there, some of them dug in.

An armored attack, photographed through the vision port of a tank.

The *15. Panzer-Division* moved out to attack the ridge on 1 September, reinforced by *Panzer-Regiment 5*. They initially made good progress and a portion of the British 22nd Armoured Brigade was eliminated, but the shortage of fuel on the part of the Germans began to be felt. When it became known that the Italian supply ships with the fuel had been sunk and the promised logistical support could no longer be guaranteed, Rommel called off the attack on 2 September and ordered a withdrawal to the west. An immediate British counterattack in the sector of the *90. leichte Division* was turned back.

The Axis forces reached their original lines of departure on 3 September, six days after the start of operations.

The Royal Air Force dropped nearly 9,000 bombs during the battle, and the 8th Army lost 68 tanks. The losses of *Panzer-Regiment 5* were relatively low. On 10 September, the regiment reported: 3 *Panzerbefehlswagen III's*, 14 *Panzer II's*, 30 *Panzer III's* (short), 29 *Panzer III's* (long), 5 *Panzer IV's* (short) and 10 *Panzer IV's* (long). The largest losses had occurred among the light-skinned vehicles.

The British superiority in numbers of tanks, the British air superiority (with constant air attacks day and night), and the lack of fuel on the part of the Axis forces had all contributed decisively to the outcome of the battle. The failed effort to break through the British positions at Alam Halfa signaled the end of German and Italian offensive operations in Libya and Egypt.

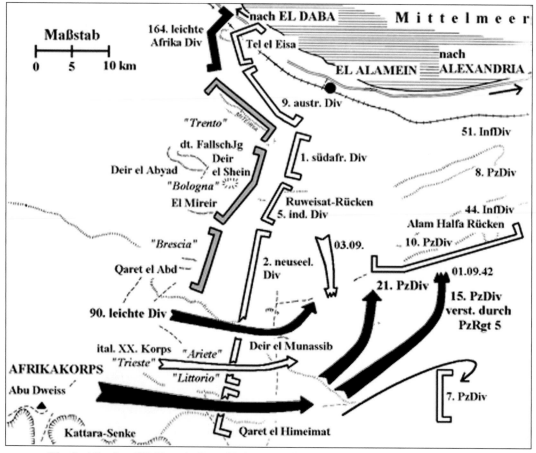

The 2nd Battle of El Alamein from 29 August to 3 September 1942 (The "6-Day-Race").

On 12 September, the *21. Panzer-Division* issued the following order-of-the-day:[38]

In addition to *Generalmajor* von Bismarck, numerous brave officers, noncommissioned officers and enlisted personnel, Knight's Cross recipient *Hauptmann* Kiehl, the commander of the *I./Panzer-Regiment 5*, was also killed

According to official records,[39] Kiehl had been awarded the Knight's Cross on 6 July 1942 as the leader of a combat element within *Panzerarmee Afrika*. He had received the German Cross in Gold as an *Oberleutnant* in the 4th Troop of *Aufklärungs-Abteilung 3 (mot.)*.

Let us hear from *Dr.* Salmayr again and his experiences during the "6-Day-Race" (excerpts):[40]

It was directed that the English El Alamein position be rolled up and the advance continued into Egypt. We were already dreaming of Alexandria and Cairo . . .

We wanted to advance into the minefields and then roll them up from the rear. The assembly areas were occupied very furtively. During the night, only one company would advance south and then prepare the camouflaged positions for the next company. The tanks were dug in deeply and covered with camouflage nets. Under the death penalty, it was forbidden to walk around in the open during the day. Final conference with the commander: go easy on

fuel and ammunition. How could that mean anything good for an attack?

We took off at night. We moved across two steep slopes and through the lanes in the minefields. As we were doing that, we were bombed. The division commander was killed. Attack against English tanks in the morning. Not a lot happened, thank God, since the new company commanders didn't have a firm grip on their guys and the radios weren't working at all. I started to doubt a good outcome for the matter. We encountered superior numbers of English tanks at a strongpoint. We raced like monkeys across a hill, down into a depression and then toward the enemy on the slope across the way. The beast were actually buried all the way up to the turrets. We were received by raging tank, antitank-gun and antiaircraft fire. By the time we looked around, several of our tanks had already been finished.

I received a call for help from the 8th Company and was in the process of moving around the 7th Company when my left track was shot off. Since everyone was pulling back and only the adjutant and the battalion commander were ahead of me, I had to dismount and abandon the tank. My tunic over my shoulder, the two medical bags in my hands, I walked back, covered by a withdrawing tank.

The enemy fire, at that point starting to include artillery, was really nice. It was a miracle that even more did not happen. I mounted the tank with the badly wounded. The tank commander, a *Feldwebel*, had lost contact and was looking for his friends in the wrong direction. I was able to straighten him out and, fortunately, we found our

38. Author's Note: Daily logs of the *21. Panzer-Division*, Operations, dated 12 September 1942.

39. Author's Note: Documents from the Army Personnel Office concerning the award of the Knight's Cross, sequence number 1,036.

40. Author's Note: Selmayr, 33ff.

badly plucked battalion. As best as I can remember, we lost eleven tanks. I mounted *II/07*.

The English air force then started to attack. We had never experienced anything quite like that before. They constantly flew past us in air-show formation and dropped their loads wherever there were even just a few vehicles close together. My tank shook in every corner. Directly in front of me, the tank of a company commander was hit right on the turret. The commander and the loader were badly wounded; both of them died later. The gunner and the radio operator had critical wounds. Other than a few field dressings, I no longer had any dressing material. My supplies had remained behind in the other tank, after all, and the dressing material I had in the bags had already been used in the morning and last night for smaller injuries and wounds. I set the wounds with shovels and camouflage material and sent the people to the rear.

But the night exceeded that which had happened previously. The "fun" lasted from nine in the evening until five in the morning. Everything was constantly lit up by parachute flares; the bombers buzzed through the poisonous skies and the bombs fell constantly. Vehicles were burning everywhere; ammunition and fuel went up in the air. My small *Panzer II* was wobbling like crazy. A nerve-wracking situation. Two men from the trains, who had come forward with rations and had sought cover under a tank, were badly wounded. When I received the call for help, the first thing I did was search out my ambulance to see whether it was still usable. We were lucky, and the evacuation proceeded rapidly.

The offensive had failed. We were stranded in the desert without fuel and exposed to the bombs. We slowly received fuel and pulled back.

After the conclusion of the 2nd Battle of El Alamein, the Axis forces took great efforts to improve and expand their own positions. Approximately half a million mines, shells and bombs were used to that end to create minefields, referred to as "devil's gardens." It was intended for the mine barriers to hold up the anticipated British frontal attack. Montgomery's eleven divisions also mined the areas in front of their sectors. The use of mines in front of the El Alamein positions was on an order of magnitude greater than anywhere else during the Second World War. The forward edge of the defensive area was to the west of the minefields, with the staging areas for the formations two to three kilometers farther west. Antitank guns and artillery pieces were dug in so deeply that only their barrels jutted over the edge of the emplacements. The armored and mechanized divisions were held back in the rear area as mobile reserves. When the enemy's main effort was identified, those uncommitted forces were then available to reinforce threatened sectors of conduct immediate counterattacks. In the middle of September, the *21. Panzer-Division* and the *Ariete* Armor Division were located in the southern sector of the front, approximately fifteen kilometers behind the front, which was occupied by the *Brescia, Folgore* and *Pavia* Infantry Divisions.

On 19 September, *Generalmajor* von Randow became the new division commander. The next day, the suspension of leaves that had been in effect since 20 May was lifted. The number of soldiers that were able to leave the North African theater of war was small, however, due to the limited lift capacity of the available transport aircraft.

Rommel's health took a turn for the worse. On 22 September, he left Africa for Germany for a few weeks of sick leave. *General der Panzertruppe* Stumme was given acting command of *Panzerarmee Afrika*. In case the British launched their offensive, Rommel intended to immediately return to Africa. Personnel replacements arrived from the mainland, but they suffered the first few weeks under the heat and tropical diseases and illnesses. Frequently, 30 to 40 percent of the arriving personnel had to be admitted to a field hospital.[41]

Aerial reconnaissance indicated that in September alone, a total of sixty-nine freighters, tankers and transporters entered the harbors of Alexandria and Suez. Approximately 200,000 tons of materiel arrived in Egypt on those ships. Despite success on the part of the German submarine force, 80 to 90 percent of the Allied convoys reached their destination harbors. Of great importance to the British was the delivery of the new American M4 tank, colloquially known as the "Sherman," in large numbers. The

41. Author's Note: Aberger, 267.

main armament, a 7.5-centimeter main gun, was no longer mounted in a sponson. Instead, it was in a fully rotating turret. The "Sherman" was superior to the *Panzer III* and the equal of the *Panzer IV* (long).

In contrast to the British, the logistical situation of the Axis forces worsened dramatically. For September, Rommel had requested 9,000 tons of ammunition, 12,000 tons of fuel and 6,000 tons of rations. Actually delivered were 1,000 tons of ammunition, 5,000 tons of fuel and 2,000 tons of rations. Likewise, tanks, artillery pieces, antitank guns, weapons and vehicles of all types were only transported across the Mediterranean in limited numbers. That month, 22,000 tons of supplies were sunk. Without the considerable amounts of spoils-of-war the field army had captured, the Axis forces would have been immobilized as early as August. The war in Africa started to become primarily one of logistics, and the Britons won the competition for better supply by a wide margin.

Under the circumstances outlined above, it was impossible for the Axis forces to stockpile for any

American Shermans arrive in Egypt for the British forces.

major operations. As a result, the Italian and German forces waited in the Alamein position without hopes for an improvement of the supply situation and in expectation of a British offensive.

Moreover, operational and tactical options were reduced when the enemy dominated the air space and was able to bomb at will. The overwhelming combat power of the enemy air force played a significant role in the fighting that was to come.

An Italian supply ship has been torpedoed and starts to sink astern. Note the disruptive campuflage pattern, intended to disrupt the aim of submarines.

6. Knight's Cross Recipients of Panzer-Regiment 5 in the Period from July to September 1942

The extraordinary achievements of the regiment are reflected in the award of a number of decorations to officers who especially distinguished themselves. In 1942, four officers of the regiment received the Knight's Cross to the Iron Cross, the same number as in the previous year. They were *Oberleutnant* Rocholl, *Oberleutnant* Riepold, *Oberstleutnant* Mildebrath and *Oberst* Müller.

The awards were approved between July and September 1942. In all, some thirteen soldiers and officers were awarded the Knight's Cross to the Iron Cross while serving with the regiment or its follow-on formation, *Panzer-Abteilung 5*.

Here are some details:[42]

Rolf Rocholl

Born: 8 December 1918

Killed: 23 August 1943 (Eastern Front)

Submitted for the Knight's Cross: 24 July 1942

Award of the Knight's Cross: 28 July 1942

Duty Position: Acting Commander of the *2./Panzer-Regiment 5*

Rank: *Oberleutnant*

Rolf Rocholl was promoted to *Hauptmann* during the fighting at El Alamein. His final assignment in Africa was with the field army headquarters, where he served as a liaison officer. At the beginning of April 1943, he returned to Germany to start training as a general-staff officer.

On 31 August 1943, he was posthumously awarded the Oak Leaves to the Knight's Cross of the Iron Cross for service as the commander of the 3rd Battalion of *Grenadier-Regiment 569* of the *328. Infanterie-Division*. He was the 287th member of the German Armed Forces to receive that award at the time. Rocholl also received the German Cross in Gold (4 April 1942).

Josef Otto Riepold

Born: 10 October 1915

Killed: 17 June 1942 in Africa

Submitted for the Knight's Cross: 24 July 1942

Award of the Knight's Cross: 29 July 1942

Duty Position: Commander of the *5./Panzer-Regiment 5*

Rank: *Oberleutnant*, promoted to *Hauptmann* posthumously

---

42. Author's Note: Federl, *Die Ritterkreuzträger der Deutschen Panzerdivisionen 1939–1945, Die Panzertruppe.*

Werner Mildebrath

Born: 20 June 1904

Died: 2 June 1984

Submitted for the Knight's Cross: 8 August 1942

Award of the Knight's Cross: 12 August 1942

Duty Position: Commander of *I./Panzer-Regiment 5*

Rank: *Oberstleutnant*

Born in Bodenbach (Sudetenland) on 20 June 1904, Werner Mildebrath entered the *Reichswehr* after successful completion of college preparatory studies in April 1925. At the end of 1928, he was commissioned as a *Leutnant*.

Mildebrath was a member of the *Panzertruppe* from the "get-go." He participated in courses at the armor school at Kama in the Soviet Union in 1932 and 1933 and was then assigned to the *Kraftfahrlehrkommando Zossen*, from which *Panzer-Regiment 5* was formed on 15 October 1935.

Mildebrath served as the commander of the regiment's 1st Battalion in Africa. From 25 November to 28 February 1942, he served as the acting commander of the regiment.

When he was wounded in the back by shrapnel, he was flown to a military hospital in Greece on 5 November 1942. He was then transported to Vienna and treated at the reserve hospital in Meissen until the middle of December 1942. He was then released for duty to *Panzer-Ersatz-Abteilung 5* in Neuruppin.[43]

From the spring of 1943 until the end of the war, he was assigned to the staff of *Generaloberst* Guderian, where he served as the assistant chief-of-staff for the Inspectorate of Armored Forces. He was promoted to *Oberst* on 1 October 1943. He assisted in the establishment of armored formations, the modernization of armor training and the testing and introduction of infrared night vision devices.

Oberstleutnant Mildebrath receives the Knight's Cross in Africa.

---

43. Translator's Note: 5th Armor Replacement Detachment.

The preliminary award certificate for Mildebrath's Knight's Cross. It was signed by *Generalfeldmarshall* Keitel of the Army High Command on 12 August 1942.

Gerhard Müller

Born: 19 December 1896

Died: 10 April 1977

Submitted for the Knight's Cross: 5 September 1942

Award of the Knight's Cross: 9 September 1942

Duty Position: Commander of *Panzer-Regiment 5*

Rank: *Oberst*

Gerhard Müller was born the son of a doctor on 19 December 1896 in Breslau. He entered military service as an officer candidate with the Silesian *Infanterie-Regiment 154*. From the beginning of 1916 until the end of the Great War, he served on the Western Front. Following the war, he served as an *Oberleutnant* in the Upper Silesian Border Protection Service.

On 20 January 1920, he joined the police and was transferred into the Army on 1 October 1935 as a *Hauptmann*. On 1 November 1938, he became the commander of *Panzerabwehr-Abteilung 33*, serving with it in the campaign in Poland. He distinguished himself during the campaign in the West as an *Oberstleutnant* commanding the advance guard of the *33. Infanterie-Division*. During the campaign in the East, he commanded the 1st Battalion of *Panzer-Regiment 33* of the *9. Panzer-Division* and was badly wounded in the first engagement of the division in that campaign on 29 June 1941. He lost his left arm and was no longer considered to be able to serve in the field.

Despite that, he asked for an assignment at the front and became the commander of *Panzer-Regiment 5* in Africa as an *Oberst* on 1 March 1942. In the recommendation for the Knight's Cross, the armored engagements northwest of Sidi Muftah (2 June 1942), the entry into Tobruk (20 June 1942) and the counterattack south of the rear of the El Ruweisat Ridge (22 July 1942) were singled out. For him, the award of the Knight's Cross not only represented recognition of his leadership skills but also the success of the brave men of his regiment.

Müller left Africa at the end of 1942 and became the chief-of-staff of the Directorate for Motorization in Berlin. He later saw service as the acting commander of a division in France and the Soviet Union. At the end of the war, *Generalmajor* Müller was the assistant military commander of Pilsen.

7. 23 October to the End of December 1942: The 3rd Battle of El Alamein and the Retreat to Tripolitania

On 1 October, the forces in Africa were again redesignated: *Panzerarmee Afrika* became the *Deutsch-italienische Panzerarmee*.[44] The allocation of forces remained unchanged.

Montgomery avoided risk and relied on the certain numerical superiority of his forces. After the considerable reinforcements received from September to the middle of October, the 8th Army was ready. It had eleven divisions, including four armored ones. At Montgomery's disposal were 195,000 men, 1,029 tanks, 908 artillery pieces, 1,451 new and heavy antitank guns and 800 aircraft. Opposing him among the Italian and German forces were 104,000 men (50,000 Germans and 54,000 Italians), 210 German and 300 Italian tanks, 500 artillery pieces (including 40 8.8-centimeter *Flak*) and 300 aircraft.[45]

With regard to the tanks, it should be stressed that the British had more than 500 tanks with a 7.5-centimeter main gun. Of those, 400 were Shermans. The Germans could field only 38 *Panzer IV's* (long), which were their only equivalent combat vehicle.[46] The unequal force ratios in terms of tanks, the British air dominance and the completely inadequate logistical situation of the German fighting forces were the contributing factors to the ultimate defeat of the Axis forces.

At 2140 hours on 23 October, the 3rd Battle of El Alamein started with an artillery preparation on the Italian and German positions. At the time, *Panzer-Regiment 5* had the following operational tanks:[47] 6 *Panzerbefehlswagen III's*, 19 *Panzer II's*, 53 *Panzer III's* (short), 43 *Panzer III's* (long), 7 *Panzer IV's*

44. Translator's Note: German-Italian Armored Field Army.

45. Author's Note: Aberger, 278ff.

46. Author's Note: Hans Hinrichs, *"El Alamein" in Europäische Wehrkunde*, vol. 10/82, 452.

47. Author's Note: Jentz, *Die deutsche Panzertruppe*, vol. 2, 9.

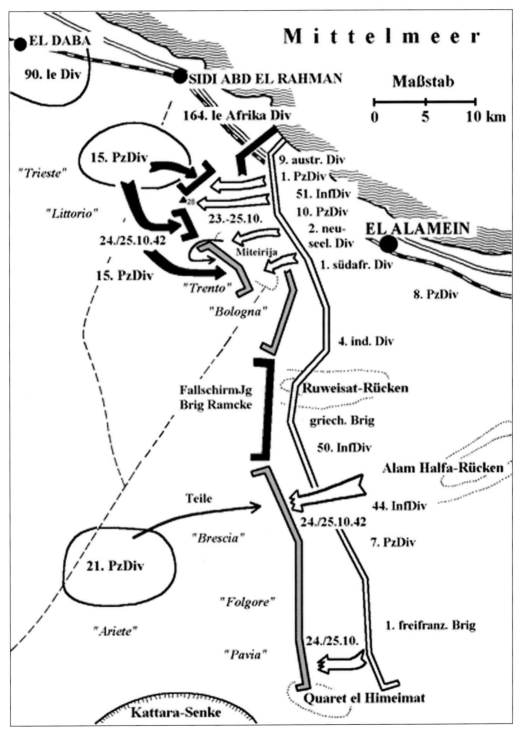

The development of the situation around El Alamein from 23 to 25 October 1942.

(short) and *15 Panzer IV's* (long). This total of 143 tanks represented only 69 percent of the authorized strength of the regiment.

The British infantry then moved out to attack in the northern sector of the front. Initially, the attack succeeded in taking little ground. On 24 October, *General der Panzertruppen* Stumme wanted to get a personal impression of the fighting and went to the front. At Hill 28, his vehicle received enemy fire. The general was flung out and suffered a heart attack. Until Rommel arrived on 25 October, *Generalleutnant Ritter* von Thoma led the Axis forces. Von Thoma had been given command of the *DAK* on 17 September.

At 0630 hours on 24 October, a British infantry attack in the area of Quaret el Himmeimat was turned back by the Italians. The same day, the enemy conducted a feint to the south against the *Brescia* Division; the British attack bogged down in the mine obstacles. It had been intended for the feint to deceive the Axis leadership into believing the main attack was in the south.

On 25 October, Montgomery launched the British 1st and 10th Armoured Divisions against the northern sector of the front after massive employment of artillery and airpower. The enemy broke into the defenses and occupied an area ten kilometers wide and five kilometers deep, with his lead attack elements reaching Hill 28.

The *15. Panzer-Division* undertook several counterattacks on 24 and 25 October and prevented an expansion of the penetration. However, the division lost 88 tanks in its attacks and, on the evening of 25 October, only had 31 operational tanks left.

On 26 October, the *21. Panzer-Division* received orders to move north. After a night march, it reached the area south of the Miteirija Ridge the next morning. *Panzer-Regiment 5* was being led by *Oberstleutnant* Mildebrath, since *Oberst* Müller was on leave. *Hauptmann* Rettemeier assumed acting command of the 1st Battalion from Mildebrath.

During the afternoon of 27 October, the *90. leichte Afrika-Division* attacked the enemy on Hill 28 without success. The *DAK,* as well as the *Ariete* and *Littorio* Armored Divisions, attacked British positions in the area of the Miteirija Ridge and to the northwest. After taking about three kilometers, the attacks bogged down in the face of the enemy's fire. British bomber formations attacked the Axis forces without interruption.

On 28 October, *Panzer-Regiment 5* was able to hold its positions against British tank attacks; at the onset of darkness, the regiment was withdrawn from the line. On 29 October, there were no large-scale enemy attacks along the front. On that day, the regiment reported the following operational tanks: 19 *Panzer II's,* 53 *Panzer III's* (short), 43 *Panzer III's* (long), 7 *Panzer IV's* (short) and 15 *Panzer IV's* (long).

On 30 and 31 October, elements of both the *21. Panzer-Division* and the *90. leichte Division* conducted counterattacks against enemy forces that had penetrated, encircled elements of the *164. leichte Afrika-Division* and blocked the coastal road southeast of Sidi Abd el Rahman. The encircled German forces were relieved, and the enemy was pushed back across the railway line. On the last day of October, the Axis field army had only 90 German and 190 Italian tanks left. The British, in contrast, still had more than 800.

Montgomery ordered the execution of Operation "Supercharge" on 2 November, intended to eliminate the Axis field army. After an artillery preparation from 360 guns, some 400 British tanks attacked the Axis positions to both sides of Hill 28. An additional 400 tanks were held at the ready to the east of the mine obstacles. Immediate German counterattacks—conducted by the *15. Panzer-Division* and the *21. Panzer-Division*—initially brought the British attack to a standstill, albeit at the cost of high German losses. The Germans were unable to push

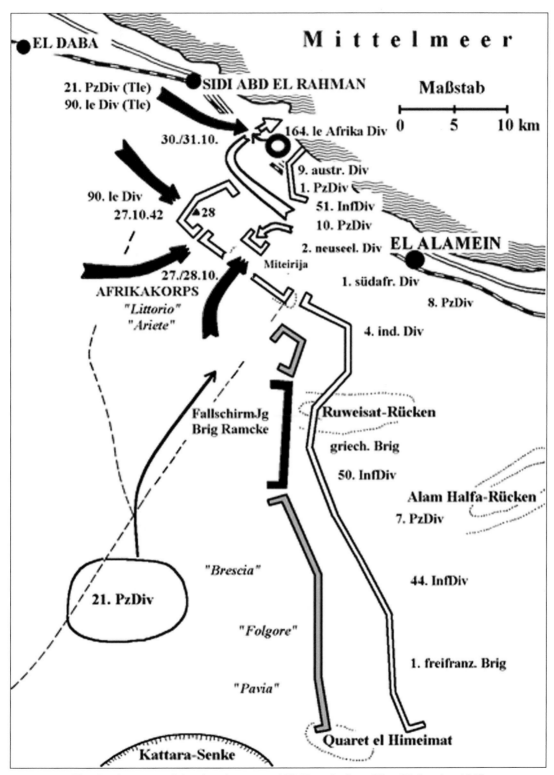

The development of the situation around El Alamein from 26 to 31 October 1942.

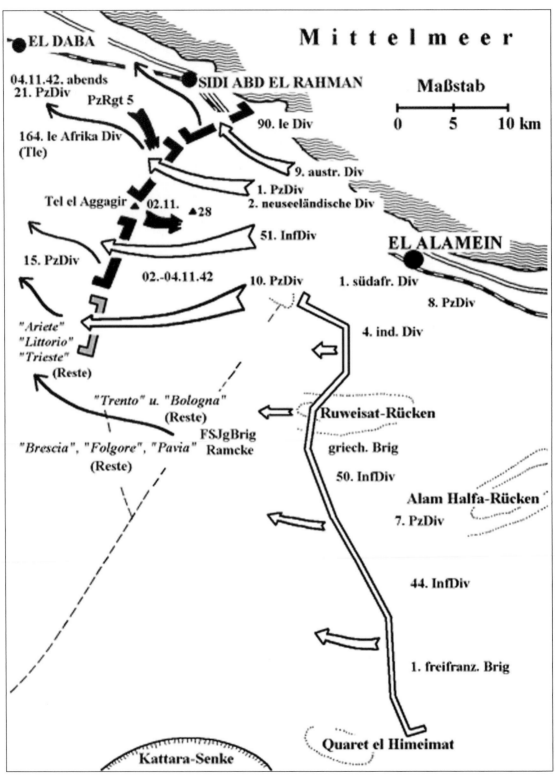

The development of the situation around El Alamein from 2 to 4 November 1942: Operation "Supercharge."

the British forces back, however. By that evening, the *DAK* had only 38 operational tanks and 24 8.8-centimeter guns, which represented the most effective weapon against the new U.S. tanks.

An order by Hitler to hold forced Rommel to rescind his directives issued on 3 November for the non-motorized elements to fall back to the Fuka area to establish new defensive positions. That same day, *Panzer-Regiment 5* conducted counterattacks against enemy forces that had penetrated. But the German and Italian forces were no longer in a position to conduct fighting that led to the substantial loss of forces. The combat power of the field army had been exhausted in the ten days of fighting.

Around 0900 hours on 4 November, the British resumed their massive armor attacks. The German tanks, which had been held in reserve up to that point, had to be committed. The British broke through the frontage of the *DAK* around Tel el Aggagir; a gap was created twenty kilometers wide and approximately fifteen kilometers deep. *Oberstleutnant* Mildebrath, who had been the acting commander of the regiment, was wounded; *Hauptmann* von Senfft zu Pilsach took his place. The commanding general of the *DAK*, *Ritter* von Thoma, was captured. *Oberst* Fritz Bayerlein, Rommel's chief-of-staff, assumed acting command of the *DAK*.

On the evening of 4 November, Rommel ordered his field army back to the area of Fuka in light of the hopeless situation. Non-motorized forces, mostly Italian infantry, remained behind, and most were captured. Rommel was able to save the remnants of his field army from destruction and captivity, however.

No general in the world could have achieved victory with the forces that Rommel had at his disposal in the 3rd Battle of El Alamein. The force ratios were too imbalanced. The British success in the battle was inevitably a consequence of its powerful materiel superiority.

Let us hear again from *Dr. Selmayr* (excerpts):[48]

Suddenly, another alert. In a wild night march, we moved to the center sector to seal off a penetration. The enemy had broken through to the left and right of the *15. Panzer-Division*; they had taken the Italians in stride . . . It was directed that we eject the enemy from the point of penetration with two companies.

As we raced over a hill and into a small depression, we received raging antitank-gun and tank-gun fire. In the blink of an eye, five tanks were burning. I dressed soldiers and attended to them as well I could. A *Leutnant* from the 6th Company was completely burned; I no longer recognized him. Even today, I can hear his hoarse, pressing question in my ear: "Doctor, will I make it . . . I have a wife and children back home." He later died at the main dressing station.

No sign of the ambulance; it turned evening. Correspondingly, I loaded the eight wounded, including the *Leutnant*, on my tank and trotted westward. I was hoping to find a main dressing station at the telegraph pole. Fortunately, I ran into an ambulance belonging to the engineers, who took my wounded. We expended some effort in trying to find the battalion. We had barely returned and wanted to eat, when the barrage fires started that shook the earth. We sometimes thought it was all over, it was booming and bursting so much outside and our small tank was really rocking back and forth with the impacts. Thank God we had no losses, despite the heavy fire. The next day, we went to the former sector of the *15. Panzer-Division* (*Panzer-Regiment 8*). The

48. Author's Note: Selmayr, 43ff.

knocked-out tanks were strewn everywhere. Tommy remained outside of our firing range, but he plastered us with his wide-ranging main guns, which were superior to ours. For the first time, we noticed the materiel superiority of the enemy. A tank officer was killed by a hit to the head from infantry fire. Due to the heat and the poor visibility—the optics were usually fouled by sand—we moved with open hatches. Usually, the tank commander also had his head out of the hatch so as to better orient himself. I did the same thing, since I could not see anything at all through my optics. As a result, we had many losses due to head wounds.

One tank was hit in front on the turret. The round entered from the front and exited from the rear—that's the power of the new Tommy tanks. From that point forward, we always placed sections of track up front on the tanks. I had to change positions several times during the day, since I was engaged, even though I always attempted to partially conceal my tank. We were constantly subjected to jamming on the radios. Tommy had captured the signals operating instructions of *Panzer-Regiment 8* and attempted to confuse us and yap his way into our radio traffic.

That evening, I talked to an artillery observer. He told me the battery had only thirty-five shells remaining and it was uncertain whether ammunition was coming forward. Great outlook—and all that before an imminent attack!

On 2 November, we moved a bit farther to the rear when my battalion was alerted to seal off a penetration. The defensive fire was too heavy; even the infantry bogged down in the enemy's fire . . . As I had moved up, *Oberleutnant* Dübois had waved to me. Now they were also bringing him back with a head wound. It was said he looked so terrible that his crew did not even want to show him to me. We tried to eject Tommy twice, but we were deflected each time. An 8.8-centimeter *Flak* moved up to support us, but it was blown apart as it unlimbered. The forward lines were hit by mortar fire. A 2-centimeter *Flak* was hit; two of the crew lay on the ground, badly wounded. I took off! We placed them on our tank despite the fire; one up front, the other to the rear. I kneeled on the side of the turret and held on to them so that they did not fall off during the movement. Then the tank took off as fast as it could. All of a sudden, Tommy took notice of us and engaged us with a battery. Always four shells at a time; sometimes to the left of us, sometimes to the right. Thank God they were really firing poorly. Of course, I still thought we were moving too slowly. I pressed myself against the turret, held on to my wounded and yelled at Krause to move faster. Finally, just as we were out of artillery range and climbing a small rise, enemy fighters raced in towards us. It was too late to stop, but they apparently did not see us, and so it turned out well. We encountered our ambulance behind the hill. A weight fell off of our chests. We transferred the wounded, took a break to eat and then trotted back to our guys.

The night remained lively. As it turned light, we pulled back to fill up, rearm and get rations. In the process we saw one of our 8.8-centimeter *Flak* shoot down an aircraft from an obstinate bunch. The crate burst into a 1,000 pieces; individual parachutes tumbled out.

All of a sudden, Senfft arrived, excited and alarmed! As we crossed the hill near the mosque, we saw what had caused that. Heading towards the south, as far as one could see, a cloud of smoke and dust; it was burning everywhere. From the east, enemy tanks in masses were advancing.

We hurried over to help our 1st Battalion and *Panzer-Regiment 8*. But what could we do? Altogether, we still numbered 30; facing us were a good 300. We received orders to counterattack. And that on a plate-flat plain . . . and, in front of us a Tommy that was not only vastly superior to us in number, but also in armor and armament. I heard Senfft radioing Mildebrath: "Attack . . . that's crazy!" Mildebrath replied: "That's true, but orders are orders!"

After only 100 meters, the first tanks were lost; the attack bogged down. The lead tank was positioned perpendicular to us and was knocked out. I moved towards it. About fifty meters away, the crew approached with two wounded. My question concerning other wounded was answered in the negative; the *Leutnant* was dead in the tank. As I later found out, the information was incorrect. The *Leutnant* was only temporarily unconscious; he crawled out of the tank under his own power, but on the enemy side. As a result, we did not see him. It was just in time before the tank went up in the air. He was later recovered by antitank personnel.

Mildebrath was wounded; Senfft assumed command of the regiment, that is, what was left of it. As far as I could tell, that was about twenty tanks. *Stabsarzt* Stockenberg was badly wounded as the result of bombs, even though there were no units in his vicinity and his position was well marked. As a result, I became the regimental physician. That night, we pulled back . . .

Violations of the Geneva Convention had been committed on both sides. Today, however, we were the black sheep . . .

On one occasion, we saw assault guns of the *Ariete* Division conduct an attack. Despite their poor armor, they advanced boldly. Of course, they were blown to bits in a miserable fashion. The Battle of El Alamein was lost; the retreat started.

A knocked-out *F2* version of the *Panzer IV* after the 3rd Battle of El Alamein.

The period from 5 November to the end of the year was marked by constant withdrawal movements on the part of the Axis forces. Around 0900 hours on 5 November, the *DAK* reached the area southwest of Fuka and transitioned to a time-phased defense. Around noon, enemy reconnaissance and armor forces attacked the *21. Panzer-Division* from the south. The attack was turned back by the last remaining tanks of *Panzer-Regiment 5*, supported by *Panzer-Artillerie-Regiment 155*.

During the night of 5–6 November, the *DAK* moved back approximately 100 kilometers and was positioned in the desert to the south of the *Via Balbia*, practically without fuel. Trucks from the *Kampfgruppen* fetched fuel from Marsa Matruk. It started to rain on the afternoon of 6 November. A period of bad weather hindered operations on the part of the Royal Air Force. That evening, *Panzer-Regiment 5* turned back an enemy encircling maneuver. That was followed by additional withdrawals.

During the morning hours of 7 November, the first elements of the *21. Panzer-Division* reached the area around Marsa Matruk, where they encountered the rearguards of the *90. leichte Division*. *Panzer-Regiment 5* had only eleven operational tanks left, 5 percent of its authorized strength. The division was able to rearm, refuel and take on rations from the depots in the town. During the night of 7–8 November, the march westward was continued.

On 8 November, there was an additional significant change in the North African theater of war. Two armored divisions and five infantry divisions comprised of 80,000 Americans and 25,000 Britons landed in Morocco in the vicinity of Casablanca and in Algiers in the vicinity of Oran and Algiers. The commander-in-chief of the Allied forces was general Dwight D. Eisenhower. The mission of that force was to advance through Tunis and on to Tripoli, so as to eliminate the Axis forces and join the 8th Army. A two-front war had started in Africa. Hitler decided to hold Africa to avoid long-lasting negative political effects with his alliance partner, Italy. Whatever was available in Italy in terms of forces was sent to Tunisia in the form of the *XC. Armee-Korps* under *General* Nehring. The first Allied armored advances on Tunis were turned back with it.

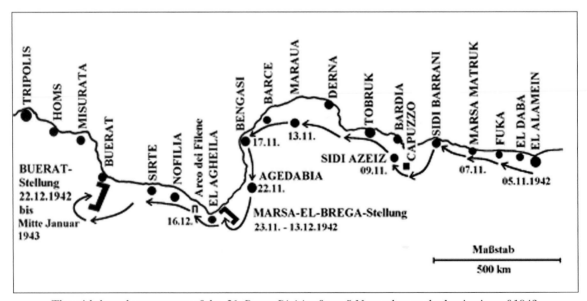

The withdrawal movements of the *21. Panzer-Division* from 5 November to the beginning of 1943.

On 9 November, the *21. Panzer-Division* reached the Sidi Azeiz area. The withdrawal then continued across the Trigh Capuzzo, the bypass road around Tobruk, through Bengasi and then Agedabia, which was reached on 22 November. Almost every other vehicle towed another. Efforts were made to avoid marching across the desert, which increased the consumption of fuel considerably. The few roads and trails were used. Long-lasting rains fell for days on end, which hampered the Royal Air Force and the elements of the 8th Army, which were only hesitantly pursuing.

Based on the low numbers of personnel and tanks—nineteen armored fighting vehicles—*Panzer-Regiment 5* reorganized itself at the time into one battalion with two companies.

From 23 November to 13 December, the *21. Panzer-Division* occupied the Marsa el Brega position. *Panzer-Regiment 5* and *Panzerjäger-Abteilung 39* were designated as the division reserve. After weeks of doing without, the soldiers finally received warm meals; the vehicles and weapons were cleaned and maintained.

On 10 December, enemy armored cars reconnoitered against the German defensive positions; that was followed by tanks on 12 December. After the initial attacks were turned back, the British attempted to bypass the Axis forces to the south. Without sufficient weapons, ammunition and fuel, the position could not be held. Consequently, Rommel ordered the evacuation of the position and the continued withdrawal.

On 16 December, the *21. Panzer-Division* passed through the Arco dei Filene and halted in the Nofilia area. That afternoon, *Panzer-Regiment 5*, together with *Panzerjäger-Abteilung 39*, helped clear up a critical situation in the sector of the *15. Panzer-Division*, which was stranded without fuel, by means of a counterattack.

On 19 December, *General der Panzertruppe* Gustav Fehn assumed command of the *DAK*. That same day, the regiment reported 21 operational tanks (10 percent of its authorized strength): 2 *Panzerbefehlswagen I's*, 1 *Panzerbefehlswagen III*, 9 *Panzer III's* (long), 5 *Panzer IV's* (short) and 4 *Panzer IV's* (long).[49]

Leapfrogging farther to the west, Sirte was reached on 20 December. For the first time since October, soldiers received mail.

When the division continued its western withdrawal on 21 December, the vehicle of the division commander ran over a mine emplaced by the British Long-Range Desert Group. *Generalmajor* von Radow and his operations officer, *Major i.G.* Heuduck, lost their lives. *Oberst* Bruer, the commander of the divisional artillery, assumed acting command of the division. That same day, *Hauptmann* von Senfft zu Pilsach was entrusted with acting command of the regiment. *Oberst* Müller had to give up command for health reasons.[50]

On the morning of 22 December, positions were occupied around Buerat. *Panzer-Regiment 5* remained there until the middle of January 1943.

Contrary to expectation, the Axis forces were not eliminated after the defeat at the 3rd Battle of El Alamein. Whenever withdrawals of that magnitude were conducted, there was always the danger of losing discipline as a result of fear and a "save yourself" mentality. For the military professional, there is nothing more distressing than the prospect of an army without discipline. That did not occur in this instance. The orderly withdrawal counts as one of Rommel's greatest achievements, since the losses sustained were slight and all of the envelopment efforts of the enemy had been thwarted. Montgomery wrote in his memoirs that Rommel's formations succeeded over and over again in escaping from the bottleneck at the last moment.[51]

49. Author's Note: Aberger, 308.
50. Author's Note: Aberger, 308.
51. Author's Note: Paul Carell, *Die Wüstenfüchse*, 357.

Of the 90,000 German soldiers at El Alamein, 70,000 made the retreat back.

On 9 December, *Generaloberst* von Arnim assumed command of the newly formed *5. Panzer-Armee* in Tunisia. At the end of 1942 and beginning of 1943, the following forces were transported to the Tunisian bridgehead:

- *10. Panzer-Division*
- *334. Infanterie-Division*
- *Division von Broich/von Manteuffel*
- *Division "Hermann Göring"*
- *999. Leichte Afrika-Division*
- *schwere panzer-Abteilung 501* (a general headquarters heavy tank battalion equipped with the newly introduced *Tiger* tank)

By the end of 1942, the *5. Panzer-Armee* had approximately 150 *Panzer III's* and *IV's* and 11 *Tigers*.

The Tunisian area of operations was different from Libya. In contrast to the bleak, seemingly endless expanses of sand and stone in Cyrenaica, there was mountainous terrain in Tunisia, in which olive orchards and fertile fields could be found. The Allies continuously attacked in the direction of Tunis. The high ground around Medjez el Bab, also known as "Christmas Mountain" or "Longstop Hill," which covered the German bridgehead to the west, was in German hands at the end of the year after hard, seesaw fighting.

The overall situation in Tunisia could be characterized as satisfactory at the time.

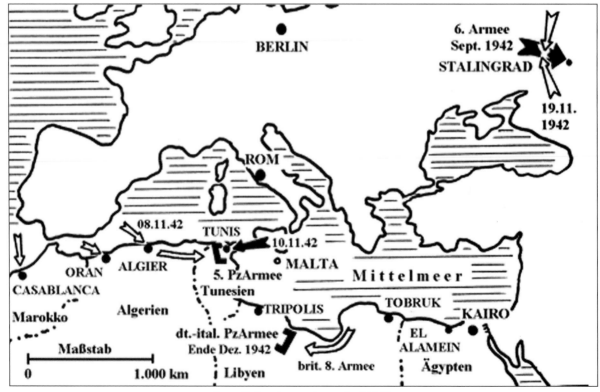

Overall situation at the end of 1942.

8. Logistics in North Africa in 1942

Supplies

When withdrawing to the Marsa el Brega position after the winter fighting of 1941, the *21. Panzer-Division* lost the majority of its trains elements with their trucks and materiel, such as tents, blankets, uniform items, and administrative capability.

After the start of the offensive on 21 January 1942, the division was partially able to make up its shortages in vehicles as spoils-of-war. At the end of February, several convoys made it through and delivered vehicles, tanks and consumable and non-consumable supplies such as signals and engineer equipment.

Resupply of fuel and ammunition remained a constant problem for the Axis leadership in Africa, especially after the advance from Tobruk to El Alamein. As a result, the 2nd Battle of El Alamein from 30 August to 4 September—the so-called "6-Day Race"—had to be broken off not as a result of losses but due to a lack of fuel. The harbors at Derna and Tobruk were constantly threatened by British naval forces and only fast individual ships could dock there. Marsa Matruk was within the effective range of the Royal Air force. Whenever ships did succeed in making it across the Mediterranean, 80 percent of the traffic went to Tripoli and Bengasi, where it had to be transloaded on trucks and transported to the front at El Alamein. Every third vehicle was driven by an unlicensed driver. The trucks themselves consumed a great deal of fuel during the movement and were also subjected to high rates of wear and tear mechanically and to the tires. Constant low-level air attacks along the few roads and trails led to losses of trucks and drivers. There were hardly any replacements for the destroyed trucks. Once the columns reached the area of operations, the convoy leaders then had the difficult task of finding the fighting forces in the desert.

As a result of the numbers of on-hand weapons and the overall supply situation, the *21. Panzer-Division* was hardly in a position to offer resistance for very long in the 3rd Battle of El Alamein. The opportunities to conduct the fight in an agile fashion and to make tactically correct decisions was limited due to the lack of fuel. The use of consumable supplies in the course of a battle lasting ten days was enormous. The main guns of the tanks of the regiment fired around 10,000 rounds.[52]

Uniform Items

Uniform items for the German soldiers in the North African theater of war had to be produced relatively quickly and under the conditions of a wartime economy. As a result, the standard was not the same as a colonial power such as England. German soldiers, tolerated by their superiors, wore a mixture

---

52. Author's Note: Aberger, 330.

Summer of 1942: a supply column on its way to the fighting troops.

of Italian, British and German uniform items. Practicality trumped uniform regulations.

In this connection, an after-action report written by the *21. Panzer-Division* in September 1942 should be mentioned. It was determined that tropical straight-leg trousers were preferred to tropical boot trousers and that lace-up shoes with fabric tongues were preferred to lace-up boots. Trousers, as well as shorts and tunics, were recommended to be tailored loosely and made out of softer material. It was also recommended that a throat scarf replace the tie. It was reported that the soldiers did not wear the pith helmet and preferred the field cap. Mosquito masks and sleeping bags were considered necessary.

Vehicular Repair

Whoever writes about the campaign in Africa cannot leave the terrific achievements of the maintenance services unmentioned. Churchill justifiably characterized the maintenance services of Rommel as a pillar of the German victories in Africa.[53] The Maintenance Company of *Panzer-Regiment 5*, with its technicians and specialists, has to be considered one of the bravest front-line units. In the middle of August 1942, the following vehicles were with the company for repair: 1 *Panzerbefehlswagen III*, 7 *Panzer II's*, 2 *Panzer III's* (long), 3 *Panzer IV's* (short) and 2 *Panzer IV's* (long).[54] The stocks of repair parts were small; there was none for captured vehicles. Vehicles considered to be total write-offs—inasmuch as they could be reached or evacuated—were cannibalized for parts. In the course of the 3rd Battle of El Alamein, the Maintenance Company was able to repair 35 tanks and returned them to the regiment.

Illustrative for all of the soldiers, technicians, civilians and officers employed in maintenance and repair duties in *Panzer-Regiment 5* was *Major* Archibald MacLean of Coll. After receiving a degree in mechanical engineering, MacLean saw service in

53. Author's Note: Carell, 343.
54. Author's Note: Aberger, 327.

1935 in the 2nd Battalion of *Artillerie-Regiment 37* in Königsberg (East Prussia). He belonged to *Panzer-Regiment 5* from 1937 until 1942, first as a *Hauptmann* and battalion maintenance officer for the 2nd Battalion and then as the regimental maintenance officer. He was widely recognized in Africa for his personal example and his well-executed evacuation of disabled tanks on the battlefield, as well as the successful repair of valuable armored fighting vehicles. He was awarded the Iron Cross, First Class, the Tank Assault Badge and the Italian Medal for Bravery. Following the campaign in North Africa, he worked as a staff officer within the Inspectorate for Armored Forces and as the division maintenance officer for the *25. Panzer-Division.*

Archibald MacLean.

Medical Care

Slightly wounded soldiers and sick personnel were generally sent to the rear on returning truck convoys. The number of ambulances was sufficient to evacuate the badly wounded. They were initially treated at the main clearing station and then sent to the field hospitals. In pressing cases, the medical flight section of the *Luftwaffe* had two *Ju 52's* and a *Fieseler Storch*. The hospitals at Naples and Athens were designated for accepting wounded who were brought in by ship or air.

Rations

As a result of their success, German soldiers were generally able to cover their ration needs until the summer of 1942 by consuming captured enemy rations. The productive wells in Egypt provided sufficient water.

After the 3rd Battle of El Alamein, the rations situation became critical. Bread rations were reduced to 300 grams per man a day (approximately 10 ounces) during the withdrawal movements; water was reduced to two liters a man. In the middle of December, the corps depot at El Agheila was blown up prematurely. Based on the already short rations being received, the soldiers were outraged. By the end of December, Christmas baked goods from Germany were issued. Unfortunately, a third of the goods received had to be destroyed since they were infected with maggots.

Rations were among the most elemental needs of the soldier in combat. A tank crew prepares a meal in an assembly area.

The final touches are applied to cakes baked by *Gefreiter* Abel in the 6th Company of the regiment.

9. Evaluation of the Campaign in Africa in 1942

After losing the winter fighting of 1941, Rommel launched a completely unexpected counterblow from the Marsa el Brega position in January 1942. Initially, the planned encirclement of the enemy in his Gazala position failed. *Panzerarmee Afrika* found itself in an extremely critical situation. The correct decision—to open the shortest route back to the supply lines through the enemy positions—created the prerequisite for going over to the offense again. The 8th Army was so decisively weakened that they could no longer deny Rommel Tobruk. Rommel had proven himself to be a bold troop leader, who was not afraid to take risks. He understood how to exploit the moment of surprise with his fast forces both tactically and operationally. The taking of Tobruk on 21 June is a magnificent example not only of combined-arms fighting but also of cooperation between the air force and the army. The offensive spirit and sense of duty of every soldier in Africa tipped the scales. The plan to take the island fortress of Malta after the capture of Tobruk was abandoned, however. That would later prove to be a fateful decision.

A lack of fuel was the constant companion of German operations in Africa. It decisively limited Rommel's freedom to maneuver, in which even advancing in the face of minimal or no resistance was handicapped, and it prevented the execution of tactically and operationally correct decisions.

Outside of El Alamein, the German and Italian forces found themselves exhausted after constantly fighting and conducting operations under extremely difficult climatic conditions and with insufficient logistical support. The British forces were in improved field positions that could not be bypassed by wide-ranging maneuvers, as they had been in the Gazala Line. In addition, they were being constantly reinforced by new formations and modern weapons systems, such as the American Sherman tank. The British air force was once again very active after moving back into the area of the Nile and increasingly exerted a decisive influence on the battlefield. At the same time, the *Luftwaffe* could only provide less and less support for the forces on the ground.

The calling off of the 2nd Battle of El Alamein ("6-Day Race") on 2 September signaled, once and for all, the transition of the Axis forces to the strategic defensive, thus representing the turning point of the campaign. The 3rd Battle of El Alamein was conducted by Montgomery in accordance with the concepts of the battles of attrition of the First World War. Avoiding all risk, he counted on a powerful materiel superiority to do the trick following the use of barrage fires. The prerequisites for that were created by the vast American deliveries. In a masterfully conducted retreat, Rommel took the remnants of his field army more than 2,000 kilometers as far as Tunisia. The withdrawal movements were dictated more by the fuel situation than pressure from the enemy. Montgomery followed very cautiously, lost a lot of time as a result and, correspondingly, missed the opportunity to end the war in Africa early.

The British victory in the 3rd Battle of El Alamein was followed by the surprise landing of the Allies in Algeria and Morocco. Both operations have to be considered as part of the overall strategic context. Their objectives were the forced evacuation of Africa by German and Italian forces, followed by an attack on the southern flank of Europe. Italy was proving to be more of a hindrance to the Germans than a help in 1942. The capabilities and means of Germany were insufficient to stop the looming defeat in Africa. It must not be forgotten that the main effort of the German leadership was not directed towards the North African theater of operations. Instead, it was the Eastern Front, where events were coming to a dramatic head (Stalingrad).

10. Overview of *Panzer-Regiment 5* in the Campaign in North Africa in 1942

The average age of those killed in Africa in 1942 was twenty-two, one year younger than the average age of 1941. Once again, it was striking how many officers and noncommissioned officers were casualties. Of the 180 killed, 59 were of that category, representing 33 percent of those fallen. By contrast, the number of officers and noncommissioned officers authorized in the TO&E was 21 percent. As a result of the high losses, it has proven impossible to draw up a list of those who occupied leadership positions within the units.

June 1942: The military cemetery next to the "White House" on the *Via Balbia* west of Tobruk.

Until 20 January 1942	Defensive operations in the Marsa el Brega position
21 January to 6 February 1942	Counterattack to retake Cyrenaica
7 February to 25 May 1942	Defensive operations in the southeastern area of Cyrenaica
1 March 1942	*Oberst* Müller assumes command of the regiment
May 1942	Receipt of the first *Panzer IV's* with the long 7.5-centimeter main gun
26 May to 19 June 1942	*Operation "Theseus,"* the battle for the Gazala position
20–21 June 1942	Capture of the fortress of Tobruk
22–30 June 1942	Pursuit of the enemy into the Marmarica and western Egypt
1–27 July 1942	1st Battle of El Alamein
30 August to 4 September 1942	2nd Battle of El Alamein (6-Day Race)
23 October to 4 November 1942	3rd Battle of El Alamein
5 November to the end of 1942	Withdrawal from the El Alamein position to the Buerat position
21 December 1942	*Hauptmann* von Senfft zu Pilsach is given acting command of the regiment

January 1942: The 8th Company of the regiment in the attack.

At the beginning of 1942, *Oberleutnant* Rettemeier assumed command of the 2nd Company. He was promoted to *Hauptmann* on 1 February 1942. He was later awarded the Knight's Cross on 5 December 1943 and, on 13 March 1944, he became the 425th member of the German Armed Forces to be honored with the award of the Oak Leaves to the Knight's Cross. Typical of the many supply impasses the Germans experienced, Rettemeier wears an enlisted *Panzer* cap in this image, a cap intended for wear on the European mainland.

An attack in February 1942. Spare tank links for added protection and "Jerry cans" of water.

A *Panzerbefehlswagen III* of the regimental headquarters in an assembly area south of Derna.

A *Panzer III* of the regiment with the longer-barreled 5-centimeter main gun.

Evening entertainment: a company sing-along.

In the assembly area in Derna. The field-made sign states: "If you want to save your sons, send beer and cigarettes." (*Wollt ihr eure Söhne retten, / Schickt Bier und Zigaretten!!!*)

Werner Fenck of the 1st Company
with a snake he dispatched.

The *Panzer III* of *Oberfeldwebel* Beucker.

A *Panzer III* of the 2nd Company with the short L42 5-centimeter gun.

A new operation is planned and discussed by means of a sandtable by the company commander of the 2nd Company, *Hauptmann* Rettemeier.

Gefreiter Günter Sauer of the 3rd Company. Note the extra stick grenades stored on the outside of the turret.

Gefreiter Edube Schwarz of the 4th Company on his *Panzer IV Ausf. F.*

The 3rd and 7th Companies were transported to Africa in the spring of 1942. Once they arrived, the regiment was almost at its authorized full strength (TO&E of 1 February 1941). The 3rd Company can be seen to the upper right; the 7th Company to the left. Both companies are in Bagnoli (Italy), waiting for transport to Africa.

A *Panzer III* of the 7th Company in Italy before the transport to Africa. Note the wear of continental *Panzer* uniforms (black) by the crewmembers.

Still in Italy: a *Panzer III* of the 7th Company.

Tankers of the 7th Company were transported to Bengasi by Italian aircraft (*SM 82*). The men have received their tropical uniforms and have added the non-regulation death's heads to the lapels, a common practice in Africa.

Panzer III's of the 7th
Company in the cargo hold
of an Italian ship.

Offloading in
Bengasi.

In the Bengasi harbor, the tanks had to be trans-loaded on ferries from the ships.

A *Panzer III* of the 7th Company prior to the fighting for the British Gazala Line.

Oberst Müller assumed command of the regiment on 1 March. Here he is seen studying documents on the rear deck of a *Panzerbefehlswagen III.*

Heinrich-Gustaf Schlieper, a radio operator on the regimental commander's command tank.

On 9 March, the former regimental commander (13 October 1937 to July 1939), Walther K. Nehring, became the commanding general of the *DAK* as a *Generalleutnant*. He remained in command until he was wounded on 31 August 1942. After the capture of Tobruk, he was promoted ahead of his peers to *General der Panzertruppen*. He received the Knight's Cross to the Iron Cross on 24 July 1941 while serving on the Eastern Front. That was followed by the Oak Leaves on 8 February 1944 (383rd recipient) and the Swords on 22 January 1945 (124th recipient). (Photograph courtesy of Christian Nehring)

May 1942: General officers meet before the attack on the British Gazala Line. From left to right: *Generalleutnant* Nehring (commanding general of the *DAK*), *General der Panzertruppen* Crüwell (assistant commander-in-chief of *Panzerarmee Afrika*) and *Generalmajor* von Bismarck (commander of the *21. Panzer-Division*).

Another view of the commanders (from left to right): Nehring, von Bismarck, *Oberst* Bruer and Crüwell.

General der Panzertruppen Crüwell led *Gruppe Crüwell* during the opening stages of the fighting for the Gazala Line. On 29 May, he was shot down while conducting a reconnaissance flight and was taken captive by the British. Behind him is *Oberleutnant* Werner Grün of *Panzer-Regiment 5*.

The morning of 27 May 1942: the Gazala Line is bypassed. *Panzer-Regiment 5* in a *Flächenmarsch* northeast of Bir Hacheim just before encountering the enemy.

A British soldier surrenders.

A knocked-out
Panzer II. Heat from
internal fires has
burnt off the paint.

Oberleutnant Günther Micklei, the signals officer of the regiment's 2nd Battalion. He was killed on 27 May 1942 at the side of his commander, *Oberstleutnant* Martin.

27 May 1942: An unpleasant surprise during the fighting for the Gazala Line was the appearance of the Grant, an American tank delivered to the British under the provisions of the Lend-Lease Agreement.

Soldiers of the regiment's 2nd Company view a knocked-out Crusader. Second from the right is the commander of the 2nd Company, *Hauptmann* Rettemeier.

The German losses were also heavy. An immobilized *Panzer IV* of the 2nd Platoon of the 4th Company of the regiment.

This *Ju 87 "Stuka"* had to make an emergency landing in the sector of the regiment due to a shot-up oil line. The damage could be repaired, and the aircraft flew back to its home base.

Spare track and sandbags help reinforce the frontal armor on this *Panzer III* of the 7th Company.

An enemy round, probably from a 2-pounder gun, was intended for the driver's port of this tank.

A break in the fighting. A *Panzer III* of the headquarters section of the 7th Company (*702*). Note the stowage of canteens and mess kits on the outside of the turret.

A drink straight from the bottle was a pleasure seldom encountered.

20 June 1942: Tanks of the regiment prepare for the attack on Tobruk.

The commanding general of the *DAK, Generalleutnant* Nehring (far left), outside of Tobruk.

Nehring briefs Rommel on his operation plan. (Photograph courtesy of Christian Nehring)

Rommel takes a short break during the fighting. He is in his personal *Sd.Kfz. 250* command vehicle, *Greif* (Griffin).

The attack on Tobruk on 20 June 1942.

Generalmajor von Bismarck (right), the commander of the *21. Panzer-Division*, listens to a report during the fighting for Tobruk.

Oberfeldwebel Schühnemann, the platoon leader of the 2nd Platoon of the 4th Company, with his crew.

Rommel in Tobruk in June 1942.

The grim reality of war: a knocked-out Crusader at the outskirts of Tobruk.

21 June 1942: Tobruk is taken. British vehicles, including two American M3 Stuarts, are abandoned on the battlefield.

Benito Mussolini visits Tobruk in July.

The turret of a knocked-out *Panzer III*.

June 1942: The military cemetery at the "White House," thirty-one kilometers west of Tobruk.

23 June 1942: The attack continues into Egypt.

The advance on El Alamein.

A camouflaged *Panzer IV* in position outside El Alamein.

A *Panzer III* receives additional protection from rocks placed in front of it. The crew prepares to set up a camouflage net as well.

The commanding general of the *DAK*, *Generalleutnant* Nehring (third from the right), talks to officers of the regiment.

Nothing much remains of this *Panzer III* after it has been cannibalized for parts for other repairable vehicles.

Top: A *Panzer IV* of the 2nd Platoon of the 8th Company.

Left: Another view of the same *Panzer IV*. The radio operator monitors radio traffic.

Near El Alamein in September 1942: Rommel's mobile command post.

The command tank of the regimental commander on the El Alamein front.

Rommel with *Ritter* von Thoma, the commanding general of the *DAK* (right) and *Generalmajor* von Vaerst, the commander of the *15. Panzer-Division* (second from right). On 22 September, Rommel left for Germany for health reasons. *General der Panzertruppen* Stumme was given acting command of the *Deusch-italienische Panzerarmee.* (Photograph courtesy of Christian Nehring)

Oberst Müller, the regimental commander. Despite the loss of an arm on the Eastern Front, Müller asked for and received combat command.

Hauptmann Werner Grün, Müller's adjutant since March 1942. He was awarded the German Cross in Gold on 25 March 1942.

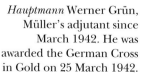

Leutnant Rudolf Wendorff, the signals officer of the 2nd Battalion, in the *Panzerbefehlswagen III* of the commander, *Hauptmann* von Senfft zu Pilsach.

Another view of Wendorff in the command tank.

A camouflaged *Panzer IV* awaits the expected British offensive.

Observing the terrain through binoculars.

The regimental commander's tank has been hit. The wooden dummy gun and the mount for the coaxial machine gun has been ripped out.

A close-up view of the damage.

7 November 1942: A *Panzer III* of the 1st Company has reached the rations depot at Marsa Matruk. The soldiers take advantage of the situation.

The regiment conducts a time-phased defense. A captured British jeep impressed into German service stops next to a *Panzer III* of the 2nd Company. Note that the soldier in the commander's cupola is wearing a pith helmet. Although issued to the soldiers, they were unpopular and rarely worn.

Despite the retreat, these German tankers from the 7th Company do not seem to have lost their sense of humor.

CHAPTER 2

Panzer-Regiment 5 in the Campaign in North Africa, 1943

1. The Creation of the "Afrika" Sleeve Title in January 1943

Preliminary remark

Starting in July 1941, the soldiers of *Panzergruppe Afrika* and, later, *Panzerarmee Afrika* wore a sleeve band bearing the inscription "*Afrikakorps.*" In the case of the Navy and the Air Force, the sleeve band simply bore the inscription "*Afrika.*" This was not an award in the traditional sense.

Date instituted, form and appearance

In his capacity as the commander-in-chief of the armed forces, Hitler dictated the introduction of a sleeve band bearing the inscription "*Afrika*" for members of all three services. This was presumably at the end of 1942, but the date is by no means certain. The German Army High Command published implementation instructions on 21 January 1943.[1]

The band was 3.3 centimeters wide, made out of khaki-colored camel hair (although there are original bands from the period that were also fabricated out of cotton), with gray cotton braid borders and the gray-white inscription "*Afrika*" framed by gray-white machine embroidered palms.

The sleeve bands were made by both German and Italian firms. As a result, there are differences in the fabric, its color tonalities and the characteristics of the embroidery.

The new sleeve bands were not immediately available; as a result, few were awarded in North Africa. Awards were generally given in the homeland to soldiers who escaped ultimate captivity in Tunisia.

Conditions of Award

For members of the Army, the award conditions fell into three categories:

- Honorable service of at least six months on African soil.[2]
- If the individual received an award for bravery, such as the Iron Cross, there were no time restrictions for employment in Africa
- Illness resulting from service in Africa that led to complete or partial reduction of suitability for service in tropical climates. The prerequisite in this case was service of at least three months.

It was permissible to award the sleeve band to those killed in action or who died in theater. The sleeve band was not allowed to be presented to foreigners.

---

1. Author's Note: *Allgemeine Heeresmitteilungen 1943*, 2nd Edition, Berlin, 21 January 1943, page 33, paragraph 60.

2. Author's Note: A *Führer* directive of 6 May 1943 later reduced the time to four months to those who served honorably in the final fighting in Tunisia.

In the case of soldiers of the former *Heeresgruppe Afrika* who were taken prisoner, a decision was to be made later, after their return, as to whether they were entitled to the sleeve band.

Recommendations for the Award and Certificates

Initially, the commanders-in-chief of the *Deutsch-italienische Panzerarmee* and the *5. Panzer-Armee* were entitled to make the award in their respective areas of operation. Effective March 1943, approval authority rested with the commander-in-chief of *Heeresgruppe Afrika*. By that time, the awards were also being distributed through replacement detachments in the homeland. During the final weeks of the campaign, few sleeve bands were award, due to the difficult supply situation and the looming end to the fighting. Most were awarded by the commander-in-chief South, processing centers or replacement detachments to soldiers who had left Africa prior to the capitulation. Awards were also presented to the next-of-kin of those who had been killed.

Awardees were presented with a certificate in DIN A5 size (approximately 5" by 7"). In addition, the award was also entered into personnel records.

On 6 October 1944, the High Command of the Armed Forces dictated that the last date for the award of the sleeve band was 31 October 1944.

Wear

The sleeve band was worn on the lower left sleeve of the uniform jacket.

Other Remarks

Sleeve bands and blank forms were to be ordered through official channels from *Heeresbekleidungsamt I* (Army Uniform Directorate) in Berlin. The awardee was to receive at least two sleeve bands, one each for the field tunic and the overcoat.

Soldiers were also permitted to wear the sleeve band on their party and state uniforms, if any.

Wilhelm Körner, recipient of the
Afrika sleeve band.

Two award certificates for the *Afrika* sleeve band for
soldiers of the regiment. The top one was prepared
by the 1st March Company of the regiment's training
and replacement detachment and the one on the
right by the detachment's 1st Training Company.
Both are dated 15 March 1943, which coincided
with the directive that the previous sleeve band—
Afrikakorps—no longer be worn and that it be turned
in. In addition to the award certificates seen here,
there were a number of other variants. The original
certificates were printed in DIN A5 format.

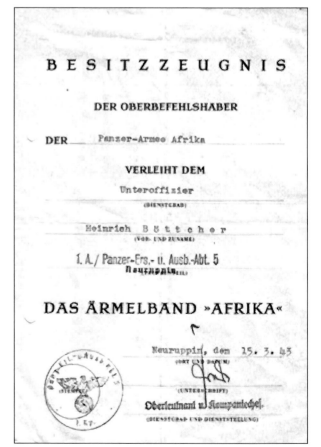

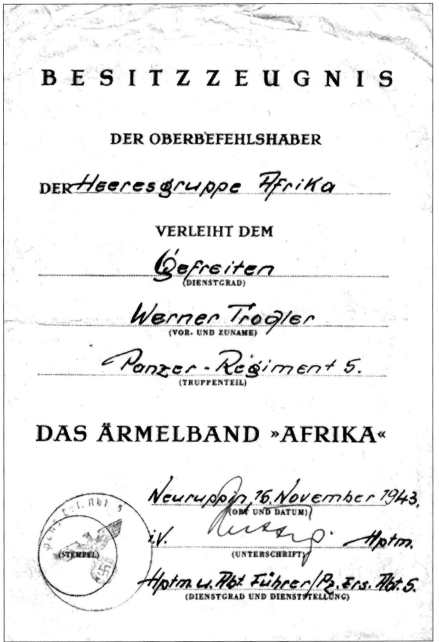

Werner Trodler in the black *Panzer* uniform and the *Afrika* sleeve band.

Gefreiter Werner Trodler's award certificate, as prepared by the training and replacement detachment in Neuruppin in November 1943.

2. From the Beginning of January 1943 to the Beginning of February 1943: The Movement of the *21. Panzer-Division* Into the Area of Operations of the *5. Panzer-Armee*; Fighting for the Passes around Faid

At the beginning of January 1943, the 8th Army continued its attack. Rommel delayed the British advance by utilizing a number of rearguards along a broad front. In addition, mine obstacles and the destruction of roads also contributed to Montgomery being unable to influence the disciplined withdrawal of the *Deutsch-italienische Panzerarmee*. On 10 January, Rommel's forces were in the Homs-Tarhuna position southeast of Tripoli. The forces that had been hurriedly brought over as the *5. Panzer-Armee* were positioned in the northern part of Tunisia.

If the Allied forces that had landed in Algeria and Morocco succeeded in taking the land bottleneck around Gabes (Tunisia), they would then be able to separate the two field armies and individually defeat them. As a result, forces were moved to that area.

Starting on 8 January, the acting division commander of the *21. Panzer-Division* was *Oberst* Hildebrandt, who was later promoted to *Generalmajor.*[3] During the afternoon of 13 January, the *21. Panzer-Division* headed north through Tarhuna (Libya) to the area north of Gabes, which was reached on 17 January. The division then became a part of *Generaloberst* von Arnim's *5. Panzer-Armee* and reported directly to it. The desert war was over for *Panzer-Regiment 5*.

Tunisia was an entirely different landscape for the soldiers. Unlike Libya, with its open terrain devoid of people, key terrain and improved roads, it was a mountainous, well-populated area with a well-

---

3. Author's Note: Aberger, 343.

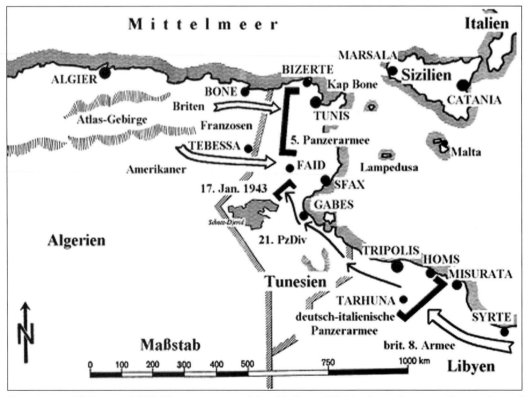

Situation on 17 January 1943: The movement of the *21. Panzer-Division* from the area of operations of the *deutsch-italienische Panzerarmee* to the sector of the *5. Panzer-Armee* in the area north of Gabes.

established road network. Large areas had vegetation with trees and bushes. Multifaceted opportunities for concealment presented themselves and allowed an unnoticed approach, even for armored forces. Large sections of land were used agriculturally for the planting of vegetables, grain and fruit. The water supply was secured by means of productive wells; in larger localities, there was even running water. The populace was friendly and helpful but largely neutral.

In a conversation with the author, Werner Grün stated that he received orders in January 1943 from the *5. Panzer-Armee* to pick up thirty brand-new *Panzer III's* (long) in Bizerta and equipping the vehicles with crews. With attached *Flak*, Grün marched from Bizerta to Faid via Sousse and Sfax. He was ordered to take and hold the pass there. Together with elements of the *10. Panzer-Division*, he succeeded against French and American resistance. When the Americans launched a counterattack, Grün fixed them to the front, while he moved out with his 1st and 2nd Companies into the enemy flank. The completely surprised enemy was shot to pieces. The next day, the knocked-out vehicles were each numbered with white paint. There was a total of fifty-three.

While the *21. Panzer-Division* was positioned in the area north of Gabes, the *Deutsch-italienische*

A G model *Panzer IV* on the march to the front in Tunisia.

Panzerarmee continued withdrawing to the northwest. During the night of 22–23 January, Tripoli was abandoned. Engineers rendered the harbor facilities unusable for a considerable period. At the end of January, Rommel occupied the Mareth position.

During the morning hours of 30 January, the *21. Panzer-Division* launched an attack into the area west of Faid. The division was divided into four *Kampfgruppen* for the operation, which was successful. The northern group took the Djebel Kralif Pass. The southern group ejected the enemy in the area around Djebel Goubrar and Djebel Rechaib. Further to the south, *Kampfgruppe Grün* attacked, reinforced by *Flak.* Grün's forces advanced west of Djebel Rechaib and turned back an enemy attack from the direction of Sidi Bou Zid. The important passes in the Faid area remained in German hands.

In the course of the fighting, 1,047 prisoners were taken and 25 tanks or armored vehicles and 15 antitank guns were either captured or destroyed. The American infantry sustained around 700 losses in killed and wounded.[4] The American forces proved themselves combat inexperienced and their leaders not yet up to the demands of the operations. For the time being, the danger of an enemy breakthrough to the coast at Sfax or Gabes was averted. On 10 February, *Hauptmann* Senfft zu Pilsach was named in the Armed Forced Daily report. *Hauptmann* Grün was selected for General Staff Officer training and left the regiment.

---

4. Author's Note: Aberger, 349.

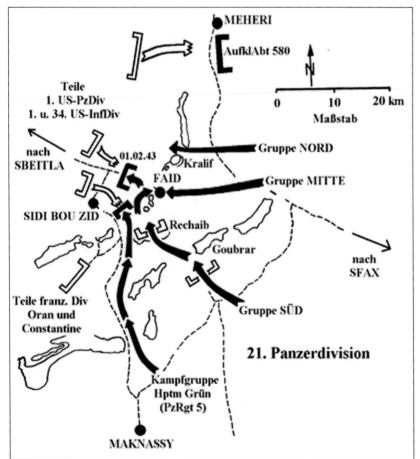

Situation from 30 January to 1 February 1943: Attack of the *21. Panzer-Division* in the Faid area.

3. Reorganization of *Panzer-Regiment 5* in February 1943 and a New TO&E for the Armored Force

On 10 January 1943, *Hauptmann* Senfft zu Pilsach transferred acting command of the regiment to *Oberst* Stenkoff, who assumed full command.[5] During the first week of February, the regiment's 2nd Battalion was consolidated with the 1st Battalion. *Panzer-Abteilung 190*, which had been in Africa since November 1942 as part of the *90. leichte Afrika-Division*, became the regiment's new 2nd Battalion.[6]

5. Author's Note: Aberger, 428.

6. Author's Note: Aberger, 350.

In January 1943, a new TO&E was introduced for the armored force. The short-barreled *Panzer III's* and *IV's* disappeared from the tables of authorization. According to *K.St.N.1175a*, dated 25 January 1943, the medium company was identified as having twenty-two tanks with the long 7.5-centimeter main gun.[7]

On 26 February, the new TO&E was approved for the regiment, but the 176 *Panzer IV's* (long) could not be issued due to the war and supply situation.

7. Author's Note: Jentz 51.

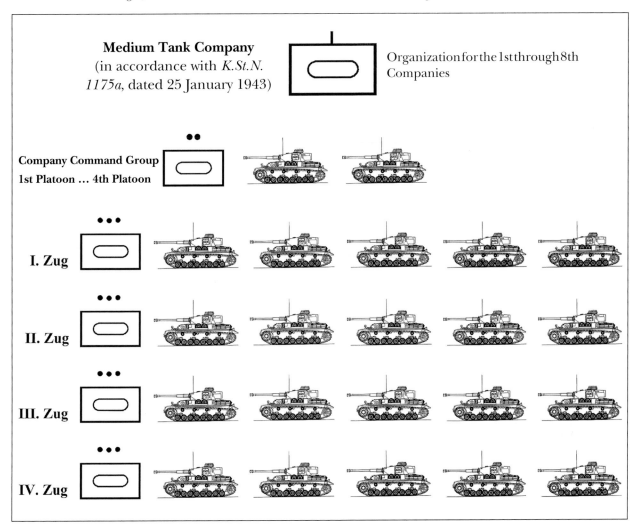

4. 14–2 February 1943: Advance on Sidi Bou Zid–Sbeitla–Sbiba (Operation "Spring Wind")

After taking Faid, the *5. Panzer-Armee* ordered an attack by the *10. Panzer-Division* and the *21. Panzer-Division* against the strong enemy forces to the west. For Operation *"Frühlingswind,"* the 21. *Panzer-Division* initially organized itself into two *Kampfgruppen*:

- *Kampfgruppe Panzer-Regiment 5* (*Oberst* Stenkoff), which consisted of the tank regiment, reinforced by elements of *Panzer-Artillerie-Regiment 155* and *Flak.*
- *Kampfgruppe Panzergrenadier-Regiment 104*, which consisted of the mechanized infantry regiment, which was also reinforced by elements of the divisional artillery and *Flak.*

The attack started at 0530 hours on 14 February. Towards noon, the *Panzer-Regiment 5* took the Sidi Bou Zid–Gafsa road and then advanced into the area west of Sidi Bou Zid. *Hauptmann* Rohr, who commanded the 1st Battalion and its fifty tanks, recalled the events as follows:[8]

We were just going around a hill from the south—the Yanks were still positioned there—when, all of a sudden, large clouds of dust and dirt could be seen off to the west. It was an American tank division, which appeared a bit too late on the battlefield. My tanks were drawn up as if on a line next to me. Behind us was the sun and the mountain with the Americans. By means of radio, I issued the best order of my life: "No firing . . . no more movement . . . only I will give the order to fire!" The Americans could not detect our tanks in the sun. It turned into a catastrophe for the enemy, when I gave the order to fire at will

at 500 meters. Seventy-eight tanks fell victim to us. We refueled and rearmed our stocks of ammunition. Rommel showed up. In the shadow of a tank, he explained his plan to us: "Immediately pursue and then continue to march as far as Algeria!"

The *10. Panzer-Division* attacked from the north in a pincer movement and took Sidi Bou Zid. Enemy forces to the east were either defeated or forced to pull back to the south. In the fighting for Sidi Bou Zid on 14 and 15 February, the U.S. 1st Armored Division lost 165 tanks and armored cars. More than 2,000 prisoners were taken.[9]

Rommel also launched an attack to the north in Operation *"Morgenluft"* ("Morning Air"), while leaving behind security forces in the Mareth position. He could see that the British 8th Army would need a few more weeks before it could continue its attack. Rommel wanted to conduct a decisive blow against the Anglo-American forces in Tunisia. He planned on cutting off the Allied forces from their logistical lines of communication by thrusting through Tebessa to the north to the coast at Bone.

It proved disadvantageous for the operation that there was no unified senior command for Tunisia. The *Deutsch-italienische Panzerarmee* and the *5. Panzer-Armee* operated independently of one another. Their efforts were rarely coordinated and molded by differing estimates of the situation. In the end, separate conduct of the fighting with different operation plans could not be blessed with success.

On 17 February, Rommel's forces took Feriana. That same day, *Panzer-Regiment 5* attacked enemy forces south of Sbeitla along a front of ten kilometers with 55 *Panzer III's* (long) and 14 *Panzer IV's* (long).[10] In a fight lasting several hours, 27 enemy tanks were knocked out without sustaining any friendly losses.

8. Author's Note: Rohr, *Geschichte einer Lübecker Familie,* vol. I, 116.

9. Author's Note: Kühn, 194.

10. Author's Note: Daily Log No. 9, *21. Panzer-Division,* Operations, 18 February 1943, Annex.

The *21. Panzer-Division* took Sbeitla at 1700 hours. The U.S. 1st Armored Division and 34th Infantry Division had sustained considerable casualties. On 18 February, the division was returned to Rommel's command. The Armed Forces High Command agreed to Rommel's proposed operation to attack in the direction of Tebessa and also allocated the *10. Panzer-Division* to him.

Leaving behind its non-motorized elements at Sbeitla, the *21. Panzer-Division* moved out to attack Sbiba at 0800 hours on 19 February with *Panzer-Regiment 5* in the lead. The attack bogged down outside the town in the face of heavy defensive fires, however. The next day, the division was pulled back to Sbeitla.

The *10. Panzer-Division*, which had been brought forward from the Fondouk-Picon area on 19 February, attacked during the evening of 20 February in the direction of Thala. It took the village, but it was then forced to pull back when the Americans committed reinforcements and reserves. Rommel's forces then attacked the Djebel Hamra pass in the direction of Tebessa. The enemy forces, likewise reinforced, could not be broken through there either. The German forces had proven to be too weak for the advance, even if the Americans were still taking losses at five times the rate of Axis forces. General Eisenhower was able to commit new, rested and full-strength forces against the exhausted and decimated German forces, In the end, they carried the day for the Allies.

By 28 February, the *21. Panzer-Division* moved back to the Faid area and then into an assembly area northwest of Gabes (Schott-Akarit position).

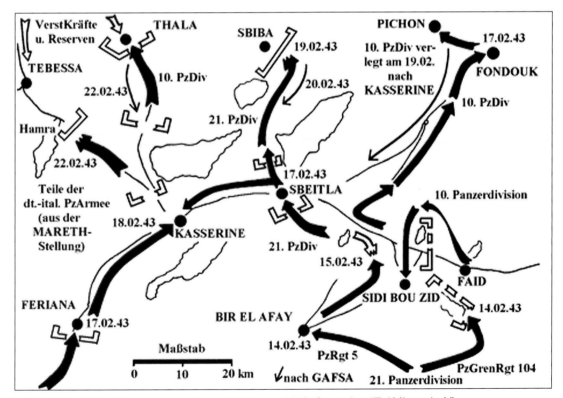

Situation from 14 to 22 February 1943: Operation "Frühlingswind."

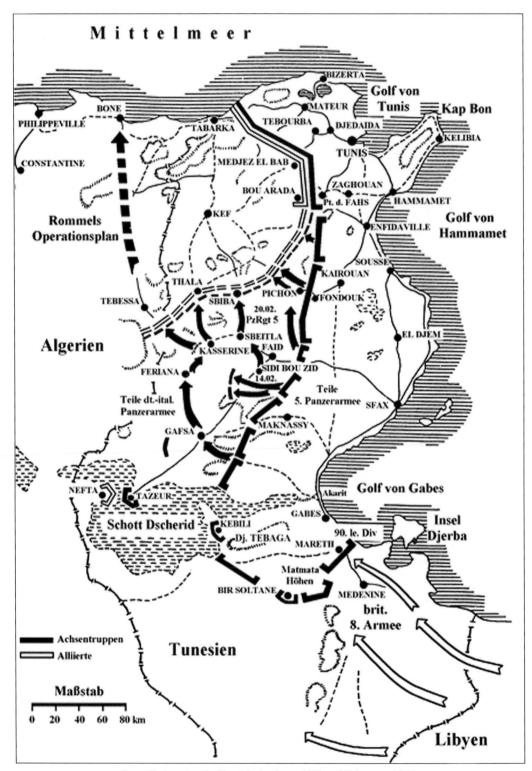

Overall situation in Tunisia in the middle of February 1943.

A Sherman captured by the 1st Battalion of the regiment in Tunisia. The inscription reads: "Do not cannibalize. For the [German Army] Weapons Branch. Captured by the *I./Pz.Rgt.5.*"

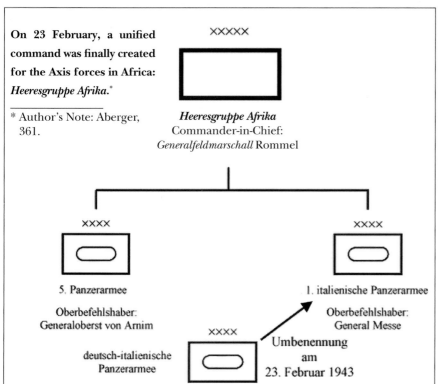

On 23 February, a unified command was finally created for the Axis forces in Africa: *Heeresgruppe Afrika.*[*]

—————————
[*] Author's Note: Aberger, 361.

XXXXX

Heeresgruppe Afrika
Commander-in-Chief:
Generalfeldmarschall Rommel

XXXX

XXXX

5. Panzerarmee

Oberbefehlshaber:
Generaloberst von Arnim

deutsch-italienische
Panzerarmee

XXXX

Umbenennung
am
23. Februar 1943

1. italienische Panzerarmee

Oberbefehlshaber:
General Messe

Deutsch-italienische Panzerarmee redesignated on 23 February as the *1. italienische Panzerarmee* (commander-in-chief: General Messe)

5. Knight's Cross Recipient of *Panzer-Regiment 5* in February 1943

The ninth and last Knight's Cross recipient of the regiment was *Hauptmann* Werner Grün.[11]

Knight's Cross of the Iron Cross.

Werner Grün
Born: 23 November 1913
Died: 5 May 2004
Recommended for the Knight's Cross: 2 January 1943
Awarded the Knight's Cross: 8 February 1943
Rank: *Hauptmann*
Duty Position: Acting commander of the 1st Battalion of *Panzer-Regiment 5*
Other High Award: German Cross in Gold (25 March 1942)

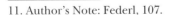

11. Author's Note: Federl, 107.

6. 6–31 March 1943: The Fighting for the Mareth Line (Operation "Capri" and the British Counteroffensive)

In contrast to *Generaloberst* von Arnim, Rommel saw his next mission in conducting an attack from the Mareth position against the 8th Army in the south so as to prevent a link-up with the Allied forces to the north. He intended to so weaken the 8th Army that Axis forces would be freed up to launch a successful attack against the Anglo-American 1st Army. Consequently, the *10. Panzer-Division* and the *21. Panzer-Division* were moved to the Schott-Akarit position at the end of February. They remained there until the morning of 3 March before moving out to the Mareth Line. On 4 March, the order was issued to attack from the Mareth Line towards Medenine.

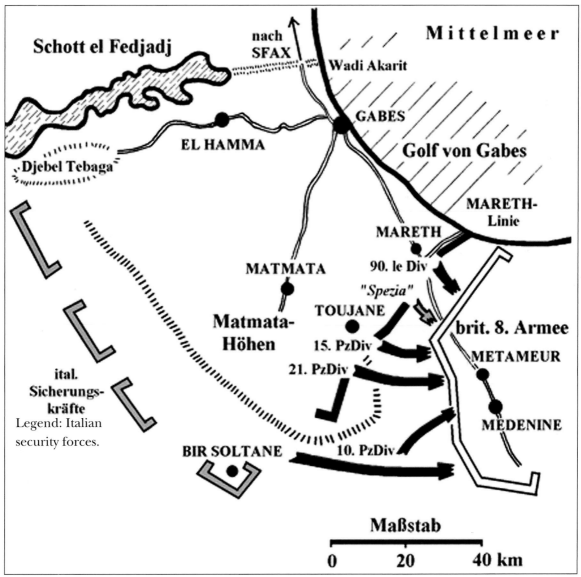

6 March 1943: Attacks by the *1. italienische Panzerarmee* from the Mareth Line against the 8th Army (Operation "Capri").

According to a report of the *21. Panzer-Division* on 4 March, *Major* Grün's 1st Battalion had twenty-eight armored fighting vehicles. The 2nd Battalion was reported to have twenty-six tanks.[12] In all, the regiment had fifty-four operational tanks.

Across from the Mareth Line, the 8th Army and its eight divisions had 80,000 men, 400 artillery pieces, 550 antitank guns and 900 tanks with large stockpiles of ammunition.[13] British engineers had emplaced approximately 70,000 mines in front of the positions.

At first light on 6 March, *Panzer-Regiment 5* started its approach to the British positions. Visibility was reduced to 3 to 4 kilometers as the result of ground fog. At 0600 hours, the German artillery preparation against the enemy positions started. Without initially encountering any resistance, the lead elements of the regiment reached an area about six kilometers west of Metameur. The tanks then ran into an expansive minefield with an antitank-gun front established behind it. The enemy was apparently well prepared for the attack. Heavy enemy artillery fire started. At that point, neither the *15. Panzer-Division* nor the *21. Panzer-Division* were able to advance any farther. Around 1600 hours, *Panzer-Regiment 5* reported it had only thirty-five operational tanks left.[14]

Although the *10. Panzer-Division* succeeded in making a penetration into the enemy's positions later in the afternoon, all of the efforts by the three armored divisions to continue the attack that day failed in the faced of the heavy defensive fires. An unusually heavy employment of antiaircraft elements on the part of the British prevented the *Luftwaffe* from providing close-in support. By evening, the three German armored divisions had lost 55 tanks out of their original 141. Of those, 40 were complete write-offs. The British losses in comparison were

12. Author's Note: Aberger, 364.

13. Author's Note: Kühn, 197.

14. Author's Note: Daily Log No. 9, *21. Panzer-Division*, Operations, 6 March 1943.

of no consequence. The attack had to be called off. During the night of 6–7 March, the attack formations returned to their lines of departure. *Panzer-Regiment 5* was fixed by enemy artillery fire until about 0400 hours on 7 March before it could start its withdrawal.

Hermann Frömbgen, a tank commander in *Panzer-Regiment 5* as the result of the incorporation of *Panzer-Abteilung 190* into the regiment at the beginning of February, wrote the following concerning the attack of 6 March:

Early on the morning of 6 March, the powerful column of tanks marched into the high plateau west of Medenine. The attack group deployed across a broad front coming out of the mountainous terrain at Matmata. Our battalion rolled along around the middle of the attack sector towards the east. We had already covered ten to fifteen kilometers without a shot having been fired. No enemy aircraft allowed themselves to be seen above us. An uncomfortable feeling came over us, since that was something out extraordinary. After all, that size combat force could not remain hidden from the enemy!

But when we had closed to about 1,000 meters of the flat ground outside of Metameur, all hell broke loose. The enemy covered us with artillery fire the likes of which we had never experienced before. Suddenly, the fighter-bombers showed up. They flitted in over the battlefield at low level and caused all sorts of mischief in our ranks. Their rockets thudded on the steel and tore it like paper.

Our company had just reached a piece of terrain that sloped somewhat downward when the enemy antitank guns also joined the fray. Out front, near our attack objective, I identified at least twelve antitank guns by their muzzle flashes. All of them were firing at our company; we returned tit for tat. *Unteroffizier* Volz, to the left of me, was knocked out. Right after that, the tank of our company commander received a direct hit. The commander's driver was killed immediately, as we were later told. Then my vehicle was hit. A return roller flew away. The next hit hammered into the engine. Our vehicle stopped!

Despite that, we continued to fire. My gunner, Gerd Hahn, fired well and knocked out three antitank guns. But then we got hit for the third time. That one hit us on the gun mantlet. A few seconds later, we received radio traffic telling us to pull back, but we were stuck and that meant only one thing: Fire, fire, fire! The barrel of our main gun had never before spit out so many rounds in such a short period of time. Then we were hit again; this time in the vicinity of the superstructure. Track links, replacement roadwheel and mud guard were flung off. Then a hard, cracking impact in the vicinity of the driver's station. The hatches flew open. Despite that, we thought we would suffocate, since thick smoke was billowing into the fighting compartment. I issued the command to bail out.

In a flash, three men were outside, seeking cover near the tank. But where were the others? Where was the radio operator? He was a really young guy, who was getting his baptism of fire with this attack. Gerd Hahn and I climbed up on the side of the tank and

found him. He had been badly wounded in the arm and had been unable to get out of his seat. With our combined strength, we lifted him up and placed him under cover next to the tank. Once again, an antitank round was hammering against the steel walls of the tank. That could be dangerous for the radio operator, so we propped him up between us in the middle and tried to get some ground between us and the tank to the rear. All of the tanks of the company that could still move had pulled back about 300 meters, where they were safe from the antitank guns. They engaged identified targets from there that were along and on the hill in front of us. Dragging the radio operator between us, we reached a slight depression through the hail of shellfire. We were at the end of our strength and, as a result of the flurry of activity associated with the rescue attempt, we had lost contact with the driver, Weber, and the loader, Pfeffer. We were hoping, however, that they had preceded us and were safe.

Unfortunately, that was not the case and had to go to the *Spieß* [15] with a heavy heart and report two missing. After we had caught our breath and had regained our strength somewhat, we tried to get out of that hell that the full fury of the artillery had unleashed. No fewer than forty guns were registered on our small sector. But our radio operator didn't want any more of it. He had been weakened by the loss of blood and was unable to leave the depression. We pulled him out by force and, sometimes carrying him, sometimes dragging him, we reached the *SPW* of the forward observer that had been assigned to us. They took us on board

---

15. Editor's Note: The equivalent of a master sergeant.

and, if we did not receive a direct hit, we were safe for the time being. After I showed the observer a few targets and briefed him on them, we used a second break in the firing to continue moving to the rear. We reached the position of the *Nebelwerfer*[16] and got to a *wadi*, where our artillery had gone into position, a short while later. We took a short break there as well. It was only there that Gerd Hahn, who had covered the 1,000 meters in his socks, since his sandals had remained behind in the tank, when I was wounded in the head. I didn't want to believe him, but when I reached back there, there was blood on my neck. Hahn checked my head and found a piece of shrapnel as big as a pea, which had penetrated into my skin through my cap and got stuck there.

We then tried to find our unit, which had to be somewhere around there. We took off right away. And it was not a moment too soon, since several fighter-bombers attacked the artillery just after we had left the *wadi*. They hammered into the *wadi* with rockets and machine-gun fire. We ran back into the *wadi* along the side and looked for cover in the crevices. When the attack was over, we hurried on. In our efforts to get back as quickly as possible, we took a shortcut, landing in a minefield. Truck drivers on the trail called out to us and alerted us to the danger. We made our way back carefully and reached the trail unscathed.

Towards noon, the two of us reached the clearing station. After we had been taken care of, we went back to the company, which had reassembled at the line of departure for the morning's attack. Only a few tanks made it back; that evening, we discovered the scope of the lost battle and voices were heard that

the attack had been betrayed ahead of time. It had been strange, after all, how heavy the fires had been that the enemy had greeted us with. It seemed as if a special "reception committee" had been established to honor us. We had wanted to deliver a heavy blow to the 8th Army; instead, we had received one. We had lost half of our tanks, and the three remaining armor divisions, which had participated in the attack, had suffered similarly. *Panzer-Regiment 5* was pulled out of its positions the next day and integrated into the Mareth position.

The last large attack of the Axis forces had ended with a defeat. *Heeresgruppe Afrika* had to recognize that its own forces were insufficient to disrupt Montgomery's approach for long. When the enemy possessed such a manifold superiority, then a limit was reached at which no matter how much personal bravery was involved on the part of the Germans, it could not be overcome.

On 9 March, Rommel flew to the *Führer* Headquarters to report on the situation. On 11 March, in recognition of his extraordinary leadership in the North African theater, Rommel became the first officer of the German Army to receive the Diamonds to the Oak Leaves with Swords to the Knight's Cross of the Iron Cross. He was only the sixth member of the German Armed Forces to be so honored up to that point. Rommel, who intended to return to the front after the award, was told to take a cure for his health.

Generaloberst von Arnim became the new commander-in-chief of *Heeresgruppe Afrika*, succeeding him in command of the *5. Panzer-Armee* was *General* von Vaerst, who had commanded the *15. Panzer-Division* during the fighting in Libya and Egypt. *General* Cramer assumed command of the *DAK* within the Italian 1st Army. The *21. Panzer-Division* remained the *DAK* reserve in the area north of Mareth until 9 March.

---

16. Translator's Note: Rocket launcher.

A *Panzer III* in the assembly area.

Von Arnim planned a graduated withdrawal of the Italian 1st Army to the Schott-Akarit position north of Gabes so as to close the gap with the *5. Panzer-Armee.* The Akarit *wadi* is about 20 kilometers north of Gabes. The bottleneck is formed by the *Schott el Fedjadj* and the Mediterranean coast. The former is a salt sea that cannot be negotiated and stretches about 150 kilometers from east to west and approaches to within 20 kilometers of the coast. The position was defined by the Akarit *wadi*, which also runs east to west, and forms the last natural barrier before the bridgehead of Tunis.

Orders issued on 12 March designated the *DAK*—at that point comprising the *10., 15.* and *21. Panzer-Divisionen*—as the mobile reserve of the Italian field army. Starting on 15 March, the *21. Panzer-Division* was employed to improve the Schott-Akarit position.

On the evening of 16 March, the 8th Army started its attack on the eastern portion of the Mareth

position with the objective of breaking through to the Sfax area. At the same time, strong British forces bypassed the line west of the Matmata Hills and American forces moved out to attack Gafsa, with the intent of reaching the coast near Sfax by advancing through Maknassy. If the efforts paid off, the Italian 1st Army would be surrounded.

On 21 March, the British 50th Infantry Division succeeded in penetrating the Mareth Line, but the penetration could be sealed off and cleared in the days that followed by the *15. Panzer-Division.* The commander-in-chief of the Italian 1st Army, General Messe, moved the *21. Panzer-Division* and the *164. leichte Division* into the El Hamma area to counter the threat to the rear of the position. After the Italian screening forces west of the Matmata Hills had been forced out of position, the enemy succeeded in breaking through the Tebaga bottleneck and taking El Hamma on 27 March. *Panzer-Regiment 5* launched a counterattack with its 77 tanks on a frontage of

Partial view of the Mareth Line, looking south. The terrain of the position favored the defense. Its major disadvantage was that it could be bypassed through the desert west of the Matmata Hills.

approximately five kilometers against around 170 enemy tanks and antitank guns.[17] Losing 23 of its tanks to the enemy's 29, the regiment succeeded in preventing the enemy from advancing to the coast. But while the losses of the enemy could quickly be made good again by dint of practically inexhaustible reserves, the loss of the German tanks was irreplaceable. The Mareth Line could no longer be held, and the Italian 1st Army ordered its evacuation. The *21. Panzer-Division* held its positions and allowed the main body of the Italian field army to reach the Schott-Akarit position. Despite considerable numerical superiority—743 British tanks versus 142 German ones—Montgomery had been unable to encircle the Italian field army and destroy it.

The U.S. 1st Army was able to take Maknassy on 22 March, but it was prevented from reaching the coast by the employment of reserves and the hurried introduction of *Tiger* tanks. The Allies did not succeed in separating the two field armies of *Heeresgruppe Afrika.* On 28 March, the Italian 1st Army reached the Schott-Akarit position. *Panzer-Regiment 5* was employed on the right flank to either side of

the Gafsa-Gabes road, defending against American attacks. *Hauptmann* Rohr later recalled:[18]

At the end of March 1943, a critical situation arose in the hilly foreland of the Atlas Mountains at El Guettar. The *21. Panzer-Division* gave me command of the remnants of *Panzer-Regiment 5.*[19] I was directed to stabilize the situation at El Guettar. Everything appeared to have been lost there. Consequently, I took my tank and moved there by map, where I was greeted with great jubilation. After we appeared, the Yanks did not attempt any further advances. But they fired continuously with everything they had. After a week, Kesselring sent me radio traffic: "My recognition for your brave performance of duty." What we did not know: The English and the Americans wanted to link up at this position. The Americans from the front out of the west. The English from the south behind us. We had prevented that until the last German soldier had come to safety from the south.

17. Author's Note: Rohr, 117.

18. Author's Note: *Oberst* Stenkoff had been transferred to the headquarters of the *5. Panzer-Armee.*

19. Author's Note: Kühn, 207.

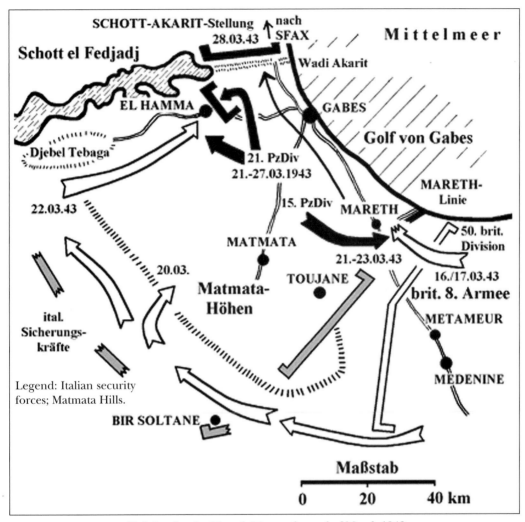

Fighting for the Mareth Line at the end of March 1943.

7. 5 April to 13 May 1943: The Final Fighting in Tunisia

On 5 April, three divisions of the 8th Army broke into the Schott-Akarit position.

A counterattack launched by the *90. leichte Afrika-Division* and the *15. Panzer-Division* prevented a breakthrough. Von Arnim ordered the Italian 1st Army to conduct a single move to the Enfidaville Position, some 80 kilometers south of Tunis, since the terrain between the two positions—nearly 200 kilometers—did not lend itself to the construction of defensive positions.

The *21. Panzer-Division* started its withdrawal movements during the evening of 6 April, after *Panzer-Regiment 5*, working together with *Panzerjäger-Abteilung 39*, was able to turn back an American armor attack into the right flank of the division. In the process, eleven Shermans were knocked out.

The division moved north through Kairouan in two *Kampfgruppen* of roughly equivalent size. The battle groups were attached to the *15. Panzer-Division* and the *10. Panzer-Division*. A period of bad weather prevented the enemy air forces from operating, with the result that the march columns were largely spared from air attacks. The *21. Panzer-Division* reached an area roughly thirty kilometers west of Enfidaville during the evening of 10 April. It was designated as the reserve of *Heeresgruppe Afrika*. The division received ordered to establish defensive positions in the area of the *Djebel Fikrine*, a sector roughly thirty kilometers across. The mountain range formed a dominant bulwark on the southwestern frontage of the Tunisian bridgehead.

Since it was not possible to occupy the defensive line continuously because of the reduced forces of the division, the forward edge of the defensive area consisted of a series of widely separated strongpoints.

Hauptmann Rohr, the last (acting) commander of *Panzer-Regiment 5*. He was wounded on 21 April and succeeded in reaching Italy on a hospital ship prior to the capitulation. No one was named to succeed him.

In the middle of April, the *21. Panzer-Division* still had a personnel strength of about 2,000 men. Efforts were made to bring personnel replacements on Italian destroyers and torpedo boats. Tanks and heavy weapons, not to mention ammunition and fuel, had not made it to Tunisia for weeks. Transport aircraft, such as the *Ju 52* and the *Me 323 Gigant*— frequently fell victim to enemy fighters. On 25 April, the division abandoned its positions without a fight along the Djebel Fikrine as a result of the over-all situation.

Generalmajor Hildebrandt transferred command of the division to *Oberst* von Hülsen, who was then promoted to *Generalmajor*, on 1 May. The division set up defensive positions in the Djebel Zaghouan area. The mountainous terrain largely dominated the area between the Mediterranean coast and the Pont du Fahs Valley. Other than occasional artillery harassment fires and individual air attacks, it remained quiet in the division sector.

What was left of the armored forces in the Tunisian bridgehead was consolidated under *Oberst* Irkens, the commander of *Panzer-Regiment 8*, who was designated the *Panzerführer Afrika*. This measure included *Panzer-Regiment 5*. This force totaled seventy operational tanks and was repeatedly committed against the masses of Allied armor. The brave tankers frequently scored considerable success. On 6 May, *Oberst* Irkens had thirty operational tanks left in his command, including the last ones of *Panzer-Regiment 5*.

On 7 May, the last tanks were moved to the airfield west of Tunis. The last remaining ammunition was fired and fuel used up, thus signaling the end of the hopeless struggle of *Oberst* Irkens and his men. The last seven tanks had to be destroyed by their crews, since there was no longer any resupply of consumables.

As a result of the heavy fighting, the northern front of the bridgehead broke apart into small

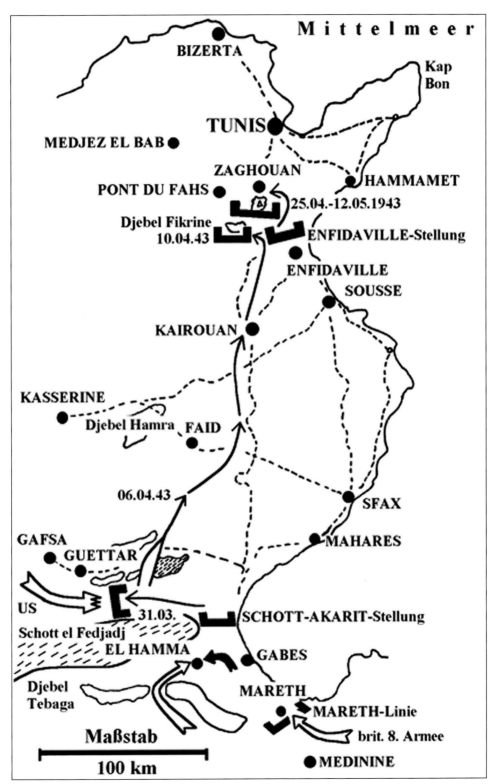

31 March to 12 May 1943: The last operations and movements of the *21. Panzer-Division* and *Panzer-Regiment 5* in Africa.

sectors, where resistance was still offered. During the afternoon of 7 May, the *5. Panzer-Armee* reported that enemy forces with approximately 1,000 tanks had broken through at Medjez el Bab and headed in the direction of Tunis, while enemy forces had also broken through further north and were headed for Bizerta. Tunis fell and the Allies then turned south into the rear of the *DAK*. The remaining ammunition was fired and the weapons and vehicles prepared for destruction.

On 12 May, the *21. Panzer-Division* surrendered, and the final resistance in the Tunis bridgehead collapsed the following day. On 13 May, the German Armed Forces announced the following:

> The heroic struggle of the German and Italian formations in Africa found an honorable end today. The last resistance of the groups fighting in the vicinity of Tunis —without water and rations for days—had to be stopped after the expenditure of all of their ammunition. In the end, they succumbed to a lack of supplies and not the assault of the enemy, who often enough had to recognize the superiority of our weapons even in this theater of war.

> Despite all that, the warriors of Germany and Italy fighting in Africa fulfilled the mission they had been given in its entirety. As a result of their resistance, which made the enemy contest every foot of ground in months of bitter fighting, they fixed extremely strong forces of the enemy in North Africa and inflicted extremely heavy losses on him in personnel and materiel. The relief that that brought to other fronts and the time that has been won has been most advantageous to the Axis powers.

Along with the end of the fighting in North Africa, *Panzer-Regiment 5* had also found its end.

8. Overview of *Panzer-Regiment 5* in the Campaign in North Africa in 1943

10 January 1943	*Oberst* Stenkoff assumes command of *Panzer-Regiment 5*
Until 13 January 1943	Defense of the Homs-Tarhuna position
13–17 January 1943	Movement into the area north of Gabes
30 January to 1 February 1943	Attack and capture of the mountain passes in the Faid area
Beginning of February 1943	Reorganization of the regiment—the 2nd Battalion is consolidated with the 1st Battalion and *Panzer-Abteilung 190* of the *90. leichte Afrika-Division* is redesignated as the new 2nd Battalion of the regiment
14–22 February 1943	*Operation "Frühlingswind"*: Advance on Sidi Bou Zid–Sbeitla–Sbiba
Until 5 March 1943	Movement into the Schott-Akarit position, followed by the Mareth position
6–7 March 1943	Operation "Capri": Attack from the Mareth position against Medenine
27 March 1943	Counterattack at El Hamma
31 March 1943	*Hauptmann* Rohr assumes acting command of the regiment
Until 6 April 1943	Defense in the Scott-Akarit position in the vicinity of El Guettar
6–10 April 1943	Withdrawal to the Enfidaville position
Until 7 May 1943	Final fighting of the regiment as part of *Kampfgruppe Oberst Irkens* in Tunisia
13 May 1943	Capitulation of *Heeresgruppe Afrika*

The average age of those who fell in Africa in 1943 was twenty-three. Once again, it is striking how many officers and noncommissioned officers made up the numbers of casualties, reaching approximately 33 percent, the same percentage as in 1942. According to the regiment's TO&E, officers and noncommissioned officers made up only 21 percent of the regiment's personnel.

According to official German sources, the following numbers of soldiers of the regiment were known to have been killed or died in Africa:

- 1941: 107
- 1942: 180
- 1943: 57
- Total fallen in Africa: 344

10. Final Observations Concerning the Campaign in Africa from 1941 to 1943

The Alliance

There was no interest at all on the part of the political leadership of the Greater German *Reich* for conducting war in North Africa. The defeat of the Italians in Libya forced Germany from a strategic viewpoint and as an alliance partner of the Axis to intervene. Moreover, Mussolini had asked for the support of German formations.

Based on Directive No. 22 of the German Armed Forces High Command, a *Sperrverband Afrika*[20] was formed, which was intended primarily to conduct defensive operations in Libya. The fact that the German formations increasingly had to bear the burden of the fighting in North Africa was due to the failure of the Italians, something that became ever more apparent. The Italians not only disappointed, they even became a burden. Wherever crises arose

20. Translator's Note: Blocking Force "Africa."

or breakthroughs occurred, it was almost always in the Italian sector. German battle groups then had to clean up the situation. Despite that, the Germans were compelled to rely on the Italians, especially with regard to logistics, and generally treated them with kid gloves, whenever possible.

German Successes

The German formations of Rommel soon garnered a reputation as a result of the fighting in the North African theater of war as an especially brave force. Even today, there is an almost legendary status associated with the *Afrikakorps*. The secret of the German success rested primarily on the leadership skill of Rommel, who was able to offset the personnel and materiel numerical inferiority of his forces for a long time through cleverly conducted offensive blows. The weaker force could become the stronger one at a decisive place by means of speed, maneuverability, surprise and deception. But this type of leadership required execution by a qualified force. The German

Illustration of a German and Italian soldier by the Italian graphic artist, Sergio Bianchi. *Die Oase*, vol. 21, issue 11 (November 1971): 14.

forces in Africa fulfilled those requirements. They had modern weapons at their disposal, as well as leadership that was oriented on the accomplishment of the mission. Superiors and subordinates formed a unit by largely overcoming differences in rank.

The leaders were up front, even Rommel in his capacity as commander-in-chief. They set a good example by going forward. The high toll extracted among the officer and noncommissioned officer corps is proof of that. Although the tables of organization and equipment only specified that every fifth soldier was an officer or noncommissioned officer, almost every third death in theater belonged to that group.

In contrast, the enemy demonstrated a lack of tactical agility over and over again, which led to numerous failures, despite an oppressive superiority in personnel and materiel. Lower and mid-level leadership was given too little freedom of action compared to its German counterpart. Instead of exploiting success, the attack spearheads frequently remained where they were after achieving local success to wait for further orders.

Employment of Armor

For both sides, the employment of armor was always the centerpiece of operations. The African desert offered almost ideal prerequisites for the execution of its operational doctrine. The elements of armor protection, fire and movement were able to be employed almost without restriction.

Rommel himself wrote: "Everything revolves around the tanks; the other formations are just a side dish."[21] Despite numerical inferiority and high losses in a struggle of attrition under the worst imaginable weather conditions, the German armored formations held their own for two years in seesaw fighting involving offensive, defensive and delaying actions against the enemy in North Africa. They

---

21. Author's Note: Rommel, *Krieg ohne Haß*, 121.

Generaloberst Rommel at the command post of *Oberst* Baade (third from the left), the commander of *Schützen-Regiment 115*.

gained valuable time and protected the southern flank of Europe. *Panzer-Regiment 5* was a part of that terrific fighting force, and it distinguished itself in an exceptional manner in North Africa.

Logistics as a Fundamental Issue of the Campaign

But bravery, courage, morale and leadership skills do not set the tone all by themselves over the long haul; logistics also has to function. Logistics does not directly affect the battle, but it influences all fighting to a greater or lesser extent.

With few exceptions, supplies for the Axis forces were always insufficient. A lack of dominance on the seas and in the air and the failure to take the island of Malta had a decisive effect.

The losses in ships, personnel and logistical items of all types in the Mediterranean was relatively high. On top of that, there was the especially long supply routes from the harbors to the front. Without the large spoils-of-war captured in 1941 and 1942, Rommel's successes would not have been possible at all. Logistics became the most pressing problem and, in the end, of decisive importance for the campaign.

The Strategic Importance of the Campaign in Africa

North Africa was considered to be a secondary theater of war for the German leadership. It was directed that time be won and the loss of Italy as an alliance partner be prevented. The opportunities that conducting warfare against England in Africa offered were either not recognized or could not be exploited, because German resources against a world of enemies were limited. It was primarily due to the adverse situation that had developed on the Eastern Front that support for the fighting in Africa was minimal. The Germans wanted to first wait for a victory over the Soviet Union before they shifted their main effort to the area of the Mediterranean. Consequently, both theaters interacted. After the

defeat at Stalingrad and the capitulation of the German and Italian forces in Tunisia in May 1943, the further course of the war was written on the horizon. Germany could not replace its personnel and materiel losses.

Losses

Approximately 250,000 German soldiers were employed in North Africa during a campaign that lasted more than two years. Of those, around 130,000 were taken prisoner in May 1943. It is estimated that more than 100,000 men were killed on both sides in the fighting conducted between 1941 and 1943. Of those, the British lost 35,470 and the Americans 16,500. In addition, there were a number of French (approximately 5,000) and citizens of other nations. Among the Axis forces, 13,748 Italians lost their lives, as well as 18,594 Germans. Thousands remained unaccounted for. The number of those lost in transit to Africa cannot be determined.

The German soldiers believed they were fighting for a good and justified cause. They cannot be held responsible for political decisions. Correspondingly, they deserve our respect and admiration. In the end, it is a sign of culture and human dignity in the face of great sacrifice.

The insignia of the *DAK* became a thing of the past on 13 May 1943.

The beginning of 1943: Railway transport of personnel replacements for *Panzer-Regiment 5. Gefreiter* König at an Italian railway station.

On freight cars in Italy.

At the airfield at Palermo, personnel await transportation to Africa in a *Ju 52*.

Moving to a new front in January 1943: *Panzer-Regiment 5* headed to Tunisia from Libya.

Hauptmann Werner Grün, the last recipient of the Knight's Cross to the Iron Cross in the regiment. He received the award on 8 February 1943 as the acting commander of the regiment's 1st Battalion. He was also a recipient of the German Cross in Gold.

A late model *Panzer III* in Tunisia has received both manmade and natural vegetation for concealment.

Rearming a *Panzer IV* of the 3rd Company after the fighting. On the left is *Gefreiter* Günter Sauer.

An American Sherman knocked out at Sidi Bou Zid seems to be attracting a lot of attention.

The crew of this Sherman was forced to bail out after being hit by a high-explosive round fired by gunner Werner Fenck of the 1st Company on 14 February 1943. The tank was not damaged and was sent to Germany for evaluation.

A *Panzer IV* of the 8th Company in an assembly area. Palm fronds are used in an effort to break up the outline of the vehicle.

February 1943: Another *Panzer IV* of the 8th Company. It appears that only single digits were used to identify the vehicles at this point.

3 March 1943: Movement from the Schott-Akarit position to the Mareth Line.

The main gun of this *Panzer IV* had to be recalibrated. Note the extra storage mounts for water and fuel cans.

21 March 1943: *Leutnant* Fortun, a platoon leader in the 8th Company, during the fighting in the El Hamma area.

Battle damage sustained to a *Panzer IV* of the 8th Company after air attacks and artillery fire.

The final fighting nears. Despite no longer being listed on the TO&E, this *Panzer IV* (short) continued to be employed in front-line service to the end.

Desperate fighting against enemy numerical superiority. A 5-centimeter *Pak 38* antitank gun in action.

A British low-level aerial attack is taken under fire.

CHAPTER 3

History of *Panzer-Abteilung 5,* 1943

1. 14 September 1943: Activation of *Panzer-Abteilung 5* in Neuruppin

After the loss of *Panzer-Regiment 5* in Tunisia, there was still a considerable number of soldiers of the former regiment who had been spared the final fighting and captivity, because they had found themselves outside of North Africa in May 1943 as convalescents or on leave. Those old "African warriors" were assigned to *Panzer-Ersatz-Abteilung 5* in Neuruppin. They were infused with the idea of not being reassigned to some other formation as replacements. Instead, they wanted to establish a new formation that would continue the tradition of the former regiment. That effort paid off in an order dated 25 August 1943 creating *Panzer-Abteilung 5*. Correspondingly, hopes were also raised that the establishment of the battalion could also lead to the re-activation of the regiment.[1]

For the activation of *Panzer-Abteilung 5*, a TO&E dated 20 June 1943 was used, which authorized issuance of assault guns in lieu of tanks.[2] The assault gun, originally designed as a close-in artillery-support weapon for the infantry, had demonstrated extraordinary success in the course of the war in combating enemy tanks. It was cheaper and easier to produce than a tank; it had a low silhouette, suitable armor protection and an effective long-barreled 7.5-centimeter main gun (L/48). In addition, the assault gun only needed a four-man crew as opposed to five crewmembers.

---

1. Translator's Note: It was common German practice to reconstitute formations that had been effectively destroyed on the battlefield. For some reason, this did not happen in the case of the formations that fought in Africa. Instead, as was the case with *Panzer-Abteilung 5*, battalions were sometimes raised that had a linkage to the former regiment, but they usually found a new "home" in the framework of a mechanized infantry division, since it was only authorized a tank battalion, as opposed to a regiment.

---

2. Author's Note: Jentz, 70.

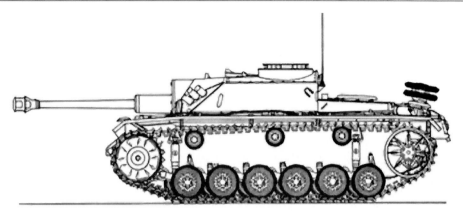

Sturmgeschütz III
(Sd.Kfz. 142/1)
G Model
Characteristics:
6 roadwheels mounted on torsion bars; 3 return rollers (chassis of a *Panzer III*).
Starting in 1943, sideskirts were outfitted at the factory.

Technical Data:[*]	
Over-all length:	7.66 meters
Over-all width (with sideskirts):	3.41 meters
Over-all height:	2.3 meters
Combat weight:	23.9 tons
Horsepower:	300
Maximum speed (road):	40 kilometers an hour
Radius of operation (road):	155 kilometers
Fuel capacity:	310 liters
Crew:	4 man
Armament:	7.5-centimeter L/48 main gun and 1 7.92-millimeter *MG 34*
Basic load of ammunition:	54 rounds
Armor:	
Hull (front):	5 + 3 centimeters
Sides:	3 centimeters
Rear:	3 centimeters
Price (without weapons):	82,500 *Reichsmark*

Used since 1943 in the assault gun battalions of the artillery and in tank battalions of mechanized infantry divisions. In some cases, also employed within the antitank battalion of infantry divisions.

---

[*] Author's Note: Walter J. Spielberger and Friedrich Wiener, *Die deutschen Panzerkampfwagen III und IV mit ihren Abarten 1935–1945*.

A G model *Sturmgeschütz III* of *Panzer-Abteilung 5* in 1943.

Organization of *Panzer-Abteilung 5*

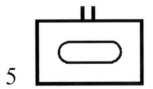

5

Signals Platoon of the Headquarters
Company of a Tank Battalion (in
accordance with *K.St.N. 1157a*, dated
20 June 1943)

3 PzKpfWg III als PzBefWg

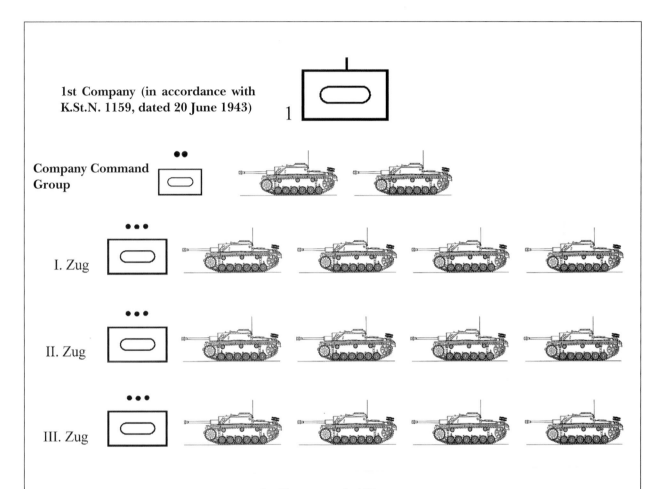

1st Company (in accordance with K.St.N. 1159, dated 20 June 1943)

Company Command Group

I. Zug

II. Zug

III. Zug

1st Platoon ... 3rd Platoon

The authorized strength in tanks and assault guns for a tank battalion organized in accordance with the TO&E dated 20 June 1943:

- 3 *Panzerbefehlswagen III's*
- 42 *Sturmgeschütz III's*

Total: 45 tanks and assault guns

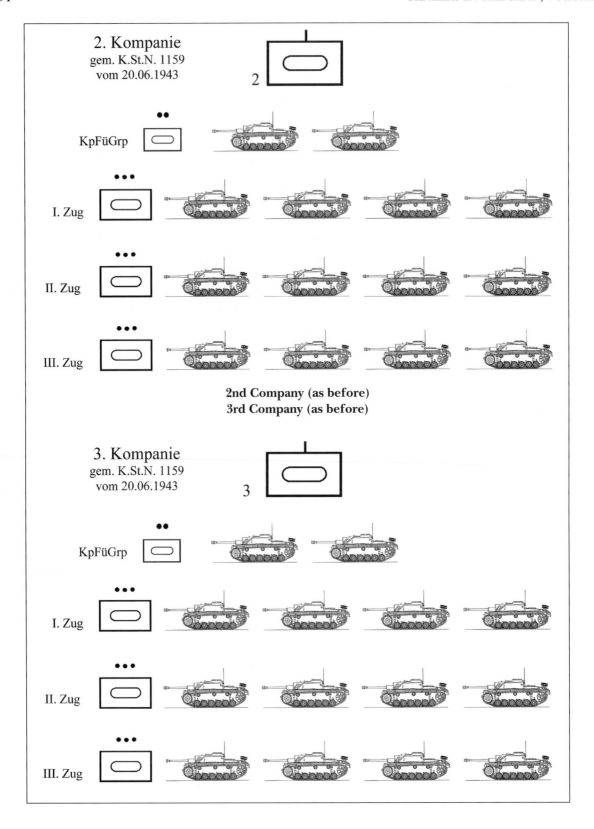

2. Kompanie
gem. K.St.N. 1159
vom 20.06.1943

2

KpFüGrp

I. Zug

II. Zug

III. Zug

2nd Company (as before)
3rd Company (as before)

3. Kompanie
gem. K.St.N. 1159
vom 20.06.1943

3

KpFüGrp

I. Zug

II. Zug

III. Zug

When taking into consideration the actual organization of the battalion in September 1943, there were apparently deviations from the theoretical organization. Statements concerning the organization contradict one another, however. There are also claims that there were four companies and not just three. In addition, the companies initially were said to have had seventeen combat vehicles as opposed to the authorized fourteen assault guns. In later after-action reports, however, the four-gun platoon organization is referenced. The battalion also received an antiaircraft platoon with three 2-centimeter four-barreled *Flak* on half-tracked vehicles.[3] There are no data available concerning the actual numbers of armored fighting vehicles issued to the battalion in September 1943.

The commander of the new battalion was *Hauptmann* Josef Rettemeier, who had been company commander of the regiment's 2nd Company in Africa in 1942. In the final fighting around El Alamein, he had assumed acting command of the 1st Battalion from *Oberstleutnant* Mildebrath.

Other leadership and staff positions were occupied as follows:

Adjutant: *Oberleutnant* Piening

Liaison Officer: *Leutnant* Zimmer

Signals Officer: *Oberleutnant* Wendler

Battalion Physician: *Stabsarzt Dr.* Müller

Company Commanders: *Oberleutnant* Köllmann, *Hauptmann* Krone, *Oberleutnant* Gast and *Oberleutnant* Frede.

Commander, Maintenance Company: *Oberleutnant (Ing)* Thüns

The lieutenants assigned had either served in Africa or already had experience on the Eastern Front. The majority of the company first sergeants, noncommissioned officer platoon leaders and tank commanders were tried-and-true service personnel from the old regiment in Africa. Most of the former enlisted personnel of the regiment were used as drivers and gunners.

In the case of personnel, almost all selections could be made based on men, who had volunteered to serve with the battalion. As a result, the new battalion had the best of prerequisites for its upcoming operations, in terms of both personnel and equipment. The cohesiveness demonstrated and the success in training during the battalion's activation phase confirmed that convincingly.

The battalion was declared operational in Neuruppin on 14 September 1943.[4] The formation was assigned to the *25. Panzergrenadier-Division*, which was authorized one tank battalion in accordance with its TO&E as a *Panzergrenadier-Division 1943*. The division consisted primarily of personnel from Wuertemberg. It had been employed on the Eastern Front as the *25. Infanterie-Division (mot)*, being re-designated and reorganized effective 23 June 1943.

---

3. Author's Note: Witthaus, correspondence to the author dated 10 January 2002.

4. Author's Note: Rettemeier, notes concerning the formation of *Panzer-Abteilung 5*, page 1.

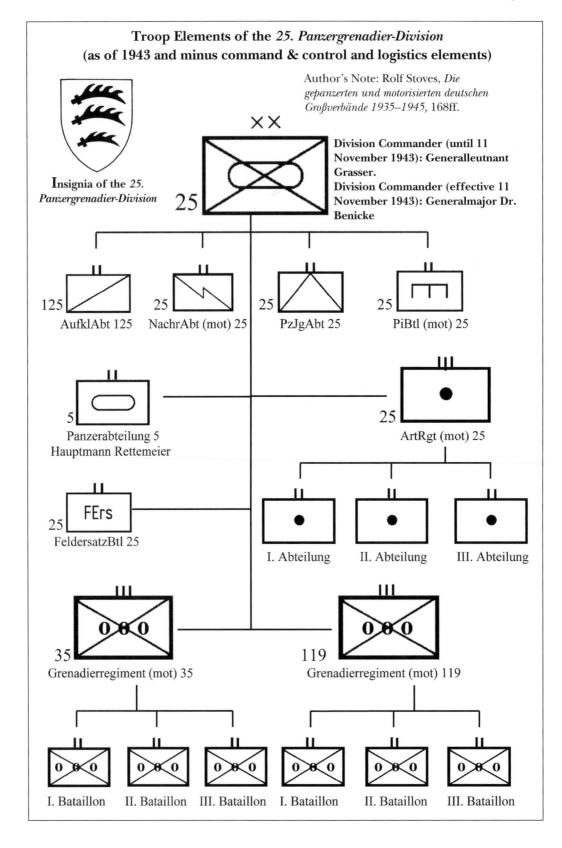

Troop Elements of the *25. Panzergrenadier-Division*
(as of 1943 and minus command & control and logistics elements)

Author's Note: Rolf Stoves, *Die gepanzerten und motorisierten deutschen Großverbände 1935–1945*, 168ff.

Insignia of the *25. Panzergrenadier-Division*

Division Commander (until 11 November 1943): Generalleutnant Grasser.
Division Commander (effective 11 November 1943): Generalmajor Dr. Benicke

125 — AufklAbt 125

25 — NachrAbt (mot) 25

25 — PzJgAbt 25

25 — PiBtl (mot) 25

5 — Panzerabteilung 5 Hauptmann Rettemeier

25 — ArtRgt (mot) 25

25 — FeldersatzBtl 25

I. Abteilung

II. Abteilung

III. Abteilung

35 — Grenadierregiment (mot) 35

119 — Grenadierregiment (mot) 119

I. Bataillon   II. Bataillon   III. Bataillon   I. Bataillon   II. Bataillon   III. Bataillon

2.10 October to the Middle of November 1943: March to the Front and Preparations for Operations

Between 10 and 15 October, *Panzer-Abteilung 5* took its leave of Neuruppin and Germany. The battalion

reached the Eastern Front by 20 October in several rail transports, where it was offloaded in Orscha in the sector of *Heeresgruppe Mitte*.

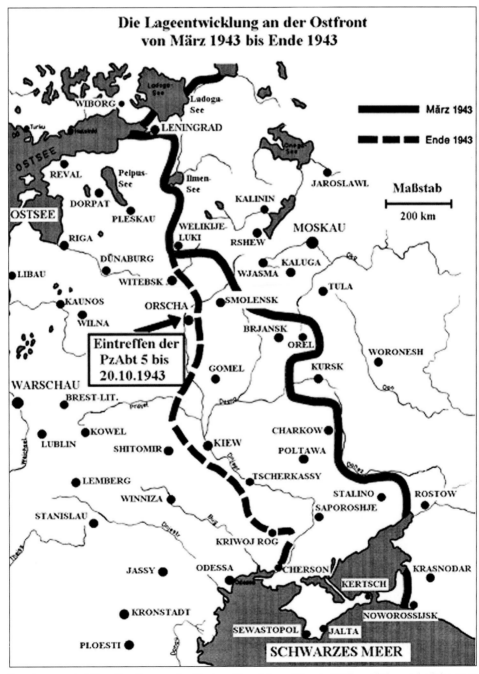

Development of the situation on the Eastern Front from March 1943 until the end of the year.

The arrival of the battalion within the sector of the *25. Panzergrenadier-Division* was greeted enthusiastically:[5]

During that dismal period of waiting, which was caused by the weather, something happened that raised spirits in the division considerably. Everyone felt as though he had been promoted one rank. *Panzer-Abteilung 5* had arrived—the division's own tank arm. What could happen to us now? It was equipped very well and also complete in terms of personnel. As it would soon turn out, it was also magnificently led by *Hauptmann* Rettemeier.

The situation did not demand the immediate employment of the battalion. As a result, several weeks were available to thoroughly prepare for upcoming operations. The battalion familiarized itself with local conditions, undertook extensive terrain reconnaissance in the anticipated areas of operations, intensified its training on weapons and equipment and conducted gunnery training, in addition to conducting officer and noncommissioned officer professional training. The training reached its climax in a live-fire exercise. In the course of the exercises, the *Flak* platoon had the opportunity to shoot down an attack Soviet aircraft, thus proving its abilities in very practical terms. Superiors at all levels of command did not miss the opportunity to form an opinion of the new tank battalion with the old "Africa warriors." Among others visiting:

_____

5. Author's Note: Boehm, *Geschichte der 25. Division*, 219.

An assault gun of the battalion's 3rd Company. In the middle is *Gefreiter* Lothar Witthaus.

- The division commander, *Generalleutnant* Grasser,
- The commanding general of the *XXVII. Armee-Korps, General der Infanterie* Völckers and
- The commander-in-chief of the *4. Armee, Generaloberst* Heinrici.

Occasional long-range Soviet artillery fire forced the battalion to leave the built-up areas and seek quarters in wooded areas. A few ambushes by partisans on the Maintenance Company west of Orscha—no serious damage was inflicted or casualties sustained—caused the establishment of a maintenance strongpoint, which was situated well for the defense and was able to withstand all attacks by the partisans.

3. 14–21 November 1943: *Panzer-Abteilung 5* in the 3rd Autobahn Battle

At the beginning of November 1943, signs of an impending Soviet offensive started appearing in the area of the Dnjepr River and west of Smolensk along the Minsk-Orscha highway. The enemy's intent was quite clear based on radio intercepts, prisoner interrogations and deserter statements: Orscha was to fall before the onset of the 1943–1944 winter. The city was only forty kilometers from the Soviets and represented an important transportation hub, as well as a crossing point over the Dnjepr. To that end, the Soviets positioned three field armies in a small area (about twenty kilometers wide). In the area around the highway and railway line along the left wing of the *25. Panzergrenadier-Division*, the Soviets positioned two armored corps, which were directed to advance on Orscha after the breakthrough had been accomplished. As a result, *Panzer-Abteilung 5* was placed in the division rear in the threatened sector as its reserve.

✠

The 14th of November proved to be the day for the baptism of fire for the tank battalion, when it participated in the 3rd *Autobahn* Battle west of Smolensk. After an especially heavy artillery preparation, the Soviets had succeeded in achieving a deep penetration along the boundary between the *25. Panzergrenadier-Division* and the *78. Sturm-Division* between the highway and the river.

The battalion launched an immediate counterattack with two companies, defeated strong enemy forces and retook the main line of resistance. The 3rd Company reinforced the infantry along the southern banks of the Dnjepr in fending off enemy attacks.

The liaison officer of the battalion, *Leutnant* Zimmer, described the first day of fighting as follows:[6]

14 November 1943: Just before the normal first call, everyone flew out of their bunker beds at 0545 hours. The Russian artillery had commenced with a mighty blow. The barrage was in unheard of intensity. That drastic wake-up call on a Sunday morning made it clear to everyone: This would be the first test for the new battalion.

We were the division reserve, with the 1st and 3rd Companies in Tscherfki between the railway line and the highway, about five kilometers behind the left wing of the division sector. There were two battalions in front of us in the main line of resistance: Along the railway line to the right was the *III./Grenadier-Regiment 119*; along the railway line on the highway to the left was *Panzer-Aufklärungs-Abteilung 125* with its three motorcycle companies. The *78. Sturm-Division* adjoined farther to the left. The tank companies were fully equipped, each with seventeen assault tanks, each of which had a long 7.5-centimeter main gun and a machine gun.

It was impossible to call the division. All of the land lines were out of commission. Because of that, the battalion commander, *Hauptmann* Rettemeier, and his liaison officer[7] went to the division command post. He received orders from the operations officer, *Oberstleutnant i.G.* Schnez, at 1100 hours: Russians had penetrated between the railway line and the highway. *Panzer-Abteilung*

5 retakes the main line of resistance in a counterattack!

The company commanders were already waiting. Short orders conference. Then the battalion formed up. Thick fog made it difficult to get oriented. Occasionally, you could only see the vehicle next to you. The battalion rolled out to the east along a frontage of about 800 meters. The companies were employed in refuse right and left formations. The battalion commander was ahead of everyone in his command tank. Behind him were the two "lashed" vehicles.[8]

You could barely see anything. The Russian artillery fire was raging. The commander continued unperturbed. He continuously gave instructions to his commanders on the radio. The left-hand company ran right into a Russian antitank-gun belt.

Firefight: Loss of [one of] the company commanders. Two tanks got stuck, but they were immediately freed up in the middle of the fighting. The battalion overcame the antitank-gun belt. Then things got really uncomfortable. All of a sudden, we were moving solely through Russian infantry. We increased our tempo and, all of a sudden, were back at the old main line of resistance. There were no friendly infantry to be seen in the trenches.

Hauptmann Rettemeier ordered us to clear the front lines as well as we could without infantry. Doing that in the fog proved difficult. Thanks to good training and constant radio contact, however, we achieved our objective.

6. Author's Note: Boehm, 221ff.

7. Translator's Note: As is typical in many German accounts, the narrator refers to himself in the third person.

8. Author's Note: Vehicles designated for the commander's use if his vehicle was shot out from under him.

New orders from the battalion commander: The companies were to leave screening forces at the main line of resistance; the main bodies were to move to Lobany, 2.5 kilometers west of the main line of resistance, and assemble! On the way back, we scouted out any and all friendly infantry there was to be found and had them mount up. A battle group of about platoon size approached us; we also had it mount up. In Lobany, we took a short stock of everything, redistributed crews and then headed off to another counterattack. As it started to turn dark, the battalion reached the old trench lines again. This time, however, the indispensible infantry was also with us. It alone was in the position to exploit the success and hold the terrain that had been captured. One tank company was echeloned to the rear to screen the endangered left flank. The other company cleared the trench line for the infantry by fire. The infantry jumped in immediately, followed our fires and completely rolled up the trench.

The battalion had completed the mission given to it by the division. The tense situation did not end, however. The division ordered the battalion to remain forward. It established all-round defensive positions at points where things could be observed behind the main line of resistance to provide its own security and safeguard the infantry. We did not know how many infiltrated Russians were still behind us. Russian T-34's rattled barely 100 meters in front of the main line of resistance; they had gotten themselves stuck in the trenches. It was impossible to deliver aimed fire. You could barely see your hand in front of your face.

Two days later: 16 November 1943

During a short period yesterday, the battalion knocked out twenty-four enemy tanks. The battalion was then moved back to a reserve position to rearm and refuel and perform maintenance.

Today, the battalion conducted a counterattack at first light so as to regain the final bit of terrain that had been lost yesterday on the extreme left wing. One of the company commanders was disabled. His tank caved in an observation bunker. The battalion commander's got one of its tracks stuck immediately thereafter in a narrow trench. It was then hit. The commander got into the last of his three command tanks, since the second one got stuck in front of a Russian observation post and was lost through fire. The battalion did not see anyone dismount. The command tank then directed the operations of the companies from an extremely good observation point. The commander committed a tank company out to the right, against thirty heavy Russian tanks that were threatening to go around us. The company hit them in the flank. Half of the Soviet tanks were stopped by the company's fires. The remainder saved themselves by moving back.

In retribution, Russian artillery placed heavy fires on the battalion. A few of the tanks suffered damage. There were some vehicles disabled. But the battalion held and, as a result, the infantry stayed in its trenches. Because we were there, the infantry received the strength to hold out. It was thankful to us. That day were set alight: 1 heavy 15.2-centimeter tank destroyer; 2 KV-I's; 2 T-34's; 1 T-60. Immobilized were: 2 T-34's; 6 KV-I's.

17 November 1943

While the positions of the *25. Panzergrenadier-Division* could be held that morning despite the bitter efforts of the enemy, the friendly forces to the left had to pull back to the superior numbers of enemy on the portion of its front adjoining ours. As a result, the left wing of the division was hanging in the air and began to crumble. A gap of 1,000 meters had been torn along the boundary. The situation was made especially difficult by the loss of means of communication. The landlines had been irreparably shot up; radio sets had been lost. The harassment fires of the Russian artillery, which lasted all day long, prevented the fixing of the damage. Messengers no longer got through, either. The only force that still had a handle on the situation and, as a result, had the opportunity to lead was the tank battalion.

The division designated *Hauptmann* Rettemeier as the commander of the left-wing sector until he could be relieved as soon as possible by *Panzer-Aufklärungs-Abteilung 125.*

He stabilized the situation through two decisive measures. Our own infantry battle groups, shrunken in size, were withdrawing as the result of the loss of small arms. The mud that was everywhere had put them, as well as some heavy machine guns and mortars, out of commission. *Hauptmann* Rettemeier had all of the machine guns in the vehicles dismounted and distributed them among the infantry battle groups, along with submachine guns, hand grenades and ammunition. Because of the lack of officers, he led them forward into the positions.

Supported by the main guns of the tanks, they aggressively occupied the main line of resistance, now freshly equipped to defend it.

The screen force on the left reported that an enemy attack from the north on the gap in the boundary was imminent. Just in the nick of time, the battalion went into position behind the gap. With all of the firepower at its disposal, it shot to pieces most of the enemy infantry advancing across a kilometer of frontage. The Russians were attacking south from Novo Selo with the intent of collapsing the left wing of the division. Following the first attack wave was a second one and, finally, a third. It was only because of commissars with pistols in their hands that they advanced across the rows of their dead and wounded comrades. Finally, we were able to breath easy. We realized on the battlefield the correctness of the radio message that the Russian commander repeatedly sent to his superiors (the division had monitored it and relayed it forward to us immediately): "Impossible to attack further! Everything bogging down in the fire of the *Ferdinands!*"[9]

For mastering the threatening situation, *Hauptmann* Rettemeier was [later] awarded the Knight's Cross [to the Iron Cross].

---

9. Translator's Note: Just as every tank that appeared on the late-war Western Front was invariably reported by Allied forces as either a *Panther* or a *Tiger*, so too was the tendency of the front-line soldiers in the East to also overestimate the size and type of German armor opposing them. The *Ferdinand* was a Porsche-designed tank destroyer armed with an 8.8-centimeter main gun that appeared in only very limited quantities due to its extremely low production run.

All further Soviet attempts to break through were repulsed through defensive efforts or counterattacks before they really even got started. The tank battalion fought together with the mechanized infantry and the divisional reconnaissance forces. In all, the battalion reported the destruction of thirty-nine enemy tanks. The Soviets suffered especially high casualties among their infantry forces. In a very narrow area between the left-hand sector of the *25. Panzergrenadier-Division* and the right wing of the friendly forces on the left, the *78. Sturm-Division*, some five divisions and an assault brigade attacked. The attack sector for each of the divisions was only 300 to 400 meters. The area was so narrow that the regiments had to be echeloned deeply behind one another.[10] On 16 November, the

enemy introduced another three divisions into the fighting. Although the German losses were painful, they were relatively small when viewed in light of the tremendous success achieved. As a result of the extraordinary achievements of the maintenance personnel, the disabled assault guns were returned to operational status after a few days.

The operations of the battalion found broad recognition. Even the commanding general of the neighboring corps, which *Panzer-Abteilung 5* had effectively supported in a crisis without receiving any orders, paid his respects by sending the soldiers personal items (chocolate, tobacco, alcohol, etc.) After a few days of quiet, the 4th Autobahn Battle erupted on 30 November.

---

10.   Author's Note: Boehm, 225.

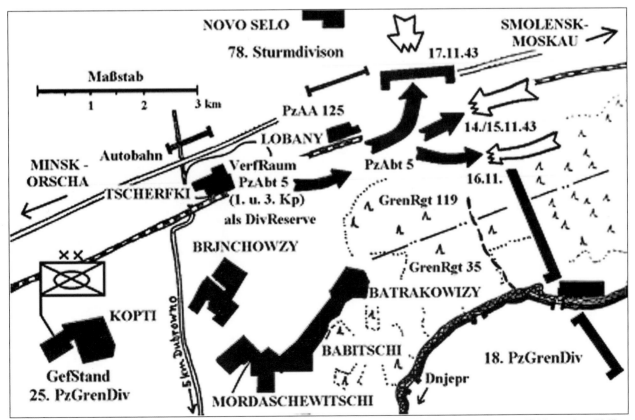

Employment of *Panzer-Abteilung 5* as the division reserve during the 3rd Autobahn Battle from 14 to 17 November 1943.

4. 30 November to 31 December 1943: *Panzer-Abteilung 5* in the 4th Autobahn Battle and the Period to the End of the Year

It was already becoming apparent in December 1943 that *Panzer-Abteilung 5* would only be available to the division on an occasional basis. A complete and fresh tank battalion late in 1943 was a stroke of luck for the battered *4. Armee*. It became a ready reserve for the field army and even the field-army group on occasion. It was given the mission of cleaning up penetrations and eliminating breakthroughs. That was also the case in the 4th Autobahn Battle. The battalion fought as part of the *18. Panzergrenadier-Division* (previously the right-hand neighbor of the *25. Panzergrenadier-Division*) starting on 30 November in the area southeast of Dubrowno. It was imperative in that sector to stabilize the hotly contested front and eliminate enemy forces that had penetrated, all the while operating under miserable weather conditions of extreme cold and snowstorms.

Oberleutnant Wilke especially distinguished himself in that fighting, although he had already stepped into the limelight in Africa as a *Feldwebel* in the 2nd Company by dint of his repeated bravery. When the battle ended on 4 December, the Soviet efforts to break through on both sides of the Smolensk-Orscha highway on the northern wing of the *4. Armee* were temporarily halted.

During that difficult and hard fighting, *Panzer-Abteilung 5* built up its self-confidence and a feeling of absolute superiority over the enemy forces it faced. As a result, the former African combatants spent their first Christmas in the Soviet Union in winter-ready quarters in a good mood. They approached the New Year with determination. What held the soldiers together was less the result of outside propaganda than the fundamental beliefs of all soldiers. Above all, it was important to them to protect their homeland from the dangers and horrors of a raging Bolshevism, the ramifications

of which they could then see with their very eyes. Oppressing many of the soldiers was the news of the increasing Allied bombing raids against the civilian populace in Germany. There were not just a few who received preferential leave to return home after their families had been bombed out.

Hauptmann Rettemeier was approved for the award of the Knight's Cross to the Iron Cross on 5 December 1943 for his bravery and decisive actions during the 3rd Autobahn Battle. A few days later, the division commander, *Generalmajor Dr.* Benicke, presented him with the award in the field. An *Afrikakorps* sleeve band can be seen on *Hauptmann* Rettemeier's black *Panzer* uniform, even though it was not technically the authorized version for this uniform.

Hauptmann Rettemeier (with binoculars) in November 1943 in his command vehicle.

On 22 June 1943, higher levels of the Tank Assault Badge—the *Panzerkampfabzeichen*—were instituted in recognition of the increasing numbers of operations that members of the tank arm were participating in. The badges were modified versions of the first level, with the appropriate minimum number of combat actions represented in the lower part of the wreath: 25, 50, 75 and 100.

CHAPTER 4

History of *Panzer-Abteilung 5,* 1944

1. Beginning of January to the Middle of June 1944: Operations in the Sectors of the *3. Panzer-Armee* and the *4. Panzer-Armee*

In two intensively conducted attacks starting at the beginning of January and at the beginning of February 1944, the Soviets attempted to take Vitebsk by employing more than sixty large formations. The Soviets ran roughshod against the self-sacrificing German divisions, which were attempting to keep the Soviets from chipping out the bulwark of the defenses of *Heeresgruppe Mitte.*

The New Year had barely started when the first offensive was launched against the positions of the *3. Panzer-Armee* southeast of Vitebsk. With short interruptions, the 1st Battle of Vitebsk lasted from 3 to 18 January.

Thanks to extremely heavy artillery support, the Soviets succeeded in crossing the road from Vitebsk to Orscha and interdicting the railway line that connected the two cities. Based on the critical situation that had developed, *Panzer-Abteilung 5* was ordered to report directly to the headquarters of the *3. Panzer-Armee.* Unfortunately, the battalion was not employed as a whole; instead, it was broken apart and attached to support several divisions and regiments to serve as "corset stays" in their defenses. As a result, individual companies and even platoons were committed. Although they had their share of local successes, they were stressed to the breaking point in both men and materiel as a result of the scattered commitment.

An impression of the fighting can be gleaned from the diary entries of *Gefreiter* Lothar Witthaus, who was assigned to the 3rd Company as a gunner (excerpts):

We moved out to the new objective with rattling tracks. The engine droned its persistent song. We rolled along the road with short intervals between us. To the right, the front thundered and hammered. It seemed like a giant mouth that could never be satisfied. We then had to leave the road, since that portion was occupied for ten kilometers by Ivan.[1] We continued forward on roads of the worst condition. By then, it had turned dark.

It turned painfully cold. That was no surprise—after all, it was the 13th of January 1944 in Russia. I tried to warm my hands off the heat of the muffler. It helped a bit. The tank driver had the worst of it. He had to pay sharp attention to the route. His hands were cramped around the steering column; his eyes riveted through the narrow vision port along the miserable road. In addition,

1. Author's Note: Witthaus is referring to the Vitebsk-Orscha road.

it was getting darker and darker. The tank commander dismounted and moved in front of the driver's station. He gave some relief to the driver by means of hand and arm signals.

From the muzzle flashes, we could tell that we had reached the positions of the friendly artillery. If only it weren't so damned dark! We continued on and reached the company after a while. *Feldwebel* Konjetzny reported in to the company commander: "3rd Platoon reports as ordered with three vehicles. *Unteroffizier* Kleinbauer has gone to the maintenance facility with main gun damage." We were directed to our positions.

Before we could go there, we had to refuel. The engine was turned off. The headsets were taken off and we dismounted. We could tell that something was going on in the area. When you had the headset on, you could not hear a lot of outside noise. The air was filled with the rattling of machine guns, from the barking of guns of all calibers and from the bursting of shells. Glowing tracer rounds placed an intertwined net over the no-man's-land. A piece of shrapnel smacked into the muck in front of me. I grabbed onto the handles of the fuel cans more tightly and swung them up to the driver. The fuel was swallowed up with a chug. We finally topped off. When we were sitting back in the vehicle, we were feeling a whole lot better. Although the armor was no life-insurance policy, it did provide a calming effect. Our platoon deployed on line so as to be prepared for any and all eventualities. Two *Panzer IV's* were inserted between us. They belonged to *Panzergrenadier-Division "Feldherrnhalle,"* whose sector we were in. The remaining nighttime hours passed

without any significant incident. With my head resting on the main gun deflector, I attempted in vain to catch a few hours of sleep.

As it turned first light, we received the combat orders we had expected. We were attached to *Feldwebel* Badalla's platoon and were directed to support an infantry battalion. We had barely entered the area of operations when we started to experience the hell of Vitebsk. It was as if you were looking into a wall of fire. Looking through the gun optics, I saw a never-ending succession of fountains of earth gush towards the sky. The shell shrapnel burst apart in glowing sprays. A constant churning and roaring was in the air. *Ratsch—Batsch.* The Russian antitank guns fired. There was constant machine-gun fire from both sides. An *MG 42* spewed its message of death towards the enemy with dizzying speed. In between, there were the impacts of artillery shells. Off to the left, I saw Russian rifle companies charging. The attack collapsed in the face of the German defensive fires. The rest of the attackers fled back. The Russians then tried on the right wing. In vain. He was unable to advance there, either. Right in front of our vehicle was a totally shot-up T-34. One of the crew lay dead next to it. A German machine-gun nest was positioned behind a pile of wood. Short bursts of fire whipped there towards the enemy from time to time. At that point, we were in the middle of a salvo of Stalin organ rockets. Muck sprayed towards the heavens all over the place and at the same time. A few shards of shrapnel smacked against the armor of the vehicle. But that did not bother us. German and Russian fighters alternated over the battlefield. Our rocket launchers howled and sent impact destructively among the enemy. *Feldwebel* Badalla radioed to my commander: "Watch out for the AT gun on the right!" Our assault gun turned with a lurch towards the target. We soon identified the bastard. The commander issued his order: "12 o'clock . . . HE . . . 300 meters . . . enemy AT . . . fire when ready!" By patting me on the back, he guided me in to the target completely. I identified the target; it was eliminated after a few rounds.

Other enemy targets were continuously engaged by us. An infantry battalion was supposed to join us for an immediate counterattack. The grenadiers claimed that there were still T-34's crawling around in the defile in front of us. Under covering fire from the other vehicles, we entered the defile. But there were no Ivan tanks to be seen anywhere. Enemy antitank guns, on the other hand, were firing industriously at us, and we took them under fire. The enemy artillery fire started to become uncomfortable. All of a sudden, there was a blow against the armor. A red glare of a flash; a flame of fire in the vehicle. I saw daylight through a cloud of smoke. Thoughts raced through my head: You can see . . . that means you're still alive! A horrific pain in my right arm and my right thigh. At first, I thought my arm was gone. I turned around on my gunner's seat. The commander had dismounted; the loader as well. I tried to pull myself up from my seat, but I got tangled up in my headphone and throat mike wires. With a jerk, I ripped loose the cables. I was filled with one thought alone: Just get out before we were blown to bits! I reached the hatch and stuck my head out. I wanted to prop myself out of the fighting compartment with my arms, but I had no grip with my right hand and sank back down inside.

"I can't get out . . . badly wounded in the arm," I called out to the driver, who was still sitting in the vehicle. He replied: "The engine's still running. I'll get behind the hill real quick. Otherwise Ivan will finish us off." We raced towards the hill at high speed. The Russian antitank guns attempted to finish us off at the last minute. I could clearly hear the short, unpleasant bark of the firing and then the immediate impact right behind the vehicle. By the skin of our teeth, we got behind the rise. Then we halted. The driver crawled up from his station. "Poor bastard!" That was the first thing he said to me when he slit open my sleeve. He then applied a tourniquet to my arm with communications cable. My arm looked terrible. A piece of shrapnel can passed completely through the lower arm. You could look right through the arm without any effort; you could see the shattered bones next to one another. But it did not appear that the artery had been damaged. It was bleeding relatively weakly. "Come on . . . get the first-aid kit, a splint and some dressing and dress me," I said in a completely calm manner to the driver. The initial shock had been replaced by a nonchalant calm. "I must have been hit in the leg as well, but it doesn't appear to be so bad . . . it's hardly bleeding at all!" I added. The driver said: "I'm going to try to get you to some type of medical facility." Although we moved very slowly, every jolt hurt like the dickens. I almost bit my lips raw so as to maintain some sort of control over the pain. After we reached the road, it was somewhat better.

There was a knocked-out T-34 in front of us on the road. My comrade called out to me: "I'm going to try to get around next to the road." But it was impossible. The tracks could not get a grip in the snow. "It's not working . . . we need to dismount."

I was unable to exit the fighting compartment with my splint through the commander's hatch. I then climbed over the gun, which had been knocked free of its mount—we had been hit right above the gun mantlet—and tried to get out through the loader's hatch. It was tough, but I was able to do it. I sat on the mudguards and then slid slowly down into the snow. The driver made it down in one move. I looked at our assault gun one more time . . . saw the large hole above the main gun. The penetration had been about seventy centimeters from my head; things could have been a lot worse. But I didn't have time for a lot of deep thinking; the pain I was suffering, which was becoming increasingly intense, took care of that. I had to find a doctor somewhere.

Off to the right of us on a steep incline, there were self-propelled guns in position. I told my comrade: "Go to the battery commander and ask whether there's a clearing station somewhere around here." After he took off, I sat down on a tree stump and attempted to bite my pain away. Shells impacting nearby did not bother me at all; right then, nothing mattered to me. After a few minutes, the driver came back with a messenger. The battery commander had made his motorcycle and sidecar combination available and had me immediately taken to the main dressing station. When my comrade had asked for

help for me, [the officer] had told him: "It is my highest honor to help a badly wounded soldier." The messenger and my driver helped me into the sidecar, then mounted themselves and raced away. The road was under heavy Russian artillery fire. I barely paid attention; nothing mattered to me.

When a troop truck received a direct hit 100 meters in front of us, I could only commiserate. The houses of a village appeared in front of us; we had moved through it the previous day. "We're there!" the messenger announced, stopping in front of a wooden house, where a Red Cross had been placed inside the door frame. Supported by my comrade, I entered. A medic led us into a room that was full of wounded. The bitter moaning of the badly wounded filled the room. A junior noncommissioned officer approached me and have me a tetanus shot. Then, two other medics cut the camouflage outer garment and the uniform.

I was placed on a stretcher and carried into the dressing room. They placed me on an operating table and opened up the dressing. Tears shot into my eyes, the pain was so intense. The doctor then arrived and examined me. I looked into his face intensely, to be able to judge the truthfulness of his diagnosis. The obvious furrows on his brow had me fear the worst. "You took a bad one, boy! You'll probably have to sacrifice your arm. The wound on your upper thigh is inconsequential." An icy shock jolted through my body. I was going to lose my arm? "Isn't there any way to save the arm?"

The surgeon shrugged his shoulders. But after thinking it over for a short while, he said: "There's an ambulance that just arrived from a hospital for special fractures. The only thing I could do for you is to send you there. I'm afraid you may not make it through the trip, however."

"In order to save my arm, *Herr Oberarzt,* I'll go through even more!"

"Fine, then. I'll see what I can do." He called out to a few medics: "The tanker goes to the special fracture hospital on the ambulance that just arrived."

I thanked both of my comrades and shook their hands. "The comradeship of the front!" I thought.

I saw them go through the door. Outside, a motor jumped to life and they rattled back towards the front in the direction of the roaring hurricane of elementary powers. Despite all that, I left that hell with a heavy heart.

✠

The number of available combat vehicles rapidly decreased, until a point was reached where the chain of command had the split-up battalion pulled out of the line when the fighting abated in order to be committed to the next Battle of Vitebsk after a short battlefield reconstitution. Starting on 3 February, the battalion was committed again, although it was not split up in its commitments. It launched two successful counterattacks against a bridgehead that the Soviets had established across the Lutchessa just south of the city. The operations gave the battalion a valuable boost. The 2nd Battle of Vitebsk ended on 17 February.

In the meantime, a new crisis started to materialize on the right wing of the *4. Armee* north of Rogatschew. Soviet attacks on the west bank of the Dnjepr were aiming towards Stary Bischoff. *Panzer-Abteilung 5* was attached back to the command and control of the *4. Armee* and reached its new area of operations in a forced march. The battalion was attached to the *XII. Armee-Korps* of *General der Infanterie* von Tippelskirch.

Panzer-Abteilung 5 moves out to conduct a counterattack with mounted infantry.

The commanding general assigned it to support the *267. Infanterie-Division* of *Generalleutnant* Drescher on 21 February.

During the two previous battles for Witebsk, the battalion had suffered considerable materiel losses. In addition, there were mechanical losses due to the long marches involved. Despite that, the formation entered combat on 23 February with approximately 30 percent of its authorized strength. Together with the grenadiers, it was able to stabilize the situation. In the meantime, the maintenance services worked at high pitch to repair the damaged armored vehicles, which inevitably arrived each day from the front. Total losses were replaced by the use of captured T-34's.[2]

As a result, the battalion was almost able to attain its authorized strength in spite of the almost uninterrupted fighting. On 26 February, it achieved considerable success when conducting

counterattacks. The operations were recognized by the commander-in-chief of the *4. Armee* in an order-of-the-day: "I offer my complete recognition to *Panzer-Abteilung 5* and its brave commander for the counterattacks launched on 26 February 1944 that were conducted with terrific élan."[3] The fighting intensified and reached its climax on 29 February, when the battalion, together with forces of the *267. Infanterie-Division*, scattered Soviet infantry attacks, knocked out the tanks supporting the attacks and eliminated a number of antitank guns and artillery pieces. As a result, the enemy was forced to call off his offensive efforts in that sector of the front.

The terrific achievement was recognized in the Armed Forces Daily Report issued on 1 March:

Excerpt from the Armed Forces Report
From the *Führer* Headquarters, 1 March 1944

2. Author's Note: Rettemeier, 5.

3. Author's Note: Rettemeier, 5.

A captured T-34 has been placed in the service of the battalion.

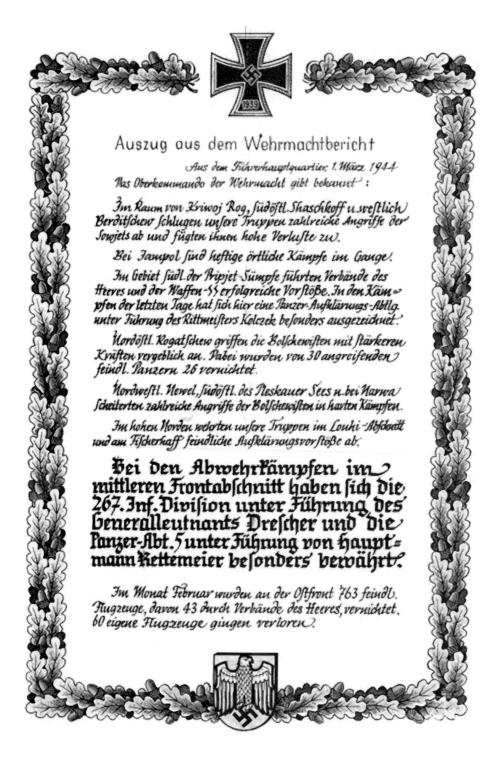

Auszug aus dem Wehrmachtbericht

Aus dem Führerhauptquartier, 1. März 1944

Das Oberkommando der Wehrmacht gibt bekannt:

Im Raum von Kriwoj Rog, südöstl. Shaschkoff u. westlich Berditschew schlugen unsere Truppen zahlreiche Angriffe der Sowjets ab und fügten ihnen hohe Verluste zu.

Bei Jampol sind heftige örtliche Kämpfe im Gange.

Im Gebiet südl. der Pripjet-Sümpfe führten Verbände des Heeres und der Waffen-SS erfolgreiche Vorstöße. In den Kämpfen der letzten Tage hat sich hier eine Panzer-Aufklärungs-Abtlg. unter Führung des Rittmeisters Kolczek besonders ausgezeichnet.

Nordöstl. Rogatschew griffen die Bolschewisten mit stärkeren Kräften vergeblich an. Dabei wurden von 30 angreifenden feindl. Panzern 26 vernichtet.

Nordwestl. Newel, südöstl. des Pleskauer Sees u. bei Narwa scheiterten zahlreiche Angriffe der Bolschewisten in harten Kämpfen.

Im hohen Norden wehrten unsere Truppen im Louhi-Abschnitt und am Fischerhalf feindliche Aufklärungsvorstöße ab.

Bei den Abwehrkämpfen im mittleren Frontabschnitt haben sich die 267. Inf. Division unter Führung des Generalleutnants Drescher und die Panzer-Abt. 5 unter Führung von Hauptmann Rettemeier besonders bewährt.

Im Monat Februar wurden an der Ostfront 763 feindl. Flugzeuge, davon 43 durch Verbände des Heeres, vernichtet. 60 eigene Flugzeuge gingen verloren.

The High Command of the Armed Forces Announces:

Our forces turned back numerous Soviet attacks in the area of Kriwoi Rog, southeast of Schashkoff and west of Berditschew, and inflicted heavy losses on the enemy.

In the area of Jampol, heavy local fighting is in progress.

In the area south of the Pripet Marshes, formations of the Army and the *Waffen-SS* conducted successful advances. In the fighting of the last few days, an armored reconnaissance battalion under the acting command of *Rittmeister* Kolczek especially distinguished itself.

To the northeast of Rogatschew, the Bolshevists attacked in vain with strong forces. In the process, twenty-six of thirty attacking enemy tanks were destroyed.

To the northwest of Newel, southeast of Lake Pleskau and around Narwa, numerous attacks by Bolshevists failed in hard fighting.

In the far north, our forces in the Louhi Sector and along the fishing bay turned back enemy reconnaissance-in-force efforts.

In the course of the defensive fighting in the central sector of the Eastern Front, the *267. Infanterie-Division*, under the command of *Generalleutnant* Drescher, and *Panzer-Abteilung 5*, under the command of *Hauptmann* Rettemeier, especially distinguished themselves.

During the month of February, 763 enemy aircraft were destroyed along the Eastern Front, 43 of them by Army formations. Sixty friendly aircraft were lost.

Fernspruch - Fernschreiben

Nachr.-Stelle 267. Jnf.-Div. | Nr. HKNX/FU 01229/30 | Befördert: an | Tag | Zeit | durch | Rolle

Vermerk: Geheim

Aufgenommen: von HKGXB | Tag 1.3. | Zeit 1300 | durch

+1300/EINS/ME/HLDXB/FU++

+1300/EINS/ME/HLDXB/FU++

Tag: 1.3.
Zeit: 1140
Dring.-Verm.

An: 257.I.D.

Absendende Stelle: AOK 4

Ich spreche der Pz.Abt. 5 und ihrem Führer, dem Hptm.Rettemeier, die wiederum durch ihren schneidigen Angriffsgeist und ihre Einsatzbereitschaft dem Gegner schwere Schläge erteilt hat, meine volle Anerkennung aus. Die Abteilung hat d amit die Kämpfe der schwerringenden Infanterie der der 257.I.D. hervorragend unterstützt und in hohem Masse an dem Abwehrerfolg Anteil. Ich werde der Abteilung eine besondere Marketenderzuweisung zukommen lassen.

gez.Heinrici, AOK 4 Ia Nr.311/44 geh.

F.d.R.:

Telegraph sent to the *267. Infanterie-Division* from the Headquarters of the *4. Armee* on 1 March:

> I extend my complete recognition to *Panzer-Abteilung 5* and its leader, *Hauptmann* Rettemeier, which once again has delivered heavy blows to the enemy as the result of its offensive élan and its dedication to duty. As a result, the battalion provided terrific support to the hard-fighting infantry of the *267. Infanterie-Division* and contributed greatly to the success of the defensive effort. I am having a special supplement of personal-demand items sent to the battalion.

/signed/ Heinrici
Headquarters, *4. Armee*
Operations (No. 311/44 SECRET)

FOR THE CORRECTNESS:
/signed/

In just three days alone, the battalion had knocked out thirty-three tanks and captured or destroyed seventy-one Soviet guns. Friendly losses were slight and could be traced back primarily to the Soviet close-air support and to losses sustained by rear-area elements as the result of partisan attacks.

On 13 March, *Hauptmann* Rettemeier received the Oak Leaves to the Knight's Cross of the Iron Cross. *Leutnant* Behrens of the 3rd Company received the Knight's Cross to the Iron Cross for his bravery and circumspect leadership.

In the weeks that followed, the battalion remained in the sector of the *XII. Armee-Korps* and worked around the clock on repairing its damaged armored vehicles. It also found some time to conduct tactical training for its officers and noncommissioned officers, as well as strengthening combat training at the company level. The rest period was short-lived, however.

In the middle of March, the Soviets gave signs of preparing for an attack between the Dnjepr and Tschaussy, which resulted in the battalion being moved to the rear of the endangered sector. The officers and noncommissioned officers became familiar with the terrain and employment options in the sector of the *18. Panzergrenadier-Division*, which they knew from the highway battles.

The battalion's combat engineer platoon improved routes to the front in light of the onset of the spring thaw. It also reinforced a few bridges to support armored vehicles in anticipation of future operations.

Early on the morning of 25 March, the anticipated Soviet offensive started with a heavy artillery preparation, not unlike that experienced in the highway battles. The Soviets succeeded in making a deep penetration into the left wing of the *18. Panzergrenadier-Division*. The immediate counterattack that was launched—initially without infantry—hit the enemy in the open and led to the destruction of the bulk of the attacking infantry and tanks and to an elimination of the immediate crisis. *Oberleutnant* Strunk's 1st Company and *Hauptmann* Frede's 3rd Company especially distinguished themselves during that round of fighting. Both of the companies initiated a pursuit of the fleeing Soviets. By doing so, they took the necessary ground and won the necessary time for *Grenadier-Regiment 467* (*Oberst* Meiners) of the *267. Infanterie-Division* to arrive in the afternoon and close the gap in the line.

The constant enemy attacks over the next few days were generally turned back before they even really got started. In that, the tankers were helped by the infantry, with whom they had formed good bonds ever since the fighting north of Rogatschew. The fighting found its conclusion in a surprise attack conducted at night that was jointly executed on the night leading into Easter Sunday by the battalion and *Oberst* Meiners's regiment. The deeply echeloned Soviet defensive system was broken through deeply,

An assault gun of the battalion during the winter fighting of 1943–44.

which led to an improvement of the front line trace. Newspapers and radio again reported on the successes of the battalion. The battalion's operations in the sectors of the *3. Panzer-Armee* in the area around Witebsk and the *4. Armee* to the west of Smolensk and along the field army's southern wing likewise came to an end.

The battalion had not only distinguished itself in all situations, but it had also contributed significantly in maintaining the German front lines. The battalion had made a name for itself within the sector of *Heeresgruppe Mitte*. The tankers with the *Afrika* sleeve band felt the high respect they were accorded wherever they appeared.

After several reassignments to different areas of the front, the battalion received a well-deserved rest period. In May, it finally wound up in the Orscha area again, where it was reunited with its parent division. It was in the same sector of the front where it had first seen combat in the East in the fall of 1943.

2. The Knight's Cross Recipients of *Panzer-Abteilung 5* from December 1943 Until March 1944[4]

Josef Rettemeier
Born: 17 September 1914 in Niederrollendorf (Bonn)
Died: 19 December 1997
Recommended for the Knight's Cross: 29 November 1943
Awarded the Knight's Cross: 5 December 1943
Rank: *Hauptmann*
Duty Position: Commander of *Panzer-Abteilung 5*
Oak Leaves to the Knight's Cross to the Iron Cross
425th Recipient
Recommended for the Oak Leaves: 6 March 1944
Awarded the Oak Leaves: 13 March 1944

Josef Rettemeier was assigned to *Kraftfahr-Abteilung 6* on 1 April 1934. On 20 April 1936, he was

4. Author's Note: Federl, *Die Ritterkeuzträger der Deutschen Panzerdivisionen 1939–1945, Die Panzertruppe.*

commissioned as a *Leutnant*. He initially served as a antitank platoon leader, later as the commander of an antitank company. He participated in the campaign in the West as part of *Panzerjäger-Abteilung 50* of the *9. Panzer-Division*. At the beginning of April 1942, he was reassigned to Africa, where he assumed command of the 2nd Company of *Panzer-Regiment 5*. He was promoted to *Hauptmann* on 1 February of that same year. During the third battle at El Alamein, Rettemeier assumed acting command of the 1st Battalion. He was badly wounded during the fighting and transported back to Germany. After his convalescence, he assumed command of *Panzer-Abteilung 5* on 14 September 1943. On 1 April of the same year, he was promoted to *Major*. In the fall of 1944, Rettemeier was transferred to the 1st Battalion of *Panzer-Lehr-Regiment 130*, where he assumed command. During the fighting in Lorraine, he was again wounded. He saw the end of the war as a course leader at the Armor School in Erlangen. In 1956, he entered the *Bundeswehr*, retiring in 1972 as an *Oberst* and assistant division commander.[5]

---

5. Author's Note: Stockert, *Die Eichenlaubträger 1940–1945*, 205.

Hans-Georg Behrens
Born: 11 December 1921
Killed in action: 16 June 1944 (Eastern Front)
Recommended for the Knight's Cross: 5 March 1944
Awarded the Knight's Cross: 12 March 1944
Rank: *Leutnant der Reserve*
Duty Position: Acting commander of the 3rd Company of *Panzer-Abteilung 5*

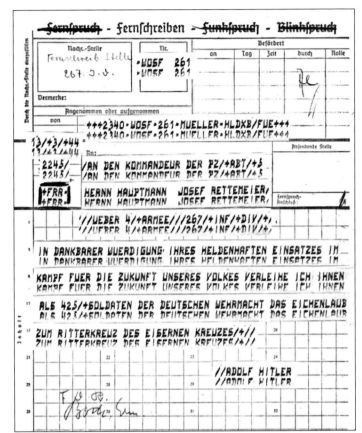

Rettemeier as a *Hauptmann* and commander of *Panzer-Abteilung 5*. As authorized by regulation, he wears his *Afrika* campaign sleeve band on his left sleeve.

Telegraph from the *Führer* on 13 March congratulating Rettemeier on his receipt of the Oak Leaves to the Knight's Cross of the Iron Cross (425th member of the armed forces to be so honored).

Major Rettemeier (first on the right), along with other recipients of the Oak Leaves, at the Obersalzberg in April 1944 to receive the award personally from the hand of Adolf Hitler.

3. 22 June to 5 July 1944: The Collapse of *Heeresgruppe Mitte* and the Disbanding of *Panzer-Abteilung 5*

Around 10 June, the intentions of the Soviet high command with regard to the sector of *Heeresgruppe Mitte* started to be recognized. There were undeniable signs of a large-scale build-up of Soviet forces. The axes of advance for the impending offensive were Brobruisk, Mogilew, Orscha and Witebsk. Weakened by the detachment of forces, the German field-army group had no appreciable reserves. *Panzer-Abteilung 5* prepared for operations in the area around Dubrowno, south of the Dnjepr, by conducting terrain reconnaissance and discussions.

The last uncertainties concerning the timing of the enemy offensive were eliminated, when partisans interdicted all of the rail lines leading into the area of operations of the field-army group on 20 June by means of extensive demolitions. The Soviet launched their offensive on 22 June. Four Soviet fronts—the equivalent of field armies—moved out, with main efforts directed at Orscha, Mogilew, Bobruisk and both sides of Witebsk. Their intent was to collapse the German field-army group's frontage.

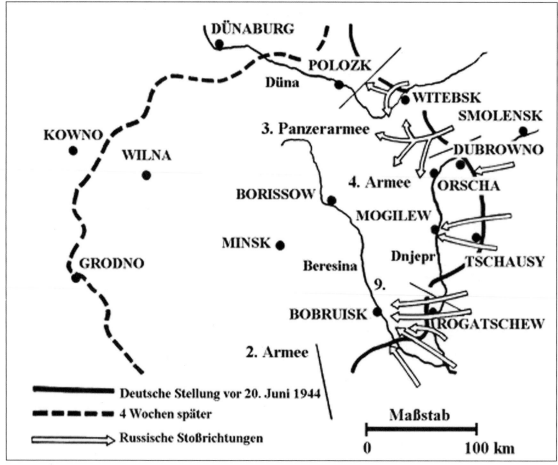

The collapse of *Heeresgruppe Mitte* in June and July 1944.
— German positions prior to 20 June 1944
— Four weeks later
→ Soviet axes of advance.
Scale: 0 – 100 kilometers

On 23 June, the enemy succeeded in breaking through on both sides of Witebsk. The 2nd Russian Front aimed for Mogilew, while the southern wing of the 3rd White Russian Front moved out against the northern wing of the *4. Armee* in the Orscha area. Portraying what happened in the events that followed—often overlapping one another—is extraordinarily difficult, because there are no daily logs, after-action reports, orders, or reports available.

Panzer-Abteilung 5 fought as part of the *25. Panzergrenadier-Division* in the area with which it was familiar. Its officer duty positions were as follows:
Commander: *Major* Rettemeier
Adjutant: *Oberleutnant* Weitland
Signals Officer: *Leutnant* Lutz
Company Commanders: *Hauptmann* Köllmann, *Oberleutnant* Strunk, *Oberleutnant* Schulze and *Hauptmann* Frede
Unassigned Officers: *Hauptmann* Krone

The battalion was initially employed as the divisional reserve. As was usually the case, the attacks at the front were initially turned back and enemy penetrations sealed off and eliminated. In the process, forty-seven Soviet tanks were knocked out on 23 June; on the next day, the battalion knocked out another twenty Soviet tanks.[6]

At the same time, however, the enemy broke through to the north between the Dnjepr and Witebsk and to the south at Mogilew, resulting in the envelopment and then encirclement of the *4. Armee*. The field-army group's front had been torn open.

The encircled divisions of the *4. Armee* entered their final round of desperate fighting. Death or wounding and captivity were often the more merciful fate for the German soldiers; those who attempted to work their way back under the most primitive of conditions were often rounded up and, in some cases, killed under shameful circumstances.

Despite the encirclement, a portion of *Panzer-Abteilung 5* was saved. When the attack spearheads of the Soviet forces approached Orscha and Mogilew in the rear of the battalion, the maintenance company and non-combat-essential elements were moved farther to the rear. Everything that was expendable was collected together so as to at least cross the Beresina and reach Minsk. Among those moving back were crews without tanks and the lightly wounded; some damaged tanks were also evacuated. Thanks to decisive leadership, it was possible to break out of the ring of encirclement with minimal personnel losses; although the ring had closed, it was not air-tight.

Until the division and, by extension, *Panzer-Abteilung 5*, was dissolved on 5 July, there was additional difficult defensive fighting, which cannot be described in detail due to a lack of references.

The soldiers who succeeded in breaking out were sent to Germany as early as August and made available for the activation of other formations.

6. Author's Note: Boehm, *Geschichte der 25. Division*, 240.

4.8 November to the End of December 1944: Reconstitution of *Panzer-Abteilung 5* and Operations in Lothringen (Lorraine)

The German Army High Command initially had *Panzer-Brigade 107* formed out of what remained of the *25. Panzergrenadier-Division*. The tank component of the brigade was *Panzer-Abteilung 2107*. The activation date was 1 August 1944.[7] On 15 and 16 September, the brigade was transported to the Western Front and fought from 18 September until 4 November in the southeastern portion of Holland in the areas of Eindhoven and Venlo. The commander of the battalion, *Major* von Plüskow, was killed in September. On 4 and 5 November, the remnants of the brigade were pulled out of the bridgehead at Venlo and rail-transported on 8 and 9 November to the Baumholder Training Area. There,

7. Author's Note: Boehm, 259.

the brigade was incorporated into *Kampfgruppe 25. Panzergrenadier-Division*, which was intended to form the nucleus of the reconstituted division of the same designation. The commander of the battle group was *Oberst* Burmeister. The former *Panzer-Abteilung 2107* was redesignated as *Panzer-Abteilung 5*. The battalion consisted of four line companies, with three of them equipped with the *Panzerkampfwagen V Panther* and one of them with the *Panzer IV*.[8] The actual number of on-hand vehicles is not known.

During the first few days of November, General Patton's U.S. 3rd Army succeeded in entering Lorraine, crossing the Mosel at Diedenhofen north of Metz and establishing bridgeheads. *Kampfgruppe 25. Panzergrenadier-Division* was committed against those forces.

8. Author's Note: Boehm, 264.

A *Panther* from *Panzer-Abteilung 2107*, which eventually was redesignated as *Panzer-Abteilung 5*.

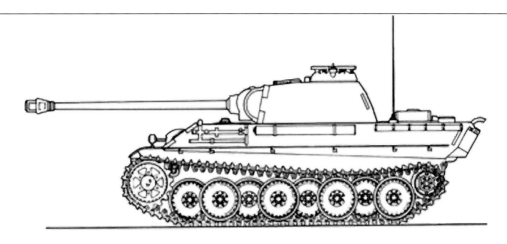

Panzerkampfwagen V "Panther"
(Sd.Kfz. 171)
Model G
Characteristics:
Interleaved running gear; long-barreled main gun; front slope, sides and turret sharply angled (similar to the T-34).

Technical Data for the Model G:*	
Overall length:	8.86 meters
Overall width:	3.43 meters
Overall height:	3 meters
Combat weight:	44.8 tons
Horsepower:	700
Maximum speed (road):	46 kilometers an hour
Radius of action (road):	177 kilometers
Fuel capacity:	730 liters
Crew:	5
Armament:	7.5-centimeter L70 main gun; 3 7.92-millimeter *MG 34's*
Basic load of main-gun ammunition:	82 rounds
Armor:	
Front hull:	8 centimeters
Sides:	4.5 centimeters
Rear:	4 centimeters

Employed starting in 1943 in increasing numbers to supplement and replace the *Panzer IV*.

It should be noted that the main gun of the *Panther*—despite its smaller caliber and lighter and smaller round—had a superior armor-penetrating capability to that of the 8.8-centimeter main gun of the *Tiger*.

* Author's Note: von Senger und Etterlin, *Die deutschen Panzer 1926–1945*, 308ff.

Kampfgruppe 25. Panzergrenadier-Division reached its area of operations with its lead elements by 11 November and attacked the Americans at 0300 hours on 12 November at Kerling, twelve kilometers northeast of Diedenhofen. Additional elements of the battle group participated in an attack against a U.S. bridgehead south of Diedenhofen in the Ückingen area. After that attack failed in the face of the very effective U.S. antitank fire and the heavy protective fires of the enemy artillery, the battle group reassembled in the Veckring area. The next attack took place on 15 November, directed against Diesdorf, east of Diedenhofen. Its intent was to prevent the U.S. bridgeheads from linking up. Once again, the tanks of *Panzer-Abteilung 5*, operating together with the assault guns of *Panzerjäger-Abteilung 25*, failed in their attack in the face of heavy antitank-gun fire. When the Americans moved out to launch an immediate counterattack, the battle group pulled back to the northeast and into the Halsdorf area, where it established a blocking position against the enemy, who was pursuing sharply.

During the night of 17–18 November, the front had to be pulled back once again. The battle group occupied positions along the high ground along the Saar on both sides of Silwingen. Things quieted down initially, since the enemy changed his direction of attack and turned north.

On 24 November, the battle group was relieved by the *19. Volksgrenadier-Division*, and it reassembled by 26 November in an area east of Merzig. The grenadiers were down to 30 percent of their authorized strength. *Panzer-Abteilung 5* had only seven operational tanks left; *Panzerjäger-Abteilung 25* reported only four assault guns.[9]

9. Author's Note: Boehm, 267.

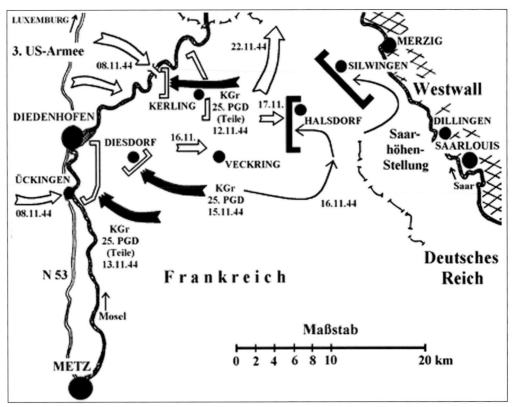

Kampfgruppe 25. Panzergrenadier-Division in Lorraine: fighting between the Mosel and the Saar from 12–24 November 1944.

Although it desperately needed to be reconstituted, the battle group was dispatched to its next combat operation on 26 November. The U.S. 4th Armored Division was threatening the right flank of the *Panzer-Lehr-Division* twelve kilometers south of Saarunion. The battle group was directed to guard the division's exposed flank, thus allowing the *Panzer-Lehr-Division* to maximize the use of its own forces in continuing its attack to the south. Although the flank guard mission of the battle group was successful and the *Kampfgruppe* was even able to advance its positions as far as the Rauweiler area by 27 November, the attack of the *Panzer-Lehr-Division* failed. At that point, the commander-in-chief of *Heeresgruppe G, General der Panzertruppen* Balck, ordered a transition to the defense east of Saarunion. *Kampfgruppe 25. Panzergrenadier-Division* pulled back to a line running

Saarunion-Mackweiler by 29 November, then moved back as far as the Bitsch area by 14 December in a series of withdrawal movements. The battle group defended successfully around Bitsch and inflicted heavy casualties on the enemy.

On 16 December, the German Ardennes offensive led to a significant change in the situation. The area around Bitsch had to be held to guard the offensive's southern flank. In hard defensive fighting, the mission was accomplished. The Americans then withdrew forces from the area to initiate countermeasures to the German offensive, and the attacks around Bitsch abated. During the night of 26–27 December, the battle group was relieved by a *Volksgrenadier* division and moved to the Pirmasens area to be reconstituted.

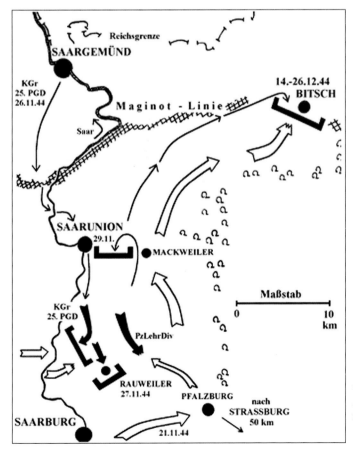

Operations of *Kampfgruppe 25. Panzergrenadier-Division* in Lorraine from 26 November to 26 December 1944, from Saarunion to Bitsch.

Cross-section view of the crew positions on a *Panther*. Seen are the tank commander, the gunner and the driver. Since the loader and the radio operator were positioned on the right-hand side of the vehicle, they are not illustrated here.

CHAPTER 5

History of *Panzer-Abteilung 5,* 1945

1. 8–28 January 1945: Offensive Operations in Northern Alsace (Operation *"Nordwind"*)

Effective 1 January 1945, *Kampfgruppe 25. Panzer-Grenadier-Division* was redesignated as a division. It consisted of the following troop elements and formations:[1]

- *Panzeraufklärungs-Abteilung 25* (minus two companies)
- *Nachrichten-Abteilung (mot) 25*
- *Panzerjäger-Abteilung 25*
- *Pionier-Bataillon (mot) 25*
- *Artillerie-Regiment (mot) 25* (minus its 2nd Battalion)
- *Panzergrenadier-Regiment 35* and *Panzergrenadier-Regiment 119* (each with only two battalions)
- *Panzer-Abteilung 5* (now equipped with assault guns and initially without its 2nd Company)

The reconstituted division was employed for the first time in that capacity as part of Operation *"Nordwind."*[2] Divisions attacked at three places between the Saar and the Upper Rhine towards the south to provide some relief to the forces that had bogged down in the Ardennes offensive in Belgium.

The *25. Panzergrenadier-Division* attacked to the left of the *21. Panzer-Division* into the northeastern portion of Alsace south of Weißenburg. The division commander, *Generalmajor* Burmeister, divided the division into an armored and non-armored group for the attack. *Panzer-Abteilung 5* formed the nucleus of the armored group, advancing on Hatten at 1100 hours on 9 January. *Hauptmann* Arendt, the battalion commander, was killed in the face of strong antitank fires.[3] After the capture of the northeastern portion of Hatten, the attack was continued in the direction of Rittershofen, but it did not succeed.

In the days that followed—until 19 January—a bitter battle of attrition ensued for the two villages, until the Americans pulled their lines back to the Moder on 20–21 January as the result of the German bridgeheads east of Hagenau.

The division then advanced into the area southwest of Sultz, successfully attacked across the Moder through the Hagenau Forest and into the area around Neuburg on 25 and 26 January and established a bridgehead there. It therefore came as a surprise on 26 January, when the division was pulled out of the line and received orders moving it to the Eastern Front. On 28 January, it reached the area around Germersheim on the Rhine and started loading on trains that same day at various railheads. The destination was Küstrin on the Oder.

---

1. Author's Note: Boehm, 271.
2. Translator's Note: Operation "Northwind".

3. Author's Note: He was posthumously awarded the Knight's Cross to the Iron Cross on 24 February for extraordinary leadership and bravery.

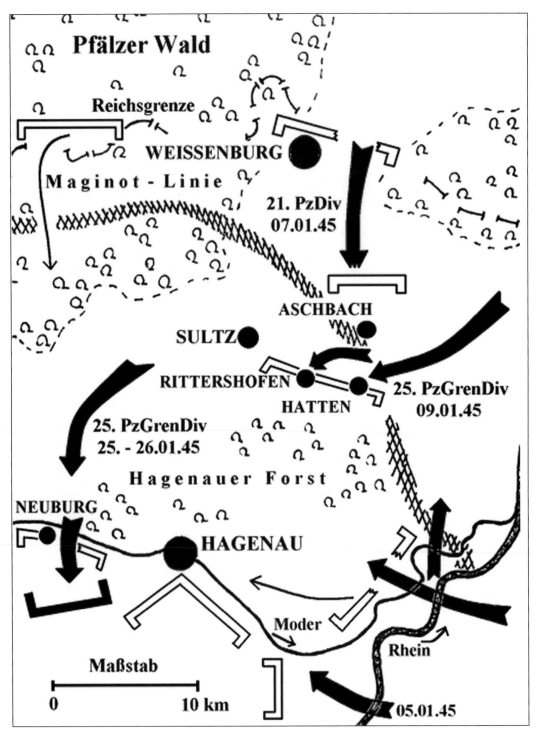

Operations of the *25. Panzergrenadier-Division* in northern Alsace from 8 to 28 January 1945 (Operation *"Nordwind"*).

2. 31 January to 30 March 1945: Fighting for Küstrin

While the division was still at the railheads, the Red Army was advancing on both sides of Küstrin without any but nominal German reserves being available to being committed against it.

Correspondingly, the division received the following order: attack east and interdict the enemy's spearheads. To that end, the division received some of the forces it had been missing since its redesignation and reconstitution. In the case of *Panzer-Abteilung 5*, it received its 2nd Company.

On 31 January, the lead elements of the division arrived in Küstrin, while the lead Soviet armored elements were already advancing into Küstrin-Neustadt. All of the troop elements of the division were immediately committed from the railhead, often without any other support. As a result of the piecemeal commitment, only local successes could be obtained. The division was unable to eliminate the Soviet bridgeheads that had already been established on both sides of the city.

Starting on 10 February, the division had the responsibility for holding open the corridor connecting the city to the west. In some cases, it was only two kilometers wide. In addition, it was responsible for supplying the city, which had been declared a "fortress," and for securing the evacuation of its civilians. The division was able to successfully execute these trying missions. All of the Soviet attacks against the corridor failed. *Panzer-Abteilung 5* and *Panzerjäger-Abteilung 25* were held back as the divisional reserves and employed as especially critical situations developed along the front.

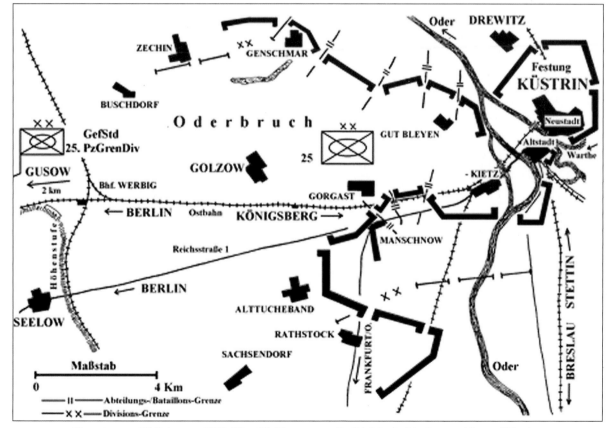

Situation on 22 February 1945: The *25. Panzergrenadier-Division* holds the corridor to Küstrin.

In the period from 18 to 22 March, the division was pulled out of the line and moved to the high ground south of Seelow above the Oder estuary as the operational reserve of the *9. Armee*.

On 22 March, the Soviets broke through in the area around Küstrin and encircled the city. The division was alerted and initiated a counterattack, along with *Panzer-Division "Müncheberg."* The initial attack objectives could be taken in a series of sharp engagements in which numerous enemy tanks were knocked out. In the days that followed, the enemy continued his attacks with new forces, which were turned back. The counterattack ended with a defensive success, although the fortress of Küstrin could not be relieved. For the time being, a breakthrough to the west along the high ground of Seelow was denied to the Soviets. The division conducted another relief attack as part of the *XXXIX. Panzer-Korps* at 0400 hours on 27 March; the attack bogged down outside of Gorgast and Genschmar. On 29 May, the Soviets took Küstrin. That brought the bitter two-month struggle for the city to a close. With the capture, the enemy possessed a bridgehead extending forty kilometers from north to south along the west bank of the Oder.

The *25. Panzergrenadier-Division* was relieved on 30 March and earmarked as the reserve for the *9. Armee*. It was moved to the area southwest of Wriezen for that purpose.

3. 31 March to 8 May 1945: Fighting North of Berlin and the End of the War

Panzer-Abteilung 5, as well as the rest of the division, was able to use the time from 31 March to 16 April 1945 for battlefield reconstitution. The division had already been considerably weakened during its fighting along the Moder bridgehead in Alsace before it arrived to the Eastern Front. Once committed to the Eastern Front, it was in action for two straight months. The mechanized infantry battalions had less than 50 percent of their authorized strengths; the tank battalion possessed only 25 percent of its authorized amount of assault guns.

On 14 April, the Soviets attacked from the bridgehead along the Oder to the west. They were able to achieve deep penetrations along *Reichsstraße 1*[4] and east of Wriezen in the days that followed. The division was employed against the enemy breakthrough at Wriezen. Although it was initially able to defend successfully, the entire front of the *9. Armee* collapsed on 18 April. The division pulled back to the northwest in a delaying action, thus avoiding landing in the pocket that was developing around Berlin. The division held a bridgehead at Eberswalde, south of the Finow Canal, from 20 to 24 April; it was then pushed back across the Oder-Havel Canal. On 25 April, the division conducted its last attack at that level in an effort to break open the encirclement around Berlin. *Panzer-Abteilung 5* was able to acquit itself well west of Oranienburg, before the division had to yield to a counterattack conducted by three enemy divisions. Contrary to orders he had received otherwise, the commander-in-chief of *Heeresgruppe Weichsal*,[5] *Generaloberst* Heinrici, ordered the division to withdraw through Mecklenburg towards the American-Soviet demarcation line, while at the same time protecting the streams of refugees heading westwards. Despite the general signs of dissolution,

4. Translator's Note: Federal Highway No. 1.
5. Translator's Note: Army Group "Vistula."

the division pulled back by bounds in an orderly and disciplined fashion and reached the Kladow area, west of Schwerin, with its last vehicles on 2 May. On the morning of 3 May, the division issued its final orders: "Destroy weapons and equipment; exfiltrate to the west into American captivity."

Towards noon on 3 May, the last four assault guns of *Panzer-Abteilung 5* reached the demarcation line along the Stör Canal, south of Lake Schwerin, and the American lines.[6] That signaled the end of the battalion for the second time.

------

6. Author's Note: Boehm, 293.

4. The Knight's Cross Recipients of *Panzer-Abteilung 5* from February to April 1945[7]

Kurt Arendt
Born: 8 October 1917
Killed in action: 9 January 1945 in the vicinity of Hatten
Posthumously awarded the Knight's Cross: 24 February 1945[8]
Rank: *Hauptmann*
Duty Position: Commander of *Panzer-Abteilung 5*

------

7. Author's Note: Federl, *Die Ritterkeuzträger der Deutschen Panzerdivisionen 1939–1945, Die Panzertruppe.*

8. Translator's Note: The Knight's Cross seen in Arendt's portrait was added by the photography studio.

Horst Giese[9]

Born: 13 October 1911

Dies: 13 July 1977

Recommended for the Knight's Cross: 7 April 1945

Awarded the Knight's Cross: 17 April 1945

Rank: *Leutnant*

Duty Position: Acting commander of the 2nd Company of *Panzer-Abteilung 5*

Other awards: German Cross in Gold (22 September 1944)

---

9. Translator's Note: It would appear that the Knight's Cross for Giese was also added at the photography studio, given the late day of his award. From a uniform perspective, Giese's tanker's jacket is an early first-pattern model that stopped being produced in 1937. Correspondingly, it was probably not his field tunic, but rather a walking-out dress-type tunic intended for wear on home leave. Also of interest is the wear of the non-standard Braunschweiger-type skulls on the collar tabs as opposed to the regulation type that can be seen in Arendt's photograph.

5. Overview of *Panzer-Abteilung 5* from 1943 to 1945

14 September 1943	Activation of *Panzer-Abteilung 5* in Neuruppin; *Hauptmann* Rettemeier designated as the first battalion commander; battalion is outfitted with assault guns and assigned to the *25. Panzergrenadier-Division*
Through 20 October 1943	Arrival at Orscha on the Eastern Front (*Heeresgruppe Mitte*)
30 November to 4 December 1943	4th Highway Battle in the Dubrowno area
January to May 1944	Operations in the sectors of the *3. Panzer-Armee* and the *4. Armee*
22 June to 5 July 1944	Collapse of *Heeresgruppe Mitte*; fighting withdrawal and the deactivation of the division and the battalion
8 November 1944	Redesignation of *Panzer-Abteilung 2107* into *Panzer-Abteilung 5*; outfitted with *Panthers* and the *Panzer IV*; battalion assigned to *Kampfgruppe 25. Panzergrenadier-Division*
12–24 November 1944	1st commitment in Lorraine between the Mosel and the Saar
26 November to 26 December 1944	2nd commitment in Lorraine in the Saarunion-Bitsch area
1 January 1945	Battle group is reorganized and redesignated as the *25. Panzergrenadier-Division*; battalion is outfitted with assault guns
8–28 January 1945	Attacks in northern Alsace in the Hatten-Hagenau area
31 January to 30 March 1945	Transfer to the Eastern Front; fighting for Küstrin
31 March to 27 April 1945	Battlefield reconstitution at Wriezen; fighting for Berlin
28 April to 3 May 1945	Withdrawal to the Soviet-American demarcation line; remnants of the division and battalion go into American captivity
8 May 1945	End of the war

APPENDIX 1

Commanders of *Panzer-Regiment 5* and *Panzer-Abteilung 5*

Panzer-Regiment 5
1935–43

Prewar period		
15 October 1935–13 October 1937	*Oberst* Zuckertort	
13 October 1937–July 1939	*Oberst* Nehring	
Campaign in Poland		
August–15 October 1939	*Oberstleutnant* Conze	Acting commander
Campaign in the West		
15 October 1939–13 October 1940	*Oberst Freiherr* von Funck	
Campaign in North Africa		
13 October 1940–30 June 1941	*Oberst* Olbrich	
1 July–25 November 1941	*Oberstleutnant* Stephan	Killed in action on 25 November 1941
25 November 1941–28 February 1942	*Major* Mildebrath	Acting commander
1 March–21 December 1942	*Oberst* Müller	
21 December 1942–10 January 1943	*Hauptmann* von Senfft zu Pilsach	Acting commander
10 January–31 March 1943	*Oberst* Stenkoff	
31 March–21 April 1943	*Hauptmann* Rohr	Acting commander; wounded and not replaced on 21 April 1943

Panzer-Abteilung 5

14 September 1943–5 July 1944	*Major* Rettemeier	

Panzer-Abteilung 5 (Reformed)

8 November 1944–9 January 1945	*Hauptmann* Arendt	Killed in action on 9 January 1945
9 January–8 May 1945	Unknown	

APPENDIX 2

Knight's Cross Recipients of *Panzer-Regiment 5* and *Panzer-Abteilung 5*

	Date of Award	Award # (Army)	Rank When Awarded	Name	Duty Position
1	15 May 1941	287	*Major*	Ernst BOLBRINKER	Commander, *I./PR 5*
2	27 June 1941	322	*Oberleutnant*	Ott-Friedrich VON SENFFT ZU PILSACH	Commander, *4./PR 5*
3	30 June 1941	321	*Hauptmann*	Kurt GIERGA	Commander, *5./PR 5*
4	30 June 1941	323	*Hauptfeldwebel*	Wilhelm WENDT	First sergeant, *5./PR 5*
5	28 July 1942	1059	*Oberleutnant*	Rolf ROCHOLL[1]	Acting commander, *2./PR 5*
6	29 July 1942	1066	*Oberleutnant*	Josef-Otto RIEPOLD[2]	Commander, *5./PR 5*
7	12 August 1942	1039	*Oberstleutnant*	Werner MILDEBRATH	Commander, *I./PR 5*
8	9 September 1942	1162	*Oberst*	Gerhard MÜLLER	Commander, *PR 5*
9	8 February 1943	1529	*Hauptmann*	Werner GRÜN	Acting commander, *I./PR 5*
10	5 December 1943	2392	*Hauptmann*	Josef RETTEMEIER[3]	Commander, *PA 5*
11	12 March 1944	2802	*Leutnant d.R.*	Heinz-Georg BEHRENS[4]	Acting commander, *3.PA 5*
12	24 February 1945	4605	Hauptmann	Kurt ARENDT[5]	Commander, *PA 5*
13	17 April 1945	5049	*Leutnant*	Horst GIESE	Acting commander, *2./PA 5*

Knight's Cross recipients who were assigned to *Panzer-Regiment 5* but received the award while assigned to other formations (incomplete listing)

Date of award	Rank	Name	Duty position when awarded; duty position within *PR 5*
3 June 1940	*Oberst*	Hermann BREITH[6]	Commander, *Panzer-Brigade 5*; commander of the *II./PR 5* from 1935 to 1938
15 August 1940	*Major*	Gerhard WENDENBURG	Commander, *Panzer-Abteilung 67*; commander of the *4./PR 5* from 1937 to 1939
31 January 1941	*Oberst*	Johannes STREICH	Commander, *Panzer-Regiment 15*; commander of the *I./PR 5* from 1935 to 1937
14 May 1941	*Major*	Theodor *Graf* SCHIMMELMANN VON LINENBURG	Commander, *II./Panzer-Regiment 15*; commander of the *6./PR 5* from 1936 to 1937
15 July 1941	*Generalmajor*	Hans *Freiherr* VON FUNCK[7]	Commander, *7. Panzer-Division*; commander of *PR 5* from 1939 to 1940
15 July 1941	*Major*	Wilhelm *Ritter und Edler* VON PETER[8]	Commander, *I./Panzer-Regiment 36*; commander of the *6./PR 5* from 1938 to 1939 and commander of the *II./PR 5* in 1940
24 July 1941	*Generalmajor*	Walther K. NEHRING[9]	Commander, *18. Panzer-Division*; commander of *PR 5* from 1937 to 1939
10 February 1942	*Oberstleutnant*	Wolfgang THOMALE	Commander, *Panzer-Regiment 27*; commander of the *1./PR 5* until 1936
6 July 1942	*Hauptmann*	Rudolf KIEHL	Leader of the combat echelon of the headquarters of *Panzer-Armee Afrika*; killed in action as the acting commander of the *I./PR 5* on 4 September 1942 at Alam Halfa
15 October 1942	*Oberstleutnant*	Johannes SCHMIDT	Commander, *I./Panzer-Regiment 27*; commander of the *2./PR 5* from 1937 to 1940
30 November 1942	*Major*	Bernhard SAUVANT[10]	Commander, *I./Panzer-Regiment 36*; assigned to the *5./PR 5* from 1935 to 1938

18 October 1944	*Major*	Hans SANDROCK	Commander, *III./Fallschirm-Panzer-Regiment "Hermann Göring"*; commander of the *1./PR 5* in Africa
18 October 1944	*Oberfähnrich*[11]	Fritz BIRNBAUM	Platoon leader in the *8./Fallschirm-Panzer-Regiment "Hermann Göring"*
12 December 1944	*Oberst*	Karl August *Freiherr* VON BÜLOW	Commander, *Panzer-Regiment 24*; commander in the *6. PR 5* from 1935 to 1936

1. Author's Note: 287th recipient of the Oak Leaves to the Knight's Cross of the Iron Cross on 31 August 1942 as a *Hauptmann* and commander of the *III./Grenadier-Regiment 569*; killed in action on 23 August 1943 in the East.
2. Author's Note: Killed in action in Africa on 17 June 1942; posthumously promoted to *Hauptmann*.
3. Author's Note: 425th recipient of the Oak Leaves to the Knight's Cross of the Iron Cross on 13 March 1944 as a *Hauptmann* and commander of *Panzer-Abteilung 5*.
4. Author's Note: Killed in action on 16 June 1944.
5. Author's Note: Killed in action on 9 January 1945.
6. Author's Note: 69th recipient of the Oak Leaves to the Knight's Cross to the Iron Cross on 31 January 1942 as a *Generalmajor* and commander of the *3. Panzer-Division*; 48th recipient of the Swords to the Oak Leaves to the Knight' Cross of the Iron Cross on 21 February 1944 as a *General der Panzertruppen* and commanding general of the *III. Panzer-Korps*.
7. Author's Note: 278th recipient of the Oak Leaves to the Knight's Cross on 22 August 1943 as a *Generalleutnant* and commander of the *7. Panzer-Division*.
8. Author's Note: Killed in action in the East on 26 September 1941.
9. Author's Note: 383rd recipient of the Oak Leaves to the Knight's Cross of the Iron Cross on 8 February 1944 as a *General der Panzertruppen* and commanding general of the *XXIV. Panzer-Korps* and 124th recipient of the Swords to the Oak Leaves to the Knight's Cross of the Iron Cross on 22 January 1945 in the same rank and capacity.
10. Author's Note: 260th recipient of the Oak Leaves to the Knight's Cross of the Iron Cross on 28 July 1943 as a *Major* and commander of *schwere Panzer-Abteilung 505 (Tiger)*.
11. Translator's Note: Officer candidate.

APPENDIX 3

German Cross in Gold Recipients of *Panzer-Regiment 5* and *Panzer-Abteilung 5*

	Date of award	Rank when awarded	Name	Formation of Assignment (according to the Federal Archives)
1	25 March 1942	*Oberleutnant*	Werner GRÜN	*PR 5*
2	25 March 1942	*Oberleutnant*	Rolf ROCHOLL	*6./PR 5*
3	25 March 1942	*Oberleutnant*	Albrecht ZORN	*I./PR 5*
4	1 May 1942	*Leutnant*	Fiete FRICKE	*PR 5*
5	1 May 1942	*Oberleutnant*	Hans SANDROCK	*I./PR 5*
6	9 October 1942	*Unteroffizier*	Adolf ASSMANN	*5./PR 5*
7	9 October 1942	*Oberfeldwebel*	Paul KUNZ	*6./PR 5*
8	9 October 1942	*Hauptfeldwebel*	Erwin LUCKOW	*4./PR 5*
9	9 October 1942	*Leutnant*	Karl-Friedrich NEUMANN	*PR 5*
10	9 October 1942	*Unteroffizier*	Arnold SCHMIED	*6./PR 5*
11	29 March 1943	*Oberleutnant*	Wolf VON SCHLIEFFEN	*II./PR 5*
12	10 May 1943	*Oberfeldwebel*	Willy GROSSE	*5./PR 5*
13	12 May 1943	*Hauptmann*	Paul KAESTNER	*PR 5*
14	12 May 1943	*Feldwebel*	Karl-Heinrich SCHUMACHER	*4./PR 5*
15	12 May 1943	*Leutnant*	Kurt WOLFF	*PR5*
16	11 December 1943	*Leutnant*	Karl-Friedrich WILKE	*3./PA 5*
17	28 April 1944	*Oberleutnant*	Jürgen STRUNK	*1./PA 5*
18	2 May 1944	*Feldwebel*	Ernst VOGLER	*3./PA 5*
19	14 February 1945	*Stabsfeldwebel*	Bruno SCHULZE	*1./PA 5*

Hans Sandrock was a commander of the *5./ Panzer-Regiment 5* in North Africa. He was awarded the Knight's Cross of the Iron Cross on 18 October 1944 as the commander of the *III./Fallschirm-Panzer-Regiment "Hermann Göring."* It was not uncommon for experienced Army personnel to be impressed into service with *Luftwaffe* ground formations. Sandrock is seen here wearing the relatively rare mouse-gray denim version of the tanker jacket.

APPENDIX 4

Logistics

It is said with some justification that logistics does not decide a battle, but it influences all of them.

The terrific achievements of *Panzer-Regiment 5* and *Panzer-Abteilung 5* would not have been possible without the self-sacrifice and dedication of those who created the prerequisites for battle: the maintenance, supply and medical forces.

The maintenance elements were constantly striving to repair disabled armored and wheeled vehicles right on the battlefield and make them operational again as soon as possible.

The supply elements were faced with the difficult mission of providing the combat elements with fuel, ammunition and rations. Those "consumable end items" had to be transported to the forces in the field under very dangerous circumstances. In North Africa, it was extraordinarily difficult to find tank companies that were on the move. In addition, the columns were often exposed to attacks from both the air and the ground.

The medical services were also exposed to extraordinary conditions, especially in North Africa. Despite that, the wounded and sick were given the greatest possible care, and the medical personnel did not shy away from danger in recovering and evacuating wounded soldiers on the battlefield.

Maintenance Services

In Africa, all of the maintenance and repair of tracked and wheeled vehicles had to be conducted without the typical infrastructure found in Europe. In the best case, tents were available. As a result of the frequent withdrawals in the desert, many had to be abandoned, however. Particularly disadvantageous for vehicular upkeep was the constant lack of replacement parts.

Oberschirrmeister Paul-Friedrich Koch, a former maintenance sergeant of the regiment, wrote the following to the author concerning maintenance and repair in the desert:

> The company maintenance contact teams were highly motivated and well versed in the technical and mechanical aspects of the tanks. In technically hopeless situations, we often demonstrated improvisational skills that are scarcely imaginable today. As is generally known, we usually supplied ourselves through vehicles that that had become disabled in the desert and were no longer capable of combat operations. That often took two days of driving in order to find the "replacement depot" by means of compass and map. Turrets that could not be repaired were swapped out at night in the main lines by means of crane vehicles. Two tanks were brought forward in front of the vehicle that was to be repaired in the event of surprise nighttime attacks. The crew of the tank that was to be repaired was notified by radio of the arrival of the new turret that night, so as to initiate the preparatory work.
>
> In order to provide better protection to the tank mechanics, we increasingly made use during the war of captured English armored

vehicles. They were then able to advance to the vehicles in the front lines that needed repair with some degree of protection from artillery fire. Those vehicles were also in radio contact with the respective company commanders. We were also able to evacuate wounded crewmembers more safely than in an unprotected field ambulance. Even wounded English soldiers, whom we were frequently able to free from being stuck in their vehicles with pry bars or save from their burning vehicles, were taken to the main clearing station in these vehicles on several occasions. We frequently heard many words of thanks from the enemy soldiers who were not too badly wounded. The maintenance facilities, which always followed us at a distance of several kilometers and, as a result, were constantly in danger, conducted their work with unimaginable courage, without being able to defend themselves while they worked.

Campaign in the West: Recovery of a *Panzer III* of the 6th Company by the regimental maintenance company.

Bourgoin, south of Lyon: Evacuation of a damaged *Panzer IV* of the 4th Company. The recovery vehicle is the massive eighteen-ton FAMO halftrack.

Another view of the evacuation, with a close-up of the flatbed trailer. Note that the trailer had steerable wheels, with a separate station at its rear for the "driver."

Africa, 1941: A disabled *Panzer III* is evacuated, but not before the maintenance personnel and members of the crew pose for a photograph.

A *Panzer III* is serviced by the maintenance company.

Working on the 5-centimeter L42 main gun of a *Panzer III.*

Unteroffizier Herbert Gräfe next to his motorcycle with sidecar. He was the leader of the maintenance contact team for the headquarters of the regiment's 1st Battalion in the spring of 1941. His team was also responsible for the regimental headquarters' vehicles.

The maintenance truck of a contact team for the 1st Battalion.

This *Panzer II* of the 2nd Company drove over a mine outside Tobruk in April 1941 and suffered suspension damage. It was abandoned in no-man's-land, where it was used during the day by a British artillery forward observer, who then left it when it turned dark. One night, *Oberschirrmeister* Koch and a tank mechanic repaired the damage and evacuated the tank back to German lines.

After the fighting for the Gazala Line and the capture of Tobruk, there was a lot of work for the maintenance company. The rear deck is being removed on this *Panzer III* for more complete access to the engine compartment.

Working on the running gear of a *Panzer III* of the 2nd Company.

A close-up of the repair efforts.

Tripoli, 12 March 1941: Military parade upon arrival and before operations in the desert. To the left are supply vehicles of the 6th Company; on the right, the 8th Company.

A supply point at the five-kilometer milestone outside Tripoli. The vehicles are topped off and complete their basic load of ammunition. Note the provisioning on the rear of the tanks for additional fuel cans.

A truck driver has just been awarded the Iron Cross, Second Class.

Gustav Gaus and the "gas station" of the 6th Company in 1941. Initially, every tank company in Africa had four dedicated fuel trucks at its disposal. Later on, they were consolidated at regimental level.

MEDICAL SERVICES

The *Sd.Kfz. 2501/8 SPW* of the regimental surgeon.

Shrapnel on the Red Cross.

Caring for a wounded soldier.

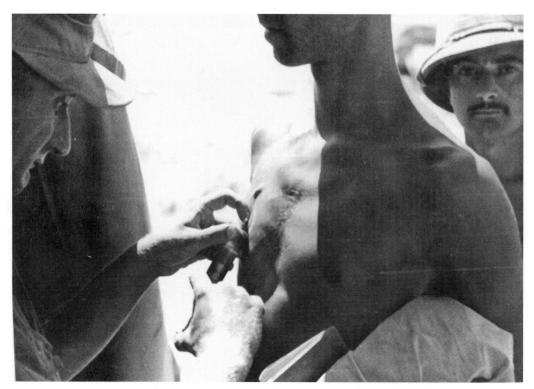

Feared but unavoidable: immunization.

A dentist conducts a field inspection.

APPENDIX 5:

Panzer-Ersatz-Abteilung 5

After mobilization in August 1939, the regiment detached two companies—the 1st Battalion's 3rd Company and the 2nd Battalion's 7th Company—to establish a replacement detachment in Neuruppin. The mission of *Panzer-Ersatz-Abteilung 5* was to train personnel replacements for the regiment.

The mosaic in front of the enlisted tent reads: "*7./PzRgt 5 / Neuruppin.*" The silhouette is of a *Panzer I* and the ubiquitous insignia of the *Panzertruppe*—the death's head—can also be seen.

Before you could become a tanker, you had to learn how to be an infantryman.

Spring 1942: Training on the *Panzer I*. To the right is an officer candidate, Karl-Friedrich König.

Mounting and dismounting drills on a *Panzer I.*

1942: Training replacements for the regiment. By this time, the *Panzer I* had disappeared from the front in a combat role.

Panzerschütze Karl-Friedrich König (at right) with an *Unteroffizier* on a *Panzer I*.

Training demonstration for recruits of the detachment: Breaking through a house wall with a *Panzer II*.

This type of demonstration was designed to create an impression of the strength and power of an armored fighting vehicle and reinforce confidence in one's weapons. I.1 actual field conditions, however, it was rare for a tank to be employed in this manner, since it was essentially "blind" against defenders on the inside of the structure.

Field training on a *Panzer II*.

The *Panzer IV.*

1942: An early version of the *Panzer III* (*Ausf. B*) with eight roadwheels is used for training within the detachment.

The same vehicle is seen with its crew for the gunnery training. Once again, a Model B *Panzer III*, easily recognizable by its four sets of roadwheels.

Gunnery training at the Döberitz Training Area. The officer observing the firing is a veteran of the campaign in Africa, as denoted by his sleeve band.

Fall 1942: Gunnery at the Döberitz Training Area with *Panzer II's, III's* and *IV's*.

The *Panzer IV* is rearmed.

This *Panzer IV Ausf. E* features supplemental armor on its front slope.

December 1943: The training detachment now has later versions of both the *Panzer III* and the *Panzer IV*, all featuring sideskirts. Although designed to protect the vehicles from hollow-charge and shaped munitions by providing standoff, the sideskirts were easily lost under field conditions.

1942: Motorcycle messengers for the regiment/battalion were trained by *Kraftfahr-Ersatz-Abteilung 3* in Rathenow. All the way to the right is *Gefreiter* Felix Kalinka, who was a motorcycle messenger assigned to the regimental headquarters company in Africa in 1942 and 1943.

APPENDIX 6:

Personnel of *Panzer-Regiment 5* Reassigned to the *I./Panzer-Lehr-Regiment 130*

After the regiment was lost in Tunisia in May 1943, remaining elements of the formation that were in Germany were reassigned to *Hauptmann* Rettemeier's *Panzer-Abteilung 5* in accordance with orders dated 25 August 1943.

In addition to *Panzer-Ersatz-Abteilung 5* in Neuruppin, there was another armored training detachment with the same numeral in Voborg (Denmark)—*Panzer-Ausbildungs- und Reserve-Abteilung 5*. Many soldiers from the former *Panzer-Regiment 5* were assigned to it as instructors and cadre personnel. Personnel from both of those detachments were used to form the 1st Battalion of *Panzer-Lehr-Regiment 130*.

Werner Simmermacher, a *Leutnant* in the 4th Company of the battalion at the time, has provided this firsthand information:

> The Headquarters Company and the 2nd through 4th Companies of the 1st Battalion of *Panzer-Lehr-Regiment 130* were activated at the Fallingbostel Training Area in the early summer of 1944 with personnel from *Panzer-Ausbildungs- und Ersatz-Abteilung 5*. The [battalion] was billeted in Camp Örbke.
>
> Based on the testing with infrared night-vision devices (*"Biwa"* and *"UHU"* devices), which were classified as SECRET, the battalion reported directly to the German Army High Command and, based on operational security reasons, had no intermediate command. As a result, the battalion did not initially belong to the *Panzer-Lehr-Division* as was the case with the 2nd Battalion.
>
> Each of the four tank companies had three platoons, each with five *Panzer V* "Panthers"; [in addition, there was a] tank for the commander and a replacement tank for him. Each of the tanks had a searchlight. The *"Biwa"* infrared night-vision device could be mounted on the tank commander's cupola. It could be traversed 180 degrees and elevated by the tank commander. The searchlight on the tank served to provide orientation and to illuminate the area to the front. A smaller infrared device with limited range was mounted at the driver's station (*"Sperber"* driver's device). There was a *"UHU" SPW* with every platoon, on which a large searchlight was mounted, which had a range of more than 1,000 meters and served to identify longer-range targets (e.g., enemy tanks). All of the searchlights were covered with red glass so that the light could not be seen with the human eye.
>
> The infrared beams of the searchlights were made visible by the *"Biwas."* The terrain looked like a snow-covered landscape after it was nearly nightfall. Enemy tanks could be identified and engaged at a distance of 800 to

1,000 meters with it. The tank commander's *"Biwa"* had aiming points similar to those in the gunner's optics, with which he could take aim.

The tank commander's *"Biwa"* was connected mechanically by two steel cables which synchronously engaged the optics of the gunner. The tank commander issued the fired command; the gunner discharged the round.

It was soon determined during live-fire gunnery that the system was not yet ready for the field. The main gun and fire-control optics of the gunner had to be calibrated with the tank commander's *"Biwa"* prior to every operation. After three to four rounds, the synchronization between the *"Biwa"* and the fire-control system no longer functioned as a result of the recoil of the main gun and vibrations and deficiencies in the mechanical transfer. The main gun and the *"Biwa"* were completely out of synchronization, with the result that there was no longer any chance of getting a hit.

A combat exercise involving the entire battalion had to be broken off, because many of the tanks had lost their orientation and there danger they might engage other tanks.

At the beginning of September—Allied forces had arrived at the western frontiers of the *Reich* by then—the Headquarters Company and the 1st through 3rd Companies, none of which had night-vision devices, were moved to the Western Front. The 4th Company remained in Fallingbostel and continued to test the *"Biwa."* The companies returned after about two months; they had turned over their tanks to other formations. After replacing the losses and issuance of new *Panthers*, the testing continued. When the Russians broke through in Hungary in November and encircled large German formations in the Budapest area, the *I./Panzer-Lehr-Regiment 130* was alerted—with the exception of a platoon, which remained behind to continue testing—to be committed for a counterattack there. The counterattack failed; the Russians continued to advance west. Our battalion turned over its remaining tanks, was pulled out of the line and then sent to the Grafenwöhr Training Area in its wheeled vehicles. It was reconstituted there with replacements and issued new tanks.

The infrared devices stored at Fallingbostel were not sent to us. The *I./Panzer-Lehr-regiment 130* was moved to the West at the end of January or the beginning of February 1945. It was committed to counterattacks in the Xanten, Cleve, Goch, Krefeld and Mönchengladbach areas, whereupon it joined the *Panzer-Lehr-Division*. After being wounded in defensive fighting between Rheydt and Mönchengladbach, I was hospitalized in Holland. The *I./Panzer-Lehr-Regiment 130* fought as part of the *Panzer-Lehr-Division* until the end in the Ruhr pocket. It was rumored that the platoon that had remained behind in Fallingbostel with the *"Biwas"* was employed with its equipment along the Oder.

The former commander of *Panzer-Abteilung 5*, *Major* Josef Rettemeier, who had become the 425th recipient of the Oak Leaves to the Knight's Cross of the Iron Cross on 13 March 1944, was given command of the 1st Battalion of *Panzer-Lehr-Regiment 130* in September 1944.

The photographs seen in this appendix show the departure of the battalion in Fallingbostel at the beginning of September 1944 to be committed on the Western front in support of *Panzer-Brigade 112*.

September 1944, Fallingbostal Training Area: The battalion forms up in front of its *Panthers*.

Hauptmann Krone (left) reports the assembled battalion to its commander, *Major* Rettemeier. All the way to the right, next to the party functionary, is the battalion adjutant, *Oberleutnant* Schwarz. All three officers were former members of *Panzer-Regiment 5*, who had fought in North Africa. All three wear the *"Afrika"* sleeve band.

The battalion commander reviews his troops.

Hauptmann Neugebauer (left) leads the color guard. Unlike the U.S. Army, color guards in the German military usually consisted of officers or senior noncommissioned officers.

Major Rettemeier gives a short talk to his battalion prior to its departure for the Western Front.

The local party functionary also addresses the soldiers. *Oberleutnant* Schwarz is seen to his commander's left. Schwarz was one of the few German soldiers to actually escape from captivity in North Africa after the capitulation in May 1943.

Another view of the ceremony. A company first sergeant can be seen in the foreground, identifiable by the two "piston rings" he wears on the sleeve of his *Panzer* tunic.

The color guards moves past the assembled formation.

Hauptmann Wulf-Werner Koch also fought in Africa with the regiment. Following the wounding of *Major* Rettemeier in October, Koch succeeded Rettemeier in command of the battalion.

The battalion's units pass in review.

Rettemeier and Schwarz. Both had been in the regiment's 2nd Company in Africa, where Rettemeier had been the company commander, first as an *Oberleutnant* and then as a *Hauptmann.*

A happy Rettemeier poses prior to getting into his staff car.

1945: Rettemeier as
a course leader at
the armor school in
Erlangen (Franconia).

Rettemeier as an *Oberst* and
commander of *Panzer-Brigade 6*
in Neustadt (Hessia) in 1968.

APPENDIX 7:

Uniform

In November 1934, a special-purpose uniform was introduced for service in armored vehicles. It consisted of protective headgear, a field jacket, trousers, a dark-green tricot shirt, black tie and lace-up boots. The field jacket and trousers were made out of heavy wool, which was kept black as a practical matter.

The field jacket had no external pockets and featured branch-color piping around the collar and the collar tabs. The branch color for the *Panzertruppe* was rose pink. Assignment to a respective formation was denoted by the addition of ciphers and numerals on the shoulder straps (enlisted and noncommissioned officers) and boards (officers). The use of these identifiers was eliminated in the course of the war. Mounted on the collar tabs was the symbol chosen for the *Panzertruppe*, the death's head, in a light-colored bright metal. The jacket was worn with an open collar. Indeed, the initial versions of the *Panzer* jacket had no provision to close the collar. As opposed to other field uniforms, junior and senior noncommissioned officers did not wear braid around the collar.

The field trousers had no piping. The trousers were cut close; they were fastened by button at the waistline and by tie strings at the cuffs.

The protective headgear consisted of a protective helmet constructed out of felt-like material covered in wool with six ventilation ports and lined in oilcloth. A beret was worn over the protective helmet.

Starting in November 1935, it was directed that the national insignia be worn on the special-purpose uniform, which meant a breast eagle on the jacket and a cap eagle on the beret.

Regimental musicians and trumpeters wore special insignia on their shoulders to denote their status, referred to in soldier's jargon as a "swallow's nest."

18 June 1935: Erich Machleb, a member of the regimental staff and the regimental band for *Kraftfahrlehrkommando Zossen* wears the special-purpose tanker's uniform. At this date, the national insignia still was not worn.

1942: *Gefreiter* Karl-Friedrich König in his black *Panzer* uniform with black *Panzer* overseas cap. The piping on the uniform and cap is rose pink in color. König wears a variant of the standard death's heads; they were referred to as *Braunschweiger-Totenköpfe*, since they were modeled on the type worn by hussar formations from Braunschweig.

In 1934, there was no black headgear for *Panzer* soldiers, with the exception of the aforementioned protective headgear. In 1941, the protective headgear—which was really never popular with the troops in the field—was replaced by a black overseas cap, which was initially introduced in 1940. Starting in 1943, the overseas cap, slightly modified and sporting a brim, was introduced. In contravention of the regulations, visor caps were sometimes worn with the black uniform, especially by officers.

Up until 1940, the black uniform was only allowed to be worn while serving on a vehicle. Starting at the end of 1940, however, less and less field-gray clothing was issued to tank crews, with the exception of the winter overcoat. Much to the joy of the tankers, the black uniform was then allowed to be worn outside of the garrison and on leave. There were numerous variations in wear when this was allowed, as can be imagined. The use of piping around the collar was discontinued when new jackets were produced in 1941, although collar-piped jackets can be seen in wear through war's end.

Unteroffizier Orlijewski was assigned to the regiment's 5th Company. While on home leave, he wore this civilian striped shirt while having a portrait and wedding photos taken in his *Panzer* uniform. He wears a later model of the *Panzer* jacket, which no longer had pink piping around the collar.

The *Panzer* uniform was worn in Germany for many different occasions and ceremonies, often combining elements of a walking-out dress uniform. *Unteroffizier* Orlijewski is seen here wearing the same uniform as before, but with a white shirt, enlisted belt and buckle and a visor cap.

The original high quality of the black wool worsened in the course of the war by the incorporation of synthetic materials. Captured stocks of wool were also used after they had been dyed black.

Eventually, not only the *Panzertruppe* but other combat and combat-support arms wore variations of the *Panzer* uniform when the unit or formation was assigned armored vehicles. A field-gray version of the uniform in wool was also produced. Some of the branches of service that wore variations of the tank uniform included: combat engineers (*Panzerpioniere*), armored/self-propelled artillery (*Panzerartillerie*), assault gunners (*Sturmartillerie*) and antitank/tank destroyer forces (*Panzerjäger/Panzerzerstörer*). Armored reconnaissance forces (*Panzeraufklärer*) wore the special-purpose black uniform from the inception of the *Panzertruppe*, however.

Unteroffizier Paul-Friedrich Koch was assigned to the 2nd Company. Starting in 1937, he was the maintenance sergeant for the regimental headquarters. He wears the first version of the *Panzer* jacket, which was authorized late in 1934. Note the "5" on the shoulder strap, denoting assignment to *Panzer-Regiment 5*.

Panzerschütze Edube Schwarz was assigned to the 4th Company. He wears the second-pattern *Panzer* jacket, which had a noticeably larger collar, which could also be closed for protection against the elements. The regimental numeral no longer appears on the shoulder straps, however.

Unteroffizier Herbert Zeidler was assigned to the 8th Company in Africa. He appears to be wearing the *Afrikakorps* sleeve band on his uniform, which was not authorized. In addition, he wears the short-lived *M42* overseas cap, which was the precursor to the billed version introduced in 1943 (*M43*).

Gefreiter Heinz Kreft had seen service in Africa, as indicated by the *Afrika* sleeve band. He made it out of North Africa. This portrait was taken in 1944, while he was assigned to *Panzer-Ersatz-Abteilung 5*. The wear of the tie was normally a requirement, although commanders could authorize an open shirt collar if temperature conditions warranted. The wear of the black overseas cap at this late date is also something of an anomaly, since one would expect a billed field cap by this time.

Oberleutnant Gerhard Fischer started his military service with the *Kraftfahrlehrkommando Zossen* in 1934. Until the end of May 1941, he was assigned to the regiment's 1st Company. He was awarded the German Cross in Gold on 28 November 1942. He received the Knight's Cross to the Iron Cross on 28 December 1943.

Obergefreiter Hans Skala was serving with *Panzer-Regiment 2* (*16. Panzer-Division*) when this photograph was taken on home leave at the end of 1944. In Africa, he was assigned to the regiment's 8th Company and served as a gunner. Note the wear of the non-regulation shirt as well as the apparent absence of shoulder straps.

Noncommissioned officers who had served in Africa. After the end of campaign in North Africa, they were reassigned to *Panzer-Ersatz-Abteilung 5* as instructors.

Gefreiter Erich Machleb was assigned to the headquarters of the regiment and a member of the regimental band. He wears the so-called *Waffenrock*, which was a combination parade and walking-out dress uniform that emphasized the branch-of-service of the wearer by its prominent use of the branch's color piping around the collar, along the front closure, on the cuffs and on trim on the rear of the jacket. The *Waffenrock* was introduced in 1934. It was field gray in color and usually made out of high-quality material, even the version issued to enlisted ranks. The cut and appearance was reminiscent of Prussian uniforms of the *Kaiser* period. It was to fit tightly and was therefore uncomfortable and unpopular with the soldiers. It was called many things in soldier jargon: "*Kaiser* Wilhelm memorial tunic"; "Sarasani"*; and "fryer tunic." When worn as a walking-out dress uniform, it was worn with stone-gray trousers (also with branch-of-service color as piping trim along the outer leg seams), lace-up shoes, a visor cap, belt and buckle and a patent-leather hanger with sheathed bayonet.

* Translator's Note: The "Sarasani" was the name of a large circus concern in Germany, not unlike Ringling Brothers in the United States. Therefore, a "Sarasani" was a circus-like costume.

Oberfeldwebel Kurt Herms was assigned to the 5th Company of the regiment. He is seen wearing an "old-style" tunic with the second level of the marksmanship badge and a Four-Year-Service ribbon. This style of tunic stems from the period of the *Reichswehr* and can be identified by pocket opening on the sides of the tunic instead of pocket flaps towards the bottom front. A branch-of-service color was also added to the front closure of the tunic, which had from six to eight buttons. In the case of noncommissioned officers, whether junior or senior, the characteristic NCO braid ran along the outside edge of the collar, as opposed to the front collar edge and bottom of the collar as was done of field tunics.

The regimental commander, *Oberst* Nehring, with his officers in February 1938 at Wünsdorf. Nehring wears on "old-style" tunic, while most of the other officers wear *Waffenröcke*. In the case of officers, material was to be used on the *Waffenrock* that "did not negatively influence the good appearance of the tunic." Great stress was place on proper fitting of the tunic. It was to be cut tightly, with no wrinkles showing. The breast eagle for officers was also silver-colored embroidery. For parades or when ordered for special occasions, a special fabric belt with silver-colored thread was worn along with a round belt buckle (as opposed to the rectangular one worn by enlisted personnel). At the beginning of the war, it was ordered that production of *Waffenröcke* cease in order to conserve materials. *Waffenröcke* already issued or purchased were allowed to be worn, however.

Gefreiter Karl-Friedrich König while assigned to *Panzer-Ersatz-Abteilung 5* in 1942. He wears a later version of the standard four-pocket field tunic with visor cap. The four-pocket tunic was introduced in 1933 and underwent many modifications and simplifications until war's end. It was a ubiquitous garment and worn for almost all occasions. Initially issued with a dark greenish-blue collar and a field-gray base, the collar also became field gray over time. The shoulder straps were likewise initially on a dark-green base, gradually being phased out in favor of straps that were field gray in color. It is often referred to as a "four-pocket" tunic. There were openings along the waist to allow mounting hardware for load-bearing equipment. In order to allow as much freedom of movement as possible, the tunic was generally cut so as to be loose fitting, almost shirt-like, which is reflected in its German designation, the *Feldbluse* (literally: "Field blouse"). It is interesting to note that König still has the regimental numerals on his tunic, even though the practice had been phased out officially for some time.

Hauptmann Hans Sandrock in an officer version of the field blouse in June 1943. Officers were responsible for purchasing their own uniforms, for which they were given a small allowance. As a result, tailor-made uniforms are frequently encountered, although officers were also allowed to purchase enlisted uniforms (not much use was made of that option, except in the case of the black *Panzer* uniform) or continued to wear upgraded versions of their previous enlisted uniforms after commissioning. The collar patches were fashioned out of silver-wire embroidery with inserts denoting the branch-of-service. These were mounted on a dark-green base. The shoulder boards were made out of silver-colored flat cord, with branch-of-service piping around the edges. Generally, they were of the sew-in variety. The stars denoting rank were gold for officers and silver for noncommissioned officers. Note that Sandrock wears an *Afrikakorps* sleeve band, which had officially been superseded by the *Afrika* sleeve band by this time.

Hans Sandrock wearing a *Luftwaffe* tropical blouse with what appears to be an army-style billed tropical field cap. From January 1941 until November 1942, he was the commander of the regiment's 1st Company. Occasionally, he was given acting command of the 1st Battalion. From November 1942 until July 1943, he was assigned to *Panzer-Ersatz-Abteilung 5* in Neuruppin. After attending a battalion command course, he was designated as the acting battalion commander of the 3rd Battalion of *Fallschirm-Panzer-Regiment "Hermann Göring"* and given formal command in November 1943, staying in that position until 26 March 1945. He was promoted to *Major* on 1 February 1942.

At the end of the war, he was the commander of the division's replacement battalion, fighting around Oranienburg.

Feldwebel Wüstefeld wears the tropical field blouse as a member of *Panzer-Regiment 5*.

When it became apparent that German forces were to be employed in the North African theater of war, it became necessary to procure uniform items on short notice that were suitable for the climatic conditions. The "tropical uniform" was developed at the end of 1940 and beginning of 1941 and introduced in short order to the field.

The tropical field blouse was based on the continental four-pocket tunic, but it did not have a lining and was produced out of olive-green cotton. The noncommissioned officer braid on the shoulder straps as well as around the color was copper brown in color instead of the traditional silver, thus not standing out from the base color of the jacket cloth. The backing for the collar patches as well as the national insignia was also a coppery brown. The backing usually found on the collar patches and sometimes on the breast eagle was missing, with both being sewn directly to the tunic. Several versions of the tunic were produced, with the pleated pockets being the sign of an early version. There was no special uniform or insignia developed for officers, with the result that officers received enlisted uniform items, adding continental-style officer insignia, frequently sewn directly over the factory-sewn enlisted insignia.

Although the wear of the death's heads on the uniform was not authorized, it is a frequently seen variation encountered among the tankers employed there.

Unteroffizier Walter Märkisch of the regiment's 1st Company in his tropical field blouse. Unlike Wüstefeld in the previous photograph, Märkisch has not only added death's heads to his field blouse, but he has used non-standard ones as well. This type of skull was normally found on *SS* uniforms. It must be assumed that supply problems may have led to the somewhat unusual choice.

Enlisted tropical shoulder straps were always removable. They were usually finished in field-gray wool on the bottom and featured the ubiquitous branch-of-service piping on the edges.

As the result of the action of the sun and the washing of the uniform, the original relatively dark olive-green bleached out, resulting in a wide variety of brown and sand-colored tones, sometimes even approaching bone white. Since a faded uniform was the mark of an "old timer," many replacements in the field artificially aged their uniforms through the use of bleach, fuel or a solution of water and anti-contamination gas pellets.

Leutnant Wendorff was assigned to the headquarters of the regiment's 2nd Battalion and served as the battalion signals officer. He wears an enlisted tunic modified for officer wear by the addition of officer slip-on shoulder straps. Otherwise, the uniform retains all of its enlisted insignia.

During the course of the fighting in North Africa, the soldiers committed there also liked to wear uniform articles from their Italian allies or captured British stocks, with the result that there was considerable variety in the uniform wear.

In contrast to the fabrics used for the manufacture of the German tropical uniforms, the materials found in Italian and British uniforms were softer and more comfortable to wear.

1942: Wendorff in another enlisted tropical uniform modified for officer wear. In this case, "continental" collar tabs as well as a "continental" eagle (albeit apparently enlisted) are worn. This was standard for most officers. As with many soldiers, he has added death's heads; this time, yet another variant, with them being much smaller than the standard ones worn on *Panzer* uniforms.

Although a tie was prescribed for wear with the uniform (a lighter olive green), it was completely ill-suited to the environment and not worn on a daily basis.

The belts worn in the field by both officers and enlisted were similar, with the belt proper being made out of an olive-green webbing material. The buckle was finished in olive green, rectangular for enlisted and round for officers.

Leutnant Wendorff during the ship movement to Africa in the summer of 1941. He is already wearing a favorite variant of the tropical uniform: shirt-sleeve order with shorts. The tropical shirts generally had no national insignia, but did have fittings for the wear of shoulder straps or boards. The tropical shorts had a built-in web belt, as did the long tropical trousers. He wears the short tropical lace-up boots that were a combination of webbing material and leather. He has provided some firsthand details in his memoirs (excerpt):

"There were three types of trousers. Initially we received the normal long trousers, which we usually wore in Africa since they were fairly comfortable. There were also breeches, which extended to below the knee and were joined there by cotton leggings, unless, of course, you had the corresponding knee-high light tropical boots. Those trousers were also good, since you could make your way quite well through thorny vegetation in them, something that was not so uncommon. Moreover, perhaps, you felt a bit more sporty in them, more soldierly. The long trousers without the creases in them flopped around the legs in a very civilian-like manner. We usually liked that freedom and shapelessness, but not always. Finally, there were the shorts, in which you usually felt less constrained or more youthful. After all, the "Africans" were, on average, younger than the forces in Europe. Sometimes, you could have the feeling running around in your shorts that you were at some sort of field games in the Youth League or the Hitler Youth—or a tourist spending his vacation in a sunny clime so as to get a nice suntan there."

Officers, such as this combat engineer, often wore their visor caps in the beginning. In this case, it is a version particularly well liked by officer, the "old-style" field cap, which is usually called a "crusher" in English.

The pith helmet was not very well liked by the soldiers. Since it took up too much room in the fighting compartment in the armored vehicles, it was hung outside, usually being quickly lost in battle.

The tropical version of the overseas cap was much preferred to the pith helmet. Here, it is being worn by Heinrich-Gustaf Schlieper, the radio operator in the regimental command tank. The cap was produced in the same color as the rest of the tropical uniform, initially sported branch-of-color piping and had a red cotton lining.

The most frequently encountered and preferred piece of tropical headgear was the billed field cap, seen here being worn by *Hauptfeldwebel* Wendt. By washing it in fuel or a solution of water and anti-contamination tablets, the cap quickly lost its color and turned almost white.

APPENDIX 8:

Documents, Decorations, and Awards

Meißen porcelain presentation item for "special achievement" in the 2nd Battalion of the regiment sometime prior to the start of the war. In its original size, the tablet measures 8.5 x 13 centimeters and is 1 centimeter thick.

Verpflichtungsschein

Hans Braun

geboren am ___ *7. 5. 1912*

zu ___ *Myslawitz*

verpflichtet sich bis zum ___ *30. 9.* 19*35* zu allen Dienstleistungen im Reichsheer auf Grund der für das Reichsheer gültigen Gesetze, Verordnungen und Bestimmungen.

Zossen = Übungsplatz, den *23. 4. 1934*   Zossen = Übungsplatz, den *12. 4.* 19*34*

Hans Braun

(Unterschrift des sich Verpflichtenden)

Kraftfahr = Lehrkommando = Zossen

(Dienstgrad, Truppenteil)

Aushändigungsvermerk.

Eine Ausfertigung des Verpflichtungsscheins habe ich am ___ *23. 4.* 19*34* erhalten.

Hans Braun

(Unterschrift)

Die Dienstverpflichtung läuft ab

am *30. 9.* 19*35*

633. I. 34. Druck & Ehrend, Berlin SO. 26.
Din A 5

Enlistment contract from Hans-Joachim Braun, who initially served in the *Kraftfahrlehrkommando Zossen* and, after its redesignation, in the 6th and 7th Companies of the regiment. Along with other leadership personnel, he left the regiment in 1938 as an *Oberleutnant* to help establish the newly forming *Panzer-Regiment 36* of the *4. Panzer-Division* in Schweinfurt. The document was signed by the commander at the time, *Major* Harpe, who had previously been the commander of the KAMA Armor School in the Soviet Union. It is interesting to note that the official stamp used still features the national eagle of the Weimar Republic and not that of the Third *Reich.*

Hans-Joachim Braun in 1934 while assigned to the *Kraftfahrlehrkommando Zossen* as a driver.

Verpflichtungsschein!
■■■

...........*Hans* ....*Braun*...
(Vor- und Familienname)

geboren am.....*7. Mai*........................19*14*....

zu.......*Myslowitz* ......, *Kattowitz*.........................
(Ort, Kreis, Land)

verpflichtet sich zum weiteren Dienst in der Wehrmacht als Offizier nach den für die Wehrmacht gültigen Gesetzen, Verordnungen und Bestimmungen.

.*Wünsdorf*...........,den.*23. März*....19.*36*...

Unterschrift des sich Verpflichtenden:

.............*Braun*.............

.*Wünsdorf*...........,den.*23. März*....19.*36*..

Unterschrift des Kommandeurs:

.............*Braun*.............
(Dienstgrad, Truppenteil)

A u s h ä n d i g u n g s v e r m e r k.

Eine Ausfertigung des Verpflichtungsscheines habe ich
am.*23. März*.............19.*36*..erhalten.

.............*Braun*.............
(Unterschrift)

Die Dienstverpflichtung läuft ab am.*1. Mai*.....19.*37*..

Another enlistment contract for Braun, this one dated 23 March 1936. It is signed by the regimental commander at the time, *Oberstleutnant* Karl Adolf Zukertort, who was promoted to *Oberst* on 1 April 1936. In October 1937, Zukertort turned over command of the regiment to *Oberst* Walter K. Nehring. Zukertort retired from active service on 31 July 1941. As with the previous enlistment contract, the official stamp still features the Weimar eagle, even though the stamp has been updated to reflect the redesignation and it was more than three years into the National Socialist regime.

Verpflichtungsschein.

Der   **Gefreite Helmut Franz**
          (Dienstgrad, Vor- und Zuname)

der   **5./Panzer-Regiment 5**
          (Truppenteil, Dienststelle)

geboren am   **8.6.**   1918 in **Eisleben**

verpflichtet sich für ein 3. Dienstjahr

            vom 1.10. **1938**   bis 30.9. **1939**
                        (Tag)   (Tag)

zu allen Dienstleistungen in der Wehrmacht nach den für die Wehrmacht
gültigen Gesetzen, Verordnungen und Bestimmungen.

Wünsdorf, den 9.8.38.
            (Ort, Tag, Monat, Jahr)

Gefreiter   *Oberleutnant*

Aushändigungsvermerk.

Zweitschrift des Verpflichtungsscheins habe ich erhalten.

Wünsdorf, den 9.8.38.
            (Ort, Tag, Monat, Jahr)

                                                              Gefreiter.

960a. 11. 37. Amtl & Strauss, Berlin SO. 36
        Din A 5

One-year extension of an enlistment contract for *Gefreiter* Helmut Franz of the regiment's 5th Company. The document was signed on the company commander's behalf by *Oberleutnant* Bernhard Sauvant (bottom left), who later went on to become a recipient of both the Knight's Cross (30 November 1942 as the commander of the I./Panzer-Regiment 36) and the Oak Leaves (28 July 1943 as the commander of *schwere Panzer-Abteilung 505*). Sauvant also left the regiment in October 1938 to help form *Panzer-Regiment 36* of the *4. Panzer-Division* in Schweinfurt. The image at the top left is from Helmut Franz's *Wehrpaß* and indicates his assignment to the 5th Company.

Beſitz = Zeugnis

Der ___ *Panzerſchütze Baums* ___

von der ___ *2. Kompanie   Panzer-Regiment 5* ___ hat im

Schießjahr 193**8** als Anerkennung für hervorragende Leiſtungen

im Schießen das in der **II**. Schießklaſſe für *Karabiner* ausgeſetzte

Ein fache Schützenabzeichen

erworben, worüber ihm dieſes Beſitz=Zeugnis ausgefertigt wird.

___ **Wünsdorf** ___, den ___ **28. Oktober** ___ 193**8**

Hauptmann u. Kompanieführer

A 688a.   Centr.-Form.-Mag. Gustav Linke, Berlin SW19 Alexandrinenstr. 80   1295

Award certificate for the rifle marksmanship lanyard to *Panzerschütze* Oskar Baums. The original size of the document is 21x30 centimeters and is signed by the commander of the 2nd Company, *Hauptmann* Schmidt.

Gefreiter Baums as a radio operator on *Hauptmann* Schmidt's tank on 19 March 1939 in Prague.

The rifle marksmanship lanyard.

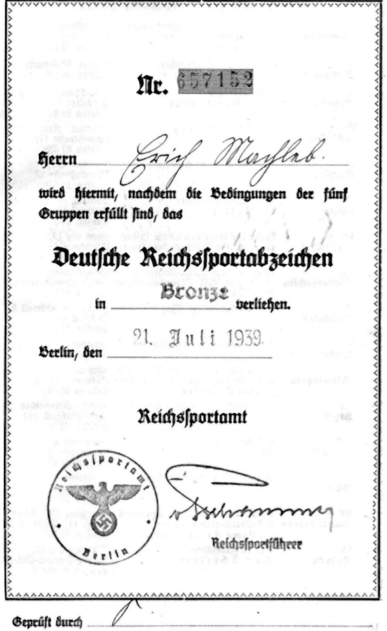

Machleb as a member of the regimental band.

Award certificate for the *Reich* Sports Badge in Bronze, which Erich Machleb was awarded on 21 July 1939. Although a civilian award, the badge was allowed to be worn on the uniform.

The *Reich* Sports Badge in Bronze.

Braun in 1941 as an *Oberleutnant* serving in *Panzer-Regiment 36* of the *4. Panzer-Division.*

Award certificate for the Service Award (4th Class) for four years of honorable service for *Leutnant* Hans-Joachim Braun of the regiment's 6th Company. The certificate was signed by the division commander, *Generalleutnant Freiherr* Leo Geyr von Schweppenburg, who served in that capacity from 12 October 1937 to October 1939. Von Schweppenburg went on to receive the Knight's Cross on 9 July 1941 as a *General der Panzertruppen* and commanding general of the *XXIV. Armee-Korps (mot.).*

The Service Award, 4th Class.

Im Namen des Führers und Reichskanzlers

verleihe ich

dem _Hauptmann Werner Hildebrath_
      (Dienstgrad, Vor- und Zuname)

8. Kompanie Panzer-Regiment 5
      (Truppe, Marineteil)

für _12_ jährige treue Dienste in der Wehrmacht die

Dienstauszeichnung _III._ Klasse

Berlin, den _31. Dezember_ 1936.

Der Kommandierende General
des Kommandos der Panzertruppen

LUTZ

General der Panzertruppen

Zukertort

Oberst u. Regts.-Kommandeur

M.S. Druck: Rbs. d. Dptr., Berlin SW 68, Kochstraße 67

Mildebrath as an *Oberst* and Knight's Cross recipient.

Award certificate for the Service Award (3rd Class) for twelve years of honorable service for *Hauptmann* Werner Mildebrath, who served as the commander of the regiment's 8th Company from 15 October 1935 to 31 May 1937. He received the Knight's Cross to the Iron Cross in Africa on 12 August 1942 as the commander of the regiment's 1st Battalion. The document was signed by *Oberst* Zukertort, the regiment's first commander.

Service Award, 3rd Class.

Im Auftrage des Führers und Reichskanzlers

Adolf Hitler

verleihe ich für hervorragende Leistungen
und opferwilligen Einsatz im Deutschen Kraftfahrsport

dem Hauptmann des Heeres Werner Mildebrath

das

Deutsche Motorsportabzeichen

Dritter Stufe

Berlin, den

30. Januar 1939

Der Führer des Deutschen Kraftfahrsports

Reichsleiter der NSDAP
Korpsführer des NSKK

Award certificate to Mildebrath for the German Motor Sports Badge in Bronze (3rd Class). Like the Sports Badge, the Motor Sports Badge was also permitted to be worn on the service uniform, even though it was ostensibly a civilian award. Right: The German Motor Sports Badge in Bronze (3rd Class).

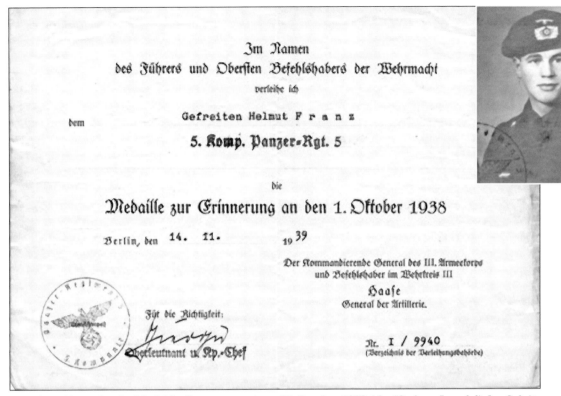

Award certificate for the Medal in Commemoration of 1 October 1938 (the "Sudeten" medal) for *Gefreiter* Helmut Franz. On service uniforms for everyday wear, the medal was represented by a ribbon.

The certificate's authenticity was verified by *Oberleutnant* Kurt Gierga, Franz's commander in the 5th Company. Gierga later went on to be awarded the Knight's Cross in Africa on 30 June 1941.

The Medal in Commemoration of 1 October 1938 (the "Sudeten" medal).

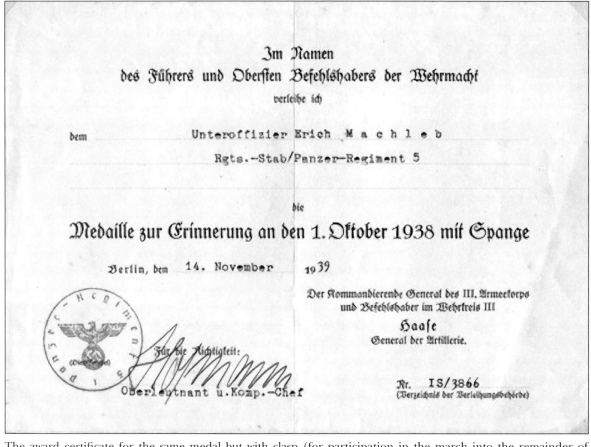

Im Namen
des Führers und Obersten Befehlshabers der Wehrmacht
verleihe ich

dem   Unteroffizier Erich M a c h l e b

Rgts.-Stab/Panzer-Regiment 5

die

Medaille zur Erinnerung an den 1. Oktober 1938 mit Spange

Berlin, den   14. November   1939

Der Kommandierende General des III. Armeekorps
und Befehlshaber im Wehrkreis III

Haase
General der Artillerie.

Für die Richtigkeit:

Oberleutnant u.Komp.-Chef   Nr. IS/3866
                                             (Verzeichnis der Verleihungsbehörde)

The award certificate for the same medal but with clasp (for participation in the march into the remainder of Czechoslovakia) to *Unteroffizier* Erich Machleb.

Machleb wearing
his award on the
Waffenrock.

The Medal in
Commemoration of
1 October 1938 with
Clasp (Prague Castle).

Besitzzeugnis

Dem

Fkm. Helmut Franz

(Dienstgr.,Vor- u.Zuname)

5./Panzer - Regiment 5

(Truppenteil)

wurde die vom ital. Oberkommando gestiftete

Erinnerungsmedaille

zum Zeichen des gemeinsamen Kampfes in Afrika
verliehen.

Afrika, den *19.1.42*   *Müller*

(Name)

(Dienstgr. u. Dienststllg.)

Major u. Abt. Führer

Award certificate for the Commemorative Medal for the Italian-German Campaign in Africa in Bronze to *Funkmeister* Helmut Franz. The certificate is signed by *Major* Müller, the acting commander of the 2nd Battalion.

Franz as an *Oberfunkmeister.*

The Commemorative Medal for the Italian-German Campaign in Africa in Bronze.

Besitzzeugnis.

Dem

Obstltn. Werner Mildebrath

Dienstgrad, Vor u. Zuname

Stab I. / Pz.-Rgt. 5

Truppenteil

wurde die vom italienischen Oberkommando gestiftete

Erinnerungsmedaille zum Zeichen des gemeinsamen

Kampfes in Afrika verliehen.

Afrika, d. 19.1.1942

Oberst u. Rgts.-Kdr.

An ornate version of the award certificate for the Commemorative Medal for the Italian-German Campaign in Africa in Bronze to *Oberstleutnant* Mildebrath, the commander of the regiment's 1st Battalion.

Mildebrath in typical tropical uniform. He has modified his cap with the addition of a metal cockade to replace the original machine-embroidered one.

The award certificate was backdated and signed by *Oberst* Müller, the regimental commander, who did not actually assume command of the regiment until 1 March 1942 (the document is dated 19 January 1942).

The silver version of the Commemorative Medal for the Italian-German Campaign in Africa.

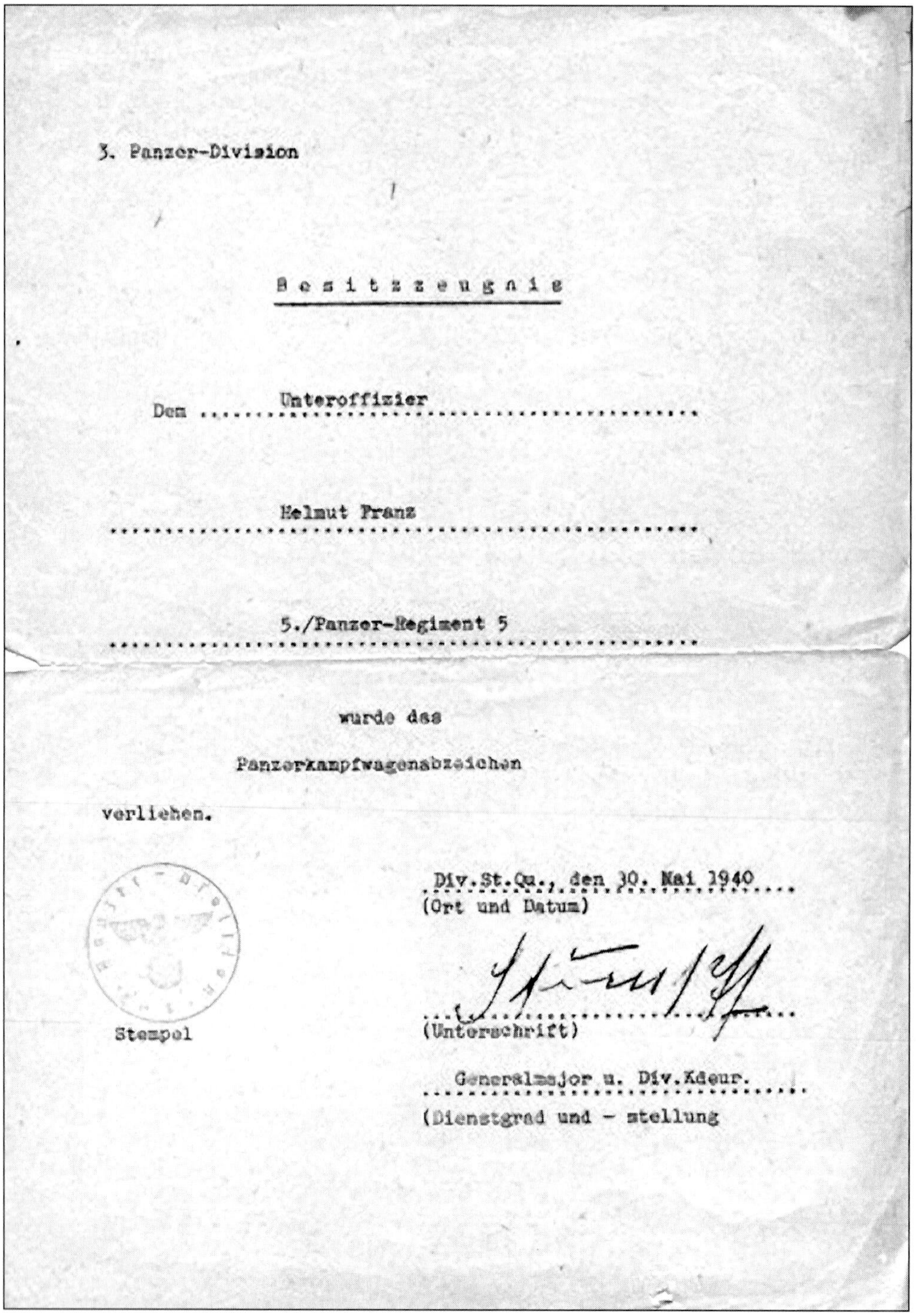

3. Panzer-Division

B e s i t z z e u g n i s

Dem .... Unteroffizier ....

.... Helmut Franz ....

.... 5./Panzer-Regiment 5 ....

wurde das

Panzerkampfwagenabzeichen

verliehen.

Div.St.Qu., den 30. Mai 1940
(Ort und Datum)

....
(Unterschrift)

Stempel

.... Generalmajor u. Div.Kdeur. ....
(Dienstgrad und - stellung

Award certificate for the Armored Combat Badge in Silver for *Unteroffizier* Helmut Franz of the 5th Company. The document is dated 30 May 1941 and was prepared by the headquarters of the *3. Panzer-Division* in mimeograph form, with the divisional commander's signature also being duplicated. Only the name, rank, unit of assignment, location and date needed to be filled in and an official stamp applied. This certificate refers to the badge as the *Panzerkampfwagenabzeichen* (Armored Fighting Vehicle Badge), the designation it had until 1 June 1940.

Armored Combat Badge in Silver.

The award certificate contains the facsimile signature of the division commander, *Generalmajor* Horst Stumpff. He served in that capacity from 15 February 1940 to 12 November 1940 and was awarded the Knight's Cross to the Iron Cross on 29 September 1941 as the commander of the *20. Panzer-Division*.

Paul-Freidrich Koch in tropical uniform as an *Oberschirrmeister*.

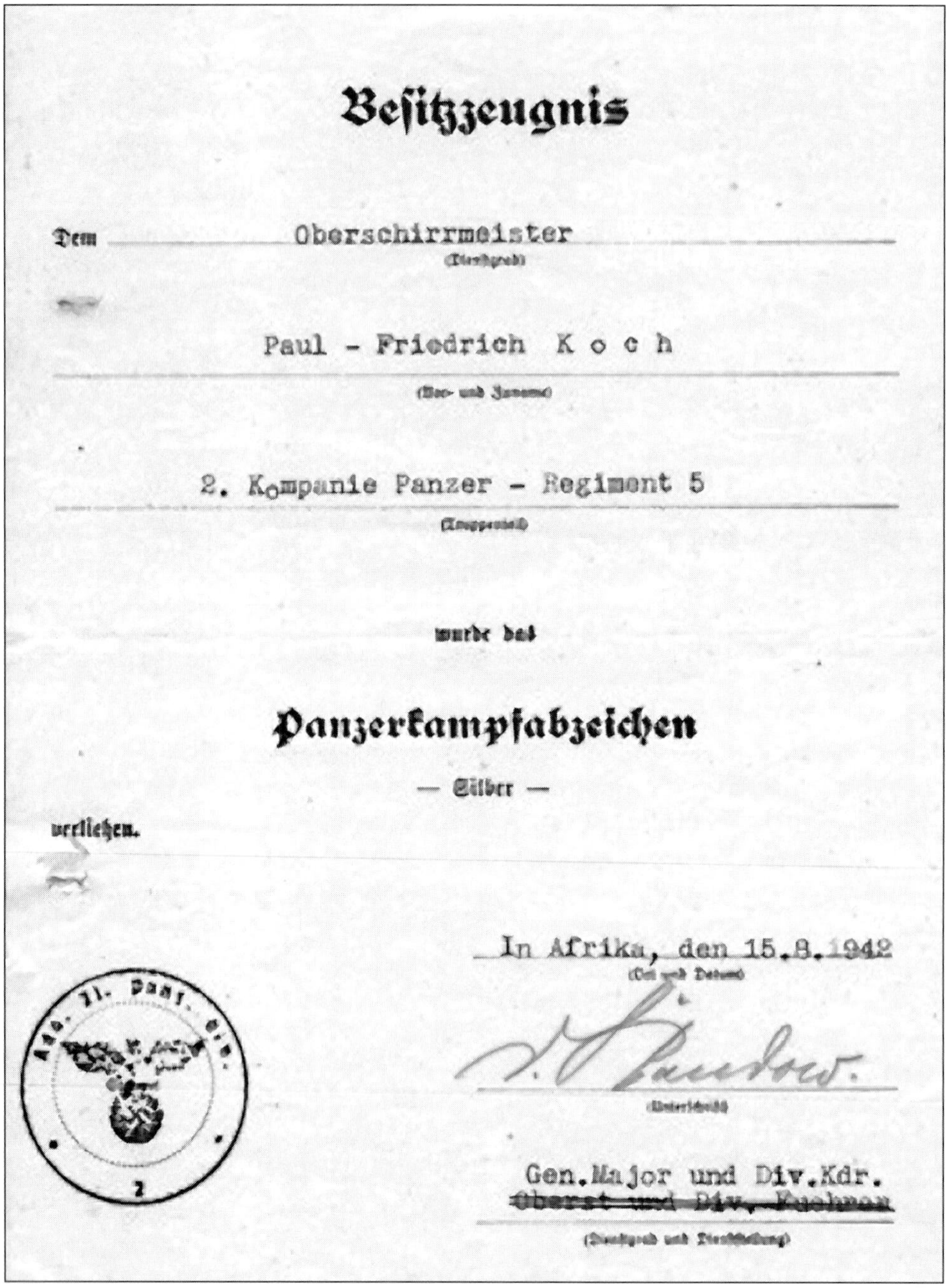

Befitzeugnis

Dem _____ Oberschirrmeister _____
(Dienftgrad)

Paul - Friedrich K o c h
(Bor- und Buname)

2. Kompanie Panzer - Regiment 5
(Truppenteil)

wurde das

Panzerkampfabzeichen

— Silber —

verliehen.

In Afrika, den 15.8.1942
(Ort und Datum)

L. v. Randow.
(Unterschrift)

Gen.Major und Div.Kdr.
~~Oberst und Div. Kochron~~
(Dienftgrad und Dienftftellung)

Award certificate for Armored Combat Badge in Silver for *Oberschirrmeister* Paul-Friedrich Koch. Koch entered service in March 1934 at seventeen years of age and was assigned to the *Kraftfahrlehrkommando Zossen*. After the formation was redesignated as *Panzer-Regiment 5* in 1937, Koch became the regimental headquarters motor sergeant. Following the capture of Tobruk, he was assigned to the 2nd Company at the end of June 1942 as its motor sergeant. He was also simultaneously the leader of the 2nd Platoon. In the fighting that followed, he was awarded the *Panzerkampfabzeichen*, which was awarded by the division and signed by the commander at the time, *Generalmajor* von Randow. After *Hauptmann* Rettemeier was wounded in the 3rd Battle of El Alamein, Koch became the acting commander of the company for short periods. He was taken prisoner in May 1943 with the surrender of *Panzer-Armee Afrika*.

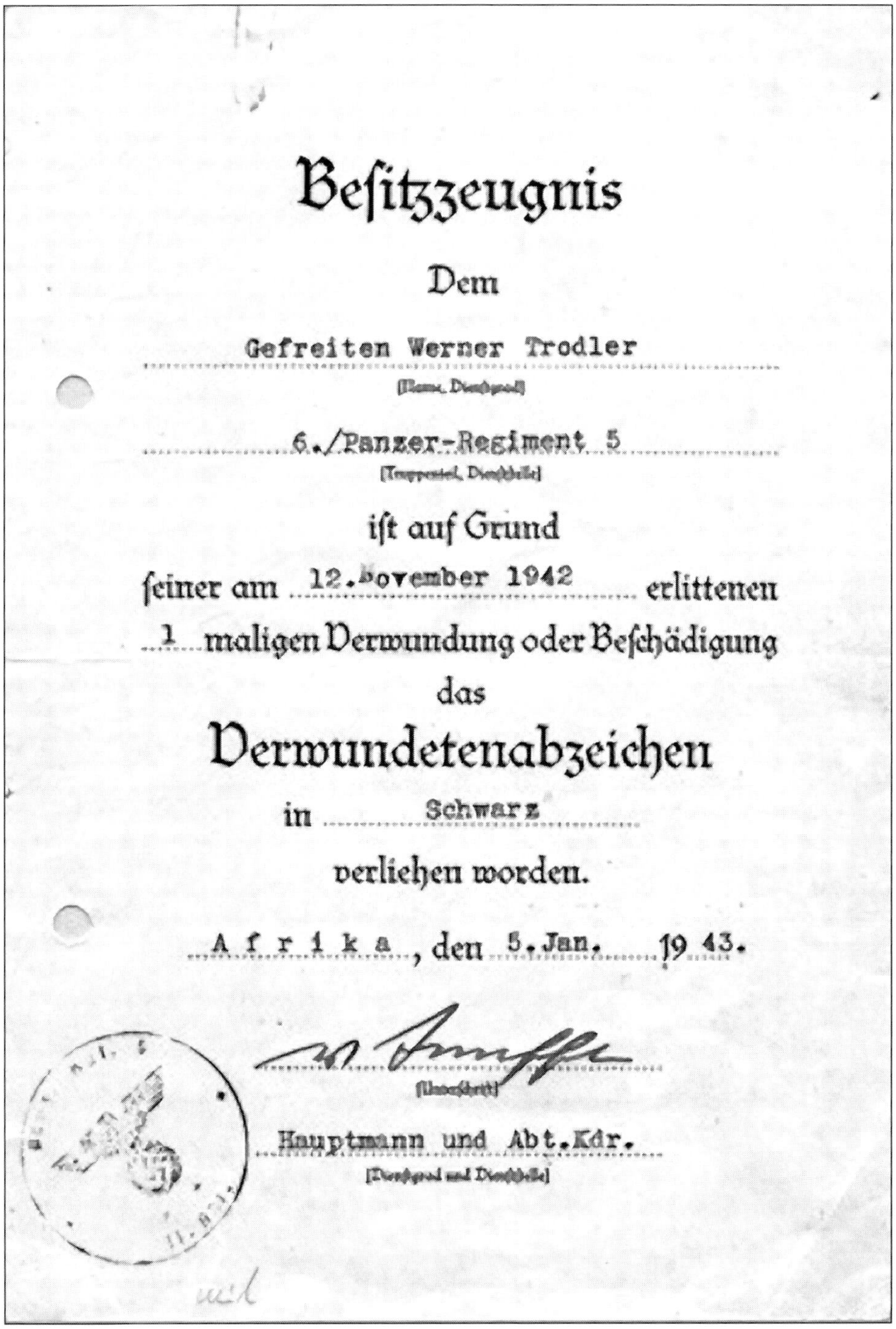

Befitzzeugnis

Dem

Gefreiten Werner Trodler

[Name, Dienstgrad]

6./Panzer-Regiment 5

[Truppenteil, Dienststelle]

ift auf Grund

feiner am 12.November 1942 erlittenen

1 maligen Verwundung oder Beschädigung

das

Verwundetenabzeichen

in Schwarz

verliehen worden.

A f r i k a , den 5.Jan. 19 43.

[Unterschrift]

Hauptmann und Abt.Kdr.

[Dienstgrad und Dienststelle]

Award certificate for the Wound Badge in Black for *Gefreiter* Werner Trodler of the regiment's 6th Company.

Gefreiter Werner Trodler

The Wound Badge in Black.

The document is signed by the battalion commander, *Hauptmann* von Senfft zu Pilsach, a later recipient of the Knight's Cross (27 June 1941). Von Senfft zu Pilsach was given acting command of the regiment on 21 December 1942, when *Oberst* Müller had to give up command due to illness. At the time the document was prepared, the regiment was in the Buerat position.

BESITZZEUGNIS

DEM

Unteroffizier Werner Fenck

(NAME, DIENSTGRAD)

Panz.Regt.5

(TRUPPENTEIL, DIENSTSTELLE)

IST AUF GRUND

13.6.42, 13.2.43 u.24.4.43

SEINER AM   ERLITTENEN

3 MALIGEN VERWUNDUNG – BESCHÄDIGUNG

DAS

VERWUNDETENABZEICHEN

IN   Silber

VERLIEHEN WORDEN.

Hamburg-Altona   , DEN 11.Nov. 194 4

Eckart

(UNTERSCHRIFT)

Oberst u. Kommandeur.

(DIENSTGRAD UND DIENSTSTELLE)

Award certificate for the Wound Badge in Silver for *Unteroffizier* Werner Fenck, who was assigned to the regiment's 1st Company in Africa. The award certificate was prepared by Military District III, headquartered in Hamburg, after Fenck suffered his third wound (dates listed on the certificate).

Fenck in the *Panzer* uniform.

The Wound Badge in Silver.

Rettemeier shortly after award of the Knight's Cross.

The Wound Badge in Gold.

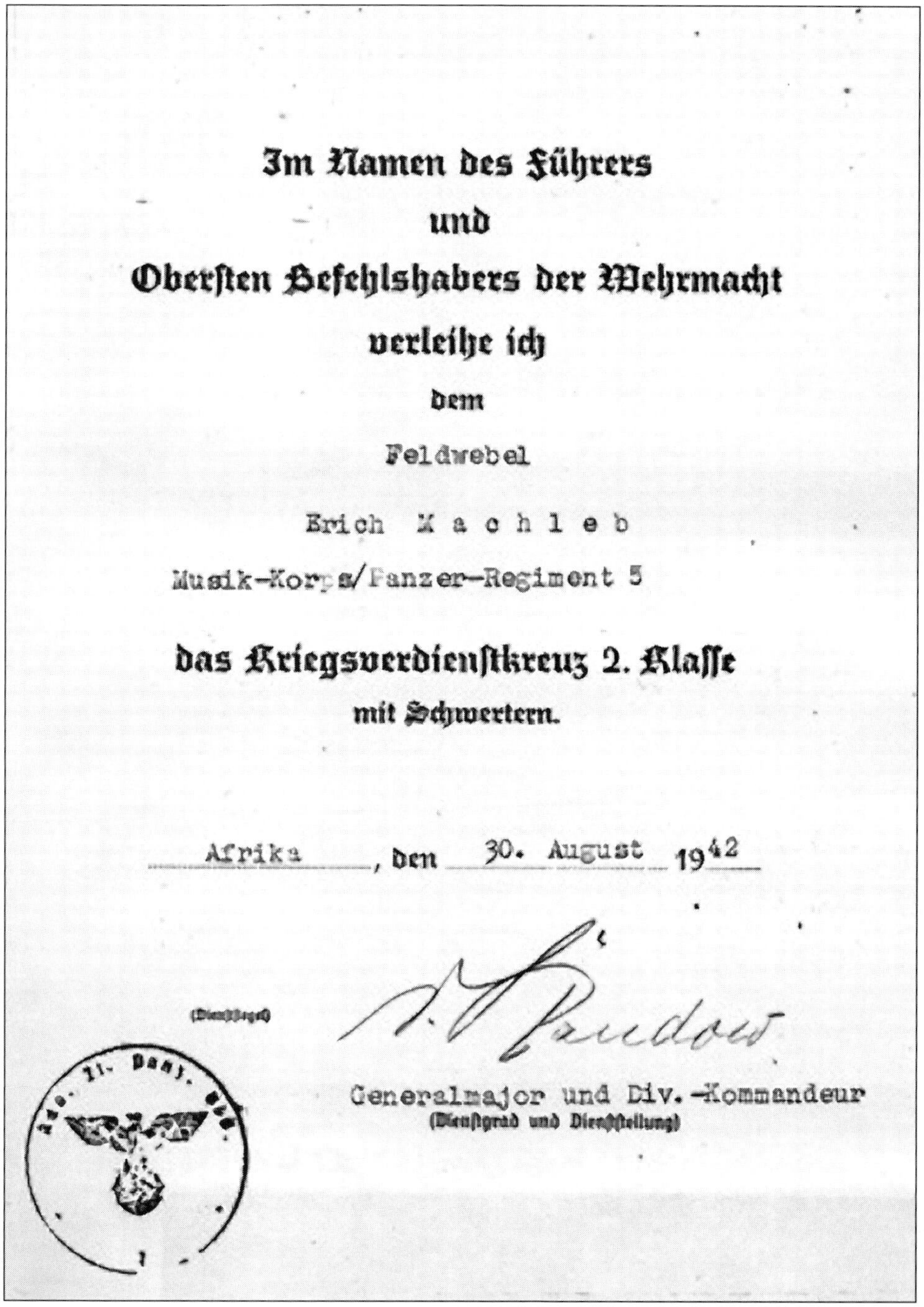

Im Namen des Führers

und

Obersten Befehlshabers der Wehrmacht

verleihe ich

dem

Feldwebel

Erich Machleb

Musik-Korps/Panzer-Regiment 5

das Kriegsverdienstkreuz 2. Klasse

mit Schwertern.

Afrika, den 30. August 1942

Generalmajor und Div.-Kommandeur
(Dienstgrad und Dienststellung)

Award certificate for the Wound Badge in Gold for *Hauptmann* Josef Rettemeier. In Africa, he was initially the commander of the 2nd Company, later becoming the acting commander of the 1st Battalion during the 3rd Battle of El Alamein. He was badly wounded during the fighting there and evacuated to Germany. Effective 14 September 1943, he became the commander of *Panzer-Abteilung 5* and was awarded the Knight's Cross to the Iron Cross in that capacity on 5 December 1943. He was the 425th recipient of the Oak Leaves to the Knight's Cross of the Iron Cross on 13 March 1944. The award certificate was signed by the division commander of the *25. Panzergrenadier-Division, Generalmajor Dr.* Benicke.

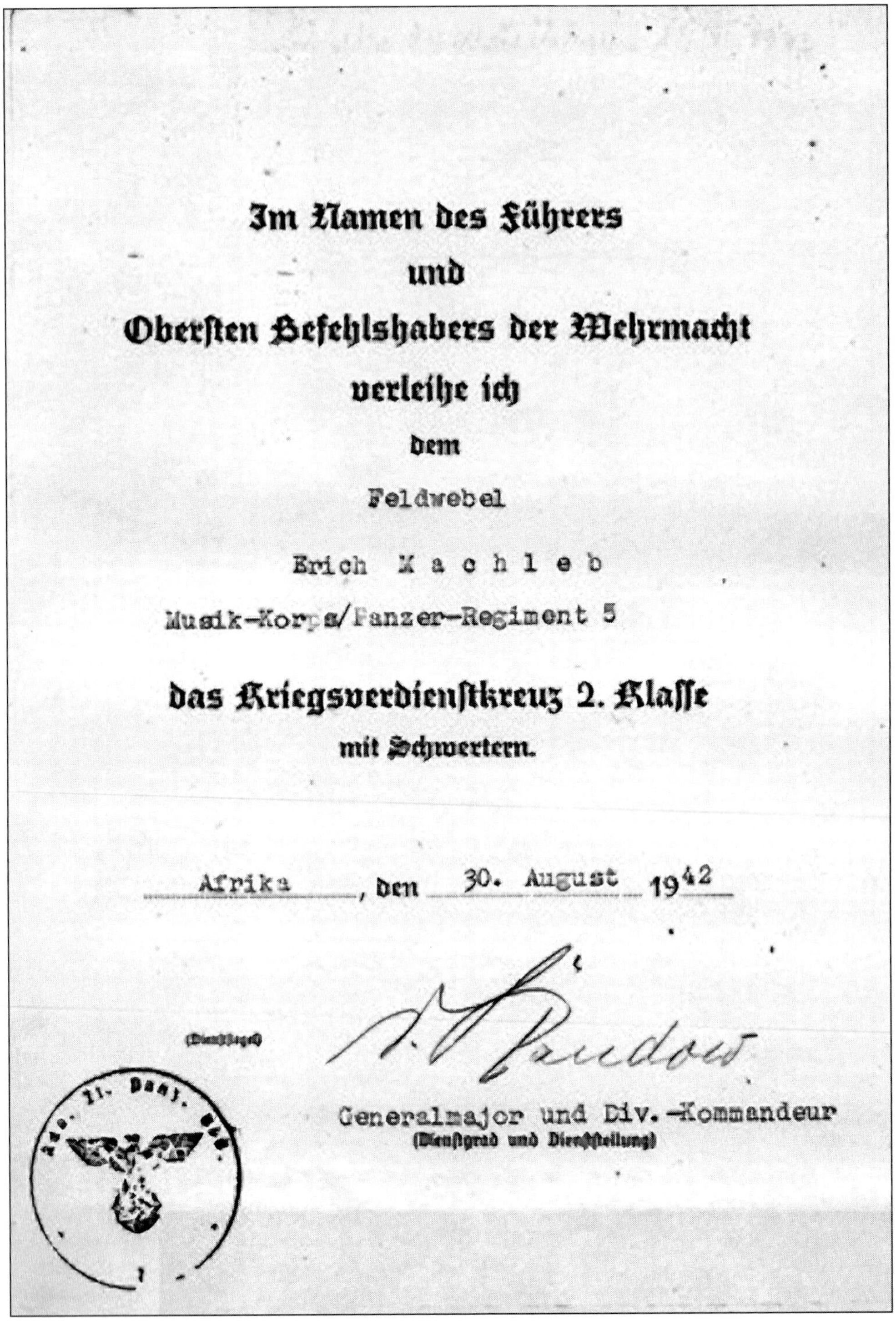

Im Namen des Führers

und

Obersten Befehlshabers der Wehrmacht

verleihe ich

dem

Feldwebel

Erich Machleb

Musik-Korps/Panzer-Regiment 5

das Kriegsverdienstkreuz 2. Klasse

mit Schwertern.

Afrika, den 30. August 1942

Generalmajor und Div.-Kommandeur
(Dienstgrad und Dienststellung)

Award certificate for the War Service Cross, 2nd Class, with Swords for *Feldwebel* Erich Machleb of the regimental band. Instead of listing his unit as the headquarters of the regiment, the document simply lists the regimental band. The document was signed by the division commander, *Generalmajor* von Randow, who was said to have a certain fondness for the band.

Machleb in tropical uniform.

The War Service Cross, 2nd Class, with Swords.

Gefreiter Heinrich-Gustav Schlieper.

Schlieper's document was signed by the commander of the *5. leichte Division*, *Generalmajor* Streich, who had been the regiment's 1st Battalion commander from 1935 to 1937. Streich was relieved of command by Rommel on 20 May 1941 due to a clash of personalities and replaced by *Generalmajor* von Ravenstein.

Im Namen des führers
und Obersten Befehlshabers
der Wehrmacht

verleihe ich

dem

Gefreiten

Heinrich=Gustaf Schlieper

Panzer-Regiment 5

das

Eiserne Kreuz 2.Klasse.

.........Afrika........,den.....6.....5.....1941

Generalmajor u. Div.-deur.
(Dienstgrad und Dienststellung)

Award certificate for the Iron Cross, Second Class, to *Gefreiter* Heinrich-Gustav Schlieper, the radio operator on the regimental commander's tank.

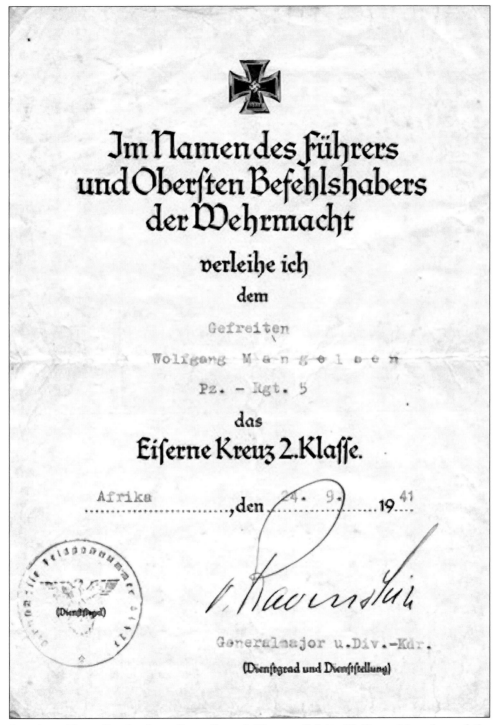

Award certificate for the Iron Cross, Second Class to *Gefreiter* Wolfgang Mangelsen of the regiment's 5th Company.

Gefreiter Wolfgang Mangelsen.

The Iron Cross, Second Class.

The document was signed by the commander of the *21. Panzer-Division*, *Generalmajor* Hans von Ravenstein. Von Ravenstein was decorated with the *Pour le mérite* in the First World War (23 June 1918) and received the Knight's Cross to the Iron Cross on 3 June 1940 as the commander of *Schützen-Regiment 4*. He replaced *Generalmajor* Streich in command of the *5. leichte Division* on 20 May 1941 and was commander of the division after its redesignation as the *21. Panzer-Division* until he was captured by the British outside Tobruk on 29 November 1941.

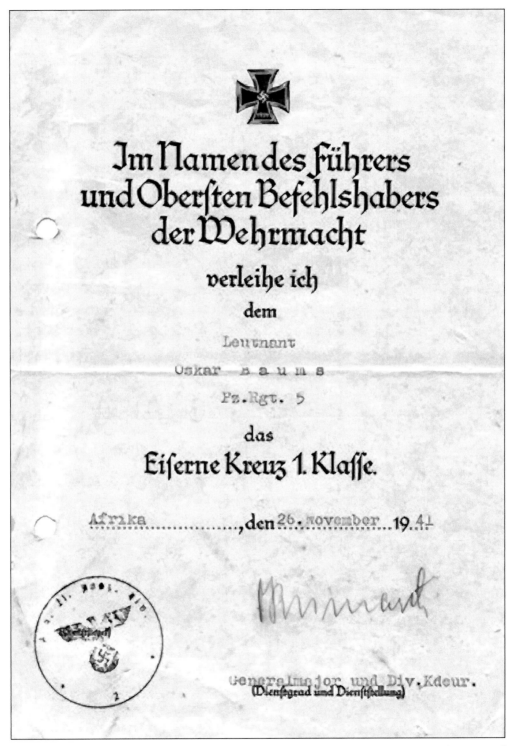

Award certificate for the Iron Cross, First Class, for *Leutnant* Oskar Baums of the headquarters of the regiment's 1st Battalion.

Oskar Baums.

The document was signed by *Generalmajor* Georg von Bismarck, the commander of the *21. Panzer-Division* from 30 January 1942 until his death in battle outside El Alamein on 31 August 1942. He had been awarded the Knight's Cross to the Iron Cross on 29 September 1940 as an *Oberst* and commander of *Schützen-Regiment 7*. The document was backdated, since von Bismarck was not in command of the division on 26 November 1941.

Helmut Franz.

Iron Cross, First Class.

Im Namen des führers
und Obersten Befehlshabers
der Wehrmacht

verleihe ich

dem

Funkmeister

Helmut F r a n z , 5./Pz.Rgt.5

das
Eiserne Kreuz 1. Klasse.

Nordafrika ,den 13. April 19 42
Der Kommandierende General
des Deutschen Afrikakorps
I. V.

(Dienstgrad und Dienststellung)
G e n e r a l l e u t n a n t .

Award certificate for the Iron Cross, First Class, to *Funkmeister* Helmut Franz of the regiment's 5th
Company.

The Franz document was signed by *Generalleutnant* Walter K. Nehring, who later received three levels of the Knight's Cross (124th Swords recipient on 22 January 1945). Nehring was the regimental commander from 1937 to 1939. At the time this document was signed, he was the commanding general of the *DAK* (9 March 1942 to 31 August 1942).

Oberstleutnant Werner Mildebrath after the receipt of his award.

The Knight's Cross of the Iron Cross.

Vorläufiges Besitzeugnis

Der Führer
und Oberste Befehlshaber
der Wehrmacht
hat

dem <u>Oberstleutnant Mildebrath, Pz.Rgt.5</u>

das Ritterkreuz
des Eisernen Kreuzes
am <u>12.8.1942</u> verliehen.

HQu OKH, den <u>12. August 1942.</u>

Das Oberkommando des Heers

i. 21.

General der Infanterie

Preliminary award certificate for the Knight's Cross of the Iron Cross for the commander of the regiment's 1st Battalion, *Oberstleutnant* Werner Mildebrath. There was also a formal presentation document for the award, which was usually presented at the *Führer* Headquarters.

As was typically the case with the Knight's Cross preliminary award documents, the certificate was signed by *General der Infanterie* Bodewin Keitel, the head of the Army's personnel office from 1 September 1939 to 30 September 1942, not to be mistaken with *Generalfeldmarschall* Wilhelm Keitel, the chief of staff of the Armed Forces High Command, who never signed the preliminary documents.

IM NAMEN DES FÜHRERS
UND OBERSTEN BEFEHLSHABERS
DER WEHRMACHT
VERLEIHE ICH
DEM

OBERLEUTNANT
ALBRECHT ZORN
KOMPANIECHEF I./P.Z. RGT. 5

DAS DEUTSCHE KREUZ
IN GOLD

HAUPTQUARTIER. DEN   25. MÄRZ 1942

OBERKOMMANDO DES HEERES

GENERALFELDMARSCHALL

Award certificate for the German Cross in Gold to *Oberleutnant* Albrecht Zorn, a company commander in the regiment's 1st Battalion. The document was signed by the chief of staff of the Armed Forces High Command, *Generalfeldmarschall* Wilhelm Keitel.

Zorn in 1940.

The German Cross in Gold, which was referred to in soldier jargon as the "scrambled egg."

Hauptmann Braun in 1943 wears the tropical uniform with the numerals of *Panzer-Regiment 36* on his shoulder boards.

Hauptquartier O.K.H., den 1.11.1941

Ich spreche dem

Oberleutnant B R A U N , Chef 1./Panzer-Regiment 36

meine besondere Anerkennung für seine hervorragenden Leistungen auf dem Schlachtfelde

in bei   N O W O M O S K O W S K

am   27. September 1941

aus.   Der Oberbefehlshaber des Heeres

Battlefield Recognition Certificate from the commander-in-chief of the Army for *Oberleutnant* Hans-Joachim Braun, who was initially assigned to *Kraftfahrlehrkommando Zossen* and was a *Leutnant* in the regiment's 2nd Battalion until 1938, when he was reassigned as cadre for the newly forming *Panzer-Regiment 36*. It was in that regiment that he received this certificate as the commander of the 1st Company.

At the start of the campaign in the East, the commander-in-chief of the Army introduced a Certificate of Recognition. It was only awarded around 2,000 times and was an unusual award in that it could not be worn. Its award was entered into the *Soldbuch*, however, and some experts claim that it was as highly valued as the award of the Knight's Cross.

The certificate seen here is the first version and was sized 22x16.1 centimeters and has an original ink signature by *Generalfeldmarschall* von Brauchitsch, the army's commander-in-chief at the time.

When Hitler assumed the function of commander-in-chief of the Army on 19 December 1941, the form changed and was henceforth called the "Recognition Certificate of the *Führer*."

ICH SPRECHE DEM
Gefreiten Heinrich-Gustaf Schlieper
Fallschirm-Jäger Rgt. 1
FÜR SEINE HERVORRAGENDEN
LEISTUNGEN
AUF DEM SCHLACHTFELDE
BEI MONTE CASSINO
MEINE
BESONDERE ANERKENNUNG AUS.

HAUPTQUARTIER·DEN *30. Januar 1944*

DER FÜHRER

DIE ERFOLGTE VERLEIHUNG
WIRD BEGLAUBIGT:

The later version of the "Recognition Certificate of the *Führer*." This one was awarded to Heinrich-Gustav Schlieper, who transferred from the Army to the *Luftwaffe*, became a paratrooper, was assigned to *Fallschirmjäger-Regiment 1* and fought at Monte Cassino. Until May 1943, he had been the radio operator on the regimental commander's tank in *Panzer-Regiment 5*.

B e s i t z z e u g n i s

Der Oberbefehlshaber

der

H e e r e s g r u p p e

A f r i k a

verleiht dem

General

Walther N e h r i n g

Kommandierende General des XC.A.K.

das Ärmelband "Afrika"

.....Gef..Stand,.den.......16..3..19 43

O b e r s t   u. Adjutant

Award certificate for the *Afrika* sleeve band awarded to *General der Panzertruppen* Walter K. Nehring on 16 May 1943. The document was signed by *Oberst* Schulte-Heuthaus, who was the adjutant of *Panzer-Armee Afrika*. Schulte-Heuthaus received the Knight's Cross as an *Oberstleutnant* on 23 January 1942, while serving as the commander of *Kradschützen-Bataillon 25* in the *25. Infanterie-Division (mot.)*. (Provided by Christoph Nehring.)

Nehring wears the
Afrika sleeve band.

The *Afrika* sleeve ban in the standard
camelhair version.

Baums as an
instructor at the
armor school in
1943.

A variation of the *Afrika* sleeve band.

BESITZZEUGNIS

DER OBERBEFEHLSHABER

DER_____Heeresgruppe Afrika_____

VERLEIHT DEM

_____Oberleutnant_____
(DIENSTGRAD)

_____Oskar Baums_____
(VOR. UND ZUNAME)

Fahnenjunker-Lehrgang 1 der Panzertruppe
(TRUPPENTEIL)

DAS ÄRMELBAND »AFRIKA«

Wischau, den 23.9.1943.
(ORT UND DATUM)

I.V.: _____
(UNTERSCHRIFT)

_____Major_____
(DIENSTGRAD UND DIENSTSTELLUNG)

Award certificate for the *Afrika* sleeve band to *Oberleutnant* Oskar Baums, who was assigned to Officer Candidate School 1 of the *Panzertruppe* at the time the award caught up to him on 23 September 1943. He originally entered military service as an enlisted man in the regiment's 2nd Company in November 1937. From March 1941 to October 1942, he was assigned first to the headquarters of the 1st Battalion and then to the regimental staff. He served as an instructor at the armor school from October 1942 until June 1944. At the end of the war, Baums was a *Hauptmann* and commander of a *Panther* company in *Panzer-Regiment 26* of the *26. Panzer-Division*, seeing service in Italy.

Dultz in 1944 while assigned to *Panzer-Regiment "Großdeutschland."* He has the regimental ciphers—an intertwined *GD*—on his shoulder boards and wears the numbered armored combat badge, an award not often seen in photographs.

The 2nd Level of the Armored Combat Award for twenty-five or more individual armored engagements. (The engagements were tracked in the soldier's *Wehrpaß*.)

A page from the military "passport"—*Wehrpaß*—of *Oberleutnant* Jürgen Dultz indicating his military awards. He entered military service on 3 December 1940 and was assigned to the headquarters company of the regiment from 25 July 1941 to 20 August 1942. On 4 August 1943, he was reassigned to the tank regiment of *Panzergrenadier-Division "Großdeutschland,"* where he was assigned until the end of the war. According to his *Wehrpaß*, he was awarded Armored Combat Badge in Silver; Italian-German Campaign medal; Iron Cross, Second Class; Iron Cross, First Class; Wound Badge in Black; Armored Combat Badge, 2nd Level (25); *Afrika* sleeve band; and Wound Badge in Silver.

Oberkommando des Heeres
Generalfeldmarschall Keitel

Berlin W 35, den
Tirpitzufer 72-76
Fernsprecher: Ortsverkehr 21 81 91
Fernverkehr 21 80 91

F.H.Qu., den 27. August 1944

Herrn

Leutnant d.R. S c h w a r z ,
Pz.Ers.Abt. 5,
N e u r u p p i n

Für die erfolgreiche Flucht aus der englischen
Kriegsgefangenschaft unter Überwindung der Meerenge von
Gibraltar, bei der Sie sich durch besondere Umsicht und
Tatkraft ausgezeichnet haben, spreche ich Ihnen meine
volle Anerkennung aus.

In Würdigung Ihres tapferen Verhaltens hat der
Führer Sie mit Wirkung vom 1.9.44 zum Oberleutnant d.R.
befördert.

Generalfeldmarschall

Certificate of recognition from *Generalfeldmarschall* Keitel to *Leutnant*
Edube Schwarz for his escape from British captivity. It reads:
Führer Headquarters, 27 August 1944
TO:
Leutnant d.R. Schwarz
Panzer-Ersatz-Abteilung 5
I especially commend you for your successful flight from
English captivity by crossing the Straits of Gibraltar, whereby you
demonstrated considerable circumspection and bravery.

In appreciation of your demonstrated bravery, the *Führer* has
promoted you to *Oberleutnant d.R.* with an effective date of 1
September 1944.

BIBLIOGRAPHY

Aberger, Heinz-Dietrich. *Die 5. (lei.)/21. Panzer-Division in Nordafrika 1941–1943.* Preußischer Militär-Verlag, Reutlingen 1994.

Barnett, Correlli. *Wüstengenerale.* Manfred Pawlak Verlagsgesellschaft mbH, Herrsching.

Bender, Roger James, and Richard D. Law. *Uniforms, Organization and History of the Afrikakorps,* 3rd edition. San José, California 1986.

Bender, Roger James, and Warren W. Odegard. *Uniforms, Organization and History of the Panzertruppe.* San José, California 1980.

Boehm, Erwin. *Geschichte der 25. Division, Kameradenhilfswerk 25 e.V.* Stuttgart 1983.

Büschleb, Hermann. *Feldherren und Panzer im Wüstenkrieg.* Kurt Vowinckel Verlag, Neckargemünd 1966.

Carell, Paul. *Die Wüstenfüchse.* Verlag Ullstein GmbH, Frankfurt (Main) and Berlin 1989.

"Das schwarze Barett Nr. 17, Nachrichtenblatt für Soldaten und Reservisten der Panzer-, Panzerjäger- und Panzeraufklärungstruppe und Organ Freundeskreis der Panzertruppe e.V." Bonn 1997.

"Datenblätter für Heeres-Waffen, -Fahrzeuge, -Gerät", Special publication W 127 of *Vierteljahresschrift "Waffen-Revue."* Publizistisches Archiv für Militär- und Waffenwesen, Karl R. Pawlas, Nuremberg 1976.

Deutsche Dienststelle für die Benachrichtigung der nächsten Angehörigen von Gefallenen der ehemaligen deutschen Wehrmacht. Listing of fallen members of Panzer-Regiment 5 (1941–1943) and Panzer-Abteilung 5 (1943–1945), Berlin 1986.

Deutsche Dienststelle für die Benachrichtigung der nächsten Angehörigen von Gefallenen der ehemaligen deutschen Wehrmacht. Listing of fallen members of Panzer-Regiment 5 (1939–1940), Berlin 2002.

Doehle, Dr. Heinrich. *Die Auszeichnungen des Großdeutschen Reichs.* Verlag E.O. Erdmenger & Co. K.G., Berlin 1945 (Licensed edition by Verlag K.D. Patzwall, Norderstadt 2000).

Döll, Rudi, former member of *Panzer-Regiment 5,* correspondence with the author, June 2000.

Esebeck, von Hanns-Gert. *Das Deutsche Afrika-Korps, Sieg und Niederlage.* Limes Verlag, Wiesbaden and Munich 1975.

Federl, Christian. *Die Ritterkreuzträger der Deutschen Panzerdivisionen 1939–1945, Die Panzertruppe,* 1st edition. VDM Heinz Nickel, Zweibrücken 2000.

Geschichte der I. Abteilung/Panzer-Regiment 5. Wilhelm Limpert, Druck- und Verlagshaus, Berlin SW 68.

Geschichte der II. Abteilung/Panzer-Regiment 5. Wilhelm Limpert, Druck- und Verlagshaus, Berlin SW 68.

Geschichte der 3. Panzer-Division, Berlin-Brandenburg, 1935–1945. Produced by the Traditionsverband der Division, Verlag der Buchhandlung Günter Richter, Berlin 1967.

287

Guderian, Heinz. *Erinnerungen eines Soldaten.* Verlag Kurt Vowinckel, Heidelberg 1951.

Haupt, Werner. *Heeresgruppe Mitte 1941–1945.* Verlag Hans-Henning Podzun, Dorheim 1968.

Heller, Rolf. *Das war der Krieg in Polen.* F.W. Peters Verlag, Berlin.

Hettler, Eberhard. *Uniformen der Deutschen Wehrmacht.* New edition in 1979 of the 1939–40 edition, published by Verlag und Gesamtherstellung Militariaarchiv K.D. Patzwall, Hamburg 1997.

Jentz, Thomas L. *Die deutsche Panzertruppe 1933–1942,* vols. 1 & 2. Podzun-Pallas-Verlag GmbH, Wölfersheim-Berstadt 1998.

Kampe, Hans Georg, Wünsdorf. *Geburts- und Entwicklungsstätte der deutschen Panzertruppen.* (Militärgeschichtliche Blätter, Schriftenreihe zur Militärgeschichte) Projekt und Verlag Dr. Erwin Meißler, Berlin 1997.

Kießlich, Dieter. *Zossen/Wünsdorf–Streifzüge durch eine alte Garnison.* Published by the Förderverein Garnisonsmuseum Wünsdorf e.V., 2nd corrected edition, Wünsdorf 1999.

Kilanowski, Heinz, former member of the *4./Panzer-Regiment 5,* correspondence with the author on 15 September 2001.

Klietmann, Kurt-G. *Auszeichnungen des Deutschen Reiches 1936–1945.* Motorbuch Verlag, 5th edition, Stuttgart 1989.

Köhler, Siegfried. *Wehrmachtberichte von den Kämpfen in Nordafrika vom 11. Januar 1941 bis 07. Februar 1942.* Self-published, Vallendar 1978.

Kuhn, Harald. *Oberleutnant und ehemaliger Kompaniechef im Panzerregiment 5, Die Ereignisse im Frühjahr und Sommer 1941 in Libyens Wüste.* No date.

Kurowski, Franz. *Brückenkopf Tunesien.* Maximilian-Verlag, Herford 1967.

———. *Die Geschichte des Panzerregiments 5.* Heinrich Pöppinghaus Verlag, Bochum 1975.

Lewin, Ronald. *Rommel.* W. Kohlhammer Verlag, Stuttgart 1969.

McGuirk, Dal. *Rommel's Army in Africa.* Century Hutchinson Ltd, London 1987.

Müller, Klaus, Oberst a.D. Dipl. Ing. *"So lebten und arbeiteten wir 1929 bis 1933 in Kama."* May 1972.

Münnich, Ralf. *Panzer in Nord-Afrika, 1941–1943.* Podzun-Pallas-Verlag, Friedberg 1977.

Nehring, Walther K., General. *Die Geschichte der deutschen Panzerwaffe 1916–1945.* Motorbuch Verlag, Stuttgart 1974.

German Armed Forces High Command. *Die Wehrmacht, Issue 22, 2nd Vol.* Berlin, 2nd November edition of 1938.

Paul, Wolfgang. *Panzer-General Walther K. Nehring,* 1st edition. Motorbuch-Verlag, Stuttgart 1986.

Piekalkiewicz, Janusz. *Krieg der Panzer 1939–1945.* Südwest Verlag, Munich 1981.

———. *Der Wüstenkrieg in Afrika 1940–1943.* Südwest Verlag, Munich 1985.

Pruett, Michael H., and Robert J. Edwards. *Field Uniforms of German Army Panzer Forces in World War II.* J.J. Fedorowicz Publishing Inc., Winnipeg 1993.

Quarrie, Bruce. *Das große Buch der Deutschen Heere im 20. Jahrhundert.* Podzun-Pallas-Verlag, Friedberg (Hessia) 1990.

Radke, Dr., Heinz. *Die Panzerbrigade 6 und ihre Garnisonen Neustadt und Stadtallendorf, Festschrift zum Treffen des Waffenrings–Kampftruppen–Kavallerie–Schnelle Truppen e.V. am 19./20. Juni 1971.* Oberschleißheim 1971.

Rettemeier, Josef, Oberst a.D. *"Niederschrift zur Geschichte der Panzerabteilung 5."* Seeboden am Millstätter See, 24 July 1974.

Ritgen, Helmut. *Die Schulen der Panzertruppen des Heeres 1918 bis zum Aufbau der Bundeswehr.* Verein der Freunde und Förderer des Panzermuseums Munster e.V./Freundeskreis Offiziere der Panzertruppen e.V., Cologne, Licensed edition from 1992.

Rohr, Heinz. *Geschichte einer Lübecker Familie, Band 1.* Lebenserinnerungen 1913–1944, Self-published, Hamburg 1994

Rommel, Erwin. *Krieg ohne Haß.* Edited by Frau Lucie-Maria Rommel and Generalleutnant

Fritz Bayerlein. Verlag Heidenheimer Zeitung, Heidenheim 1950.

Scheibert, Horst. *Kampf und Untergang der deutschen Panzertruppe 1939–1945.* Pallas-Verlag, Friedberg 1973.

———. *Paraden der Wehrmacht, Berlin 1934–1940.* Podzun-Pallas-Verlag GmbH, Wölfersheim-Berstadt 1995.

Schlicht, Adolf, and John R. Angolia. *Die Deutsche Wehrmacht, Uniformierung und Ausrüstung, 1933–1945, Band 1: Das Heer,* 1st edition. Motorbuch Verlag, Stuttgart 1992.

Schmitz, Peter and Klaus-Jürgen Thies. *Die Truppenkennzeichen der Verbände und Einheiten der deutschen Wehrmacht und Waffen-SS und ihre Einsätze im Zweiten Weltkrieg 1939–1945, Band 1, Das Heer.* Biblio Verlag, Osnabrück 1987.

Schweyher, Karl. *1941–1943, Libyen–Ägypten–Tunesien, Afrika-Artillerie-Abteilung im Afrika-Regiment 361 und im Artillerie-Regiment 190 der 90. leichten Afrika-Division, Truppenkameradschaft der ehemaligen I. Afrika-Artillerie-Abteilung 361 und 190.* Limburgerhof 1994.

Selmayr, Dr. Alfons. *Meine Erlebnisse im Weltkrieg 1939–1945.* Irschenberg 1947.

Senger und Etterlin, von F.M. *Die deutschen Panzer 1926–1945,* 4th edition. J.F. Lehmanns Verlag, Munich 1973.

Spielberger, Walter J. *Die Panzerkampfwagen I und II und ihre Abarten,* 1st edition. Motorbuch Verlag, Stuttgart 1974.

———. *Der Panzerkampfwagen III und seine Abarten,* 1st edition. Motorbuch Verlag, Stuttgart 1974.

Spielberger, Walter J., and Friedrich Wiener. *Die deutschen Panzerkampfwagen III und IV und ihre Abarten 1935–1945, Wehrwissenschaftliche Berichte, Band 2.* J.F. Lehmanns Verlag, Munich 1968.

Stockert. *Die Eichenlaubträger 1940–1945.* Verlag Friedrichshaller Rundblick GmbH, Bad Friedrichshall 1996.

Stoves, Rolf. *Die gepanzerten und motorisierten deutschen Großverbände 1935–1945.* Podzun-Pallas-Verlag GmbH, Friedberg 1986.

Witthaus, Lothar, former member of the *3./Panzer-Abteilung 5*, diary entries from January 1944.

Wolff, Dr. Kurt. *"Wir nahmen Festung, Stadt und Hafen Tobruk,"* firsthand account, written on 23 June 1942.

———. *"Panzer in Afrika,"* firsthand account written in July 1942.

PHOTO CREDITS

Heinrich Bassenge (†), *I./Panzer-Regiment 5*; Oskar Baums, Headquarters of the *I./Panzer-Regiment 5* and Headquarters of *Panzer-Regiment 5*; Heinrich Böttcher (†), Headquarters of the *II./Panzer-Regiment 5*; Hans-Joachim Braun, *Kraftfahrlehrkommando* and the *II./Panzer-Regiment 5*; Friedrich Dreeke, *7./Panzer-Regiment 5*; Jürgen Dultz (†), Headquarters of *Panzer-Regiment 5*; Werner Fenck, *1./Panzer-Regiment 5*; Gerhard Fischer, *1./Panzer-Regiment 5*; Helmut Franz, *5./Panzer-Regiment 5*; Herbert Gräfe, Headquarters of the *I./Panzer-Regiment 5*; Gustav Gaus, *6./Panzer-Regiment 5*; Günter Gielow, *8./Panzer-Regiment 5*; Werner Grün, *1./Panzer-Regiment 5*; Kurt Herms (†), *5./Panzer-Regiment 5* and regimental headquarters; Felix Kalinka (†), Headquarters of *Panzer-Regiment 5*; Paul-Friedrich Koch, Headquarters of *Panzer-Regiment 5*; Karl-Friedrich König, *8./Panzer-Regiment 5*; Erich Machleb, Headquarters of *Panzer-Regiment 5*; Walter Märkisch, *1./Panzer-Regiment 5*; Alfons Mayer, *4./Panzer-Regiment 5*; Christoph Nehring (family archives; Erwin Orlijewski (†), *5./Panzer-Regiment 5*; Adrian Pretscher, *2./Panzer-Regiment 5*; Werner Trodler (†), *6./Panzer-Regiment 5*; Hans Sandrock (†), *I./Panzer-Regiment 5*; Günter Sauer (†), *3./Panzer-Regiment 5*; Heinrich-Gustaf Schlieper (†), Headquarters of *Panzer-Regiment 5*; Edube Schwarz, *4./Panzer-Regiment 5*; Hans Skala, *8./Panzer-Regiment 5*; Josef Wegener, *2./Panzer-Regiment 5*; Rudolf Wendorff, Headquarters of the *II./Panzer-Regiment 5*; and Herbert Zeidler, *8./Panzer-Regiment 5*.